Jīva Goswāmī's

Tattva-Sandarbha

Jīva Goswāmī's

Tattva-Sandarbha

Sacred India's Philosophy of Ecstasy

Bhāvānuvāda by

Swāmī B.V. Tripurāri

Clarion Call

Other books by Swāmī B. V. Tripurāri:

Rasa: Love Relationships in Transcendence
Ancient Wisdom for Modern Ignorance

Library of Congress
Catalog Card Number: 95–083152

ISBN: 1-886069-12-3

Printed in China
through Palace Press International

To my eternal preceptor,
oṁ viṣṇupāda paramahaṁsa
parama parivrājakācārya-varya
aṣṭottara-śata-śrī śrīmad śrīla
A. C. Bhaktivedanta Swami Prabhupāda,
on the centennial anniversary of his
divine appearance in this world.

CONTENTS

Foreword .... *ix*
Preface .... *xi*
Introduction .... *xiii*
List of Abbreviations .... *xxii*

1. ŚRĪ JĪVA JĪVANĀMṚTAM 1

MAṄGALĀCARAṆA

2. INVOKING AUSPICIOUSNESS 13

PRAMĀṆA KHAṆḌA

3. IN SEARCH OF VALID EVIDENCE 31
4. THE GLORY OF ŚRĪMAD-BHĀGAVATAM 63

PRAMEYA KHAṆḌA

5. THE TRANCE OF VYĀSA 101
6. THE ULTIMATE SHELTER 145

Pronunciation Guide *183*
Glossary *185*
Bibliography *189*
Verse Index *191*
Index *195*

FOREWORD

For the past hundred years or so, since the famous oration by Swāmī Vivekananda at the 1893 World Parliament of Religions in Chicago, the Western world has been persuaded to consider Hinduism in monistic terms: all is one, all is God, you are God, I am God, we are all God. This philosophy, known as *advaita-vedānta,* was developed by Śaṅkara around 800 C.E. and is fundamentally rooted in an impersonal view of the cosmos, where all is Brahman without a second. Though actually a minority worldview in India, it continued to represent the entire tradition, especially in the hands of modern synthetic movements such as the Ramakrishna Mission, Śrī Aurobindo Ashram, and Transcendental Meditation (Maharishi Mahesh Yogi), as well as Sarvepalli Radhakrishnan.

Notwithstanding the positive effects of spreading Indian philosophy and culture, this imbalance has caused considerable misunderstanding among the American public. For instance, Hinduism in general has been victimized by the media, and especially by the evangelical Christian community which labels Hinduism in its hundreds of publications as pantheistic, impersonal, and therefore somehow evil. Yet a growing number of Westerners are becoming aware of the rich theistic, i.e. personalistic, traditions in India. In terms of census, these traditions actually constitute the majority and have roots that go way back, not merely to the nineteenth century but to India's ancient Vedic heritage.

The theistic worship of Hindu deities like Viṣṇu, Kṛṣṇa, Śiva, Durga, etc., which according to Advaita philosophy consist of inferior, illusory practices of the illiterate masses, has generated some of the most profound theological and philosophical treatises among its exponents. The scholastic precision and intuitive depth found in many of these works is unparalleled in the history of religions. Barring cultural differences, Jewish, Christian, and Islamic apologetics, as well as proponents of other traditions that espouse the worship of a personal God, would be wise to consult these works for their clarity of argument and techniques of theological presentation.

The book which you are about to read is an analysis of a medieval work that stands at the zenith of the Vaiṣṇava theological tradition. Written by Jīva Goswāmī (1513-1598), the foremost philosopher and theologian of the Gauḍīya Vaiṣṇava *sampradāya,* the *Tattva-sandarbha* is a lucid presentation of the philosophy of the *Bhāgavata Purāṇa,* which describes the teachings and pastimes of Lord Kṛṣṇa. Jīva Goswāmī is the youngest member of the famous Six Goswāmīs of Vṛndāvana, who dedicated their lives to writing and compiling works that form the theological bedrock of the Gauḍīya Vaiṣṇava tradition.

It is indeed an honor for me to preface this masterly exegesis by Swāmī B. V. Tripurāri of Jīva Goswāmī's *Tattva-sandarbha.* Any scholar who is sensitive to contemporary religious issues and interfaith dialogue will welcome this work that accurately brings forth, for the first time in the English language, the theological presuppositions and arguments of one of India's greatest theistic thinkers, comparable to Moses Maimonides in Judaism, St. Thomas Aquinas in Christianity, or Al Ghazzali in Islam. Moreover, Swāmī Tripurāri has captured the spirit of the original in a way that will be rewarding to the serious reader as well as appealing to the lay person.

Dr. Guy L. Beck
Author of *Sonic Theology: Hinduism and Sacred Sound*
Department of Religious Studies
Loyola University
New Orleans, LA

PREFACE

I embarked upon the writing this *bhāvānuvāda* of Jīva Goswāmī's treatise with a view to dive deeply into the depths of the ocean of Śrī Jīva's philosophy and thus nurture my own *jīva* (atomic soul). As the work developed, I began to feel that it was possible to write about *Tattva-sandarbha* such that those outside of the tradition of Śrī Jīva, that of Gauḍīya Vaiṣṇavism, would find it more accessible. I hope that this edition will do just that. My second hope is that it will provide an English study for the tradition's most recent generations, the bulk of whom do not speak any Indian dialect.

If this edition succeeds in its first aim, to make *Tattva-sandarbha* more accessible, this success should serve to inspire the tradition in a second sense. Should the greater philosophical and spiritually-minded public find Śrī Jīva's philosophy intriguing, they will naturally look to those who represent it for the ecstasy that Śrī Jīva philosophizes about. Śrī Jīva no doubt experienced this ecstasy, as the modern-day practitioners must in order that their practice be considered a success. When the newly interested public looks to the tradition for this success, the tradition's practitioners themselves will be further inspired to take Śrī Jīva's philosophy to heart.

Tattva-sandarbha is more than a philosophical treatise. As an introduction to Śrī Jīva's *Ṣaṭ-sandarbha,* it is a call to all *jīvas* to recognize and rise to their evolutionary potential. If we are to evolve at all, it must be spiritually, for spirit we are, not matter. How high can we fly in the spiritual sky? This is the message of Jīva Goswāmī, heralding the significance of Śrī Caitanya's descent.

The lineage of Śrī Jīva Goswāmī is a very prestigious one. My connection with it is through one of the lineage's most distinguished *ācāryas* (spiritual teachers), Śrīla A. C. Bhaktivedanta Swami Prabhupāda. On several occasions, he expressed his desire to see the *sandarbhas* of Śrī Jīva Goswāmī printed in

English. He left this task for his disciples. If he is pleased by this edition, surely so is Śrī Jīva himself and his deity, Śrī Kṛṣṇa Caitanya, who is none other than Śrī Śrī Rādhā-Kṛṣṇa.

I have been helped in this effort by both scholars and devotees. Among them I would like to express my indebtedness to my disciple Vṛndāraṇya dāsī who edited the manuscript, designed the book and cover, and saw the manuscript through to the finish. Other selfless contributors include Mañjarī Talent and Vicāru dāsa, who acted as editorial consultants; Swāmī B. B. Viṣṇu, who proofread, edited the Sanskrit, and helped compile the index along with Navadvīpa dāsa; Jai Balarāma dāsa, who helped in Sanskrit editing; Aṣṭa-sakhī dāsī, Paurṇamāsī dāsī, and Māyāpur-candra dāsa, who served as proofreaders; Rāgātmikā dāsī, who helped with data entry; and Gaurāṅga-sundara dāsa, who did research. Financial contributors include my friends at Maṇḍala Media: Rāmadāsa and Govardhana dāsa.

Among the many scholars who made suggestions, Jan Brzezinski's unsolicited suggestions were a surprize and proved to be the most comprehensive and helpful. I am also grateful to Guy Beck for his enthusiasm to write the foreword. I sense deeply that I was acquainted with both of them in a previous life. May Śrī Jīva Goswāmī bless them and all the other scholars and devotees who participated.

In *anuccheda* 180 of *Kṛṣṇa-sandarbha,* Jīva Goswāmī begs forgiveness from Śrī Kṛṣṇa for any mistake he may have made in revealing his deity's confidential *līlās*. In closing, I invoke his words with myself as the speaker in relation to this work, replacing Śrī Kṛṣṇa's name with that of Jīva Goswāmī: "May the all-compassionate Śrī Jīva Goswāmī forgive me for even the smallest wrong I may have committed."

INTRODUCTION

This book is about a book that is about a third book. The third book is about a fourth book, and the fourth book is a book about the most voluminous body of literature known to human society. Moreover, all of these books are about the same subject. Let me explain.

This book, a *bhāvānuvāda* of *Tattva-sandarbha,* is the first book. The second and third books are *Tattva-sandarbha* and *Bhāgavata Purāṇa* respectively. *Tattva-sandarbha* is a treatise explaining the significance of the *Bhāgavata Purāṇa,* also known as the *Śrīmad-Bhāgavatam.*

Śrīmad-Bhāgavatam is, among other things, the legendary Vedavyāsa's commentary on his *Vedānta-sūtra* (the fourth book). In the *Vedānta-sutra,* Vyāsa demonstrates the concordance of the Upaniṣads, Purāṇas, Itihāsas and the rest of sacred India's Vedic literature. This body of literature includes the *Mahābhārata,* which consists of one hundred thousand verses and is seven times longer than the Greek epics, *Iliad* and *Odyssey,* combined. The lengthy *Bhagavad-gītā* takes up only one chapter of the *Mahābhārata*. The Vedic literature also includes the *Rāmāyaṇa,* which, along with the *Mahābhārata,* forms the epic portion of the Vedic literature.[1]

This vast body of prose, poetry, philosophy, science, and morality, speaks ultimately of but one subject, the absolute. However, it does so from many angles of vision. Every volume is in one way or another pointing human society in the direction of its highest potential, that of transcending the limits of the human experience itself and thereby coming to know conclusively oneself and the absolute. Unfortunately, most people today are either unaware of this literary heritage or do

---

1. There is no consensus between scholars and practitioners, nor between scholars alone as to which of these literatures is "Vedic." I have cited here the view of the tradition. That all of these literatures constitute the sacred books of the Hindus is accepted by all.

not understand it to be that which it is—a veritable window to the world of pure consciousness.

The Vedic literature is known to Indologists and relatively few other scholars. At the same time, its truth remains unknown to them as well in spite of their study. Even those who accept the guidance of this scriptural legacy—practitioners who know it on its own terms—are often unable to represent the tradition with the dignity it deserves. This brings us to the second focus of this book: Śrī Jīva Goswāmī, a dignified representative of the Vedic tradition and arguably India's most important philosopher. What a shame it is therefore that he, as well as the scriptural heritage he represents, are known to so few today.

Jīva Goswāmī belongs to the Brahmā-Madhva-Gauḍīya Vaiṣṇava *sampradāya,* a spiritual lineage that traces its origins to the dawn of creation. Some five hundred years ago, this lineage was infused with deeper insights about the significance of *Śrīmad-Bhāgavatam* by Śrī Caitanya, a God-intoxicated mendicant said to be an incarnation of God (Śrī Kṛṣṇa) and more. The appellation "Gauḍīya" added to the Brahma-Madhva *sampradāya* represents Śrī Caitanya's influence on the lineage resulting in a branch of its own. This branch, however, has been likened to the tree itself, so nourishing has Śrī Caitanya's influence been to the popularization of Vaiṣṇavism in general. It is fair to say that in this century this particular lineage has indirectly brought more attention to all other branches of Vaiṣṇavism than any direct effort on the part of any of these lineages. Śrī Jīva Goswāmī is the greatest scholar of this Gauḍīya lineage. In *Tattva-sandarbha,* he has made intelligible the metaphysic upon which Gauḍīya Vaiṣṇavism rests.

As for Jīva Goswāmī's spirituality, the tradition acknowledges him to be an eternally liberated soul appearing on earth as an instrument for the will of the divine. The Gauḍīya lineage acknowledges the transcendental cowherder Śrī Kṛṣṇa to be the acme of divine existence. Śrī Jīva is seen as one of Śrī Kṛṣṇa's intimate *gopīs*, or cowherd girl servitors, who associates with him eternally in a spiritual body beyond the constraints of time and space.

In his earthly appearance, Jīva Goswāmī became a mendicant as a mere youth. Hailing from West Bengal, he followed the footsteps of his father and two uncles who, due to the influence of Śrī Caitanya, left household life to embrace the world family and the culture of divine love. As a child, Jīva Goswāmī met Śrī Caitanya. Then, seeing his elders leave prominent government positions and luxurious family lives to follow Śrī Caitanya into a life of devotion, Śrī Jīva inquired from his mother about devotional life and renunciation.

Śrī Jīva's mother did not take the boy seriously and replied that to enter such a life one must shave one's head and adopt the robe of a mendicant. But taking her words seriously, Jīva appeared before her in devotional attire. Not only did he adopt the dress of a monk, he adopted the inner heart of one as well. Shortly thereafter he left home for the spiritual pursuit.

Śrī Jīva met the eternal companion of Śrī Caitanya, the *avadhūta* Nityānanda Prabhu, in Navadvīpa, West Bengal. On Nityānanda's instruction he set out for Vṛndāvana, where his uncles had taken up residence. But first he stopped in Benares. There, under the tutelage of Madhusūdana Vācaspati, he studied all of the systems of Indian philosophy, as well as logic, Sanskrit, and other branches of knowledge.

After his education, he proceeded to Vṛndāvana, where he spent the better part of his life writing about and exemplifying the life of devotion and transcendental love. He wrote many books, his entire contribution consisting of more than four hundred thousand verses, more than that contained in all of the eighteen principal Purāṇas combined.

Jīva Goswāmī's most important literary contribution is a six part treatise, the *Ṣaṭ-sandarbha*. The *Tattva-sandarbha* is the first part. The word *sandarbha* literally means a "stringing together." In this case, it is a stringing together of verses from *Śrīmad-Bhāgavatam* to explain the inner, if not secret, spirituality that *Śrīmad-Bhāgavatam* and thereby all of the Vedic literature is ultimately pointing to. It is a spirituality that Śrī Caitanya embodied and Jīva Goswāmī gave shape to in written form. Śrī Caitanya flowed beautifully yet unapproachably like a great waterfall of love of Godhead. Śrī Jīva made a lake out of his ecstasy in the form of *Ṣaṭ-sandarbha,* such that people of this world could approach that which Śrī Caitanya personified, drink from it, and eventually swim in it, losing themselves in a tide of transcendental love.

To date, there are two translations of *Tattva-sandarbha* in English, one written by a scholar, the other by a practitioner. I am also aware of a third manuscript yet to be published. Each of the two translations in print is lacking in different ways. Stuart Elkman's, while an accurate translation, is often abstruse and difficult to access without considerable background. This is understandable in one sense, for Jīva Goswāmī wrote *Tattva-sandarbha* for an educated class of readers who were familiar with much of that which is unknown to the vast majority today. However, in his study Elkman reaches a rather far-fetched conclusion in which the modern-day followers of Śrī Caitanya and even Jīva Goswāmī himself are cast as having fabricated a philosophy centered around a misconceived notion of that which Śrī Caitanya most probably (in Elkman's mind) stood for. Conveniently, in this study Śrī Caitanya is identified more closely with the tradition of *advaita-vedānta* that Elkman himself identifies with. It is doubtful that anyone today who has made Śrī Caitanya's tradition an object of intellectual interest would agree with Elkman. Although I disagree with Elkman's conclusions, I am nonetheless indebted to him. His translation proved very helpful to me in my study.

The second translation, that of Kuśa Krata dāsa, falls short in terms of its accuracy. In some places it is wildly inaccurate as to what Jīva Goswāmī has written, yet it at the same time does not distort the overall teaching that Śrī Jīva represented. This is an interesting accomplishment. The author has entered the task of translation with a fair understanding of the tradition's devotional conclusions, fitting them in even when the actual translation is inaccurate. While I would hesitate to recommend this edition, it was the first edition of *Tattva-sandarbha* that I encountered in English, and I did derive inspiration from it.

I have not seen the third manuscript yet to be published. I am confident, however, that it will be authoritative. Śrī Satyanārāyaṇa dāsa compiled it in Śrī Vṛndāvana, the holy place most identified with the tradition. He is a practitioner and a scholar as well, and without his help it would have been impossible for me to bring out this edition. His lectures on *Tattva-sandarbha* formed the basis of my study.

This *bhāvānuvāda* has a purpose of its own, and other translations aside, it can only but add to appreciation of Jīva Goswāmī and the spiritual legacy of Śrī Caitanya. A *bhāvānuvāda* seeks to convey the feeling of a treatise. As such, this edition seeks to make *Tattva-sandarbha* as accessible as possible to those lacking a rigorous background in Indian philosophy and Vedānta in particular. Yet I have been cautious not to stray too far from the actual text so that those more familiar with this type of work will not lose interest due to what might be for them unnecessary background information.

Because *Tattva-sandarbha* is an introduction to the entire *Ṣaṭ-sandarbha*, I have in places taken the liberty to expand the seed conceptions found in the text that are developed later in full in the other five *sandarbhas*. I have done this sparingly and with an aim to help the reader understand that which is only implied in the text itself.

The *Tattva-sandarbha* has three formal divisions: *maṅgalācaraṇa, pramāṇa khaṇḍa,* and *prameya khaṇḍa.* In this study, the *pramāṇa* and *prameya khaṇḍas* have been further divided into two chapters each. *Tattva-sandarbha* consists of sixty-three *anucchedas,* or sections. It is written in Sanskrit prose and interspersed with numerous quotations from Vedic literature. I have included every verse that Śrī Jīva quotes along with its citation whenever such reference was available. Several references were not available because the verses quoted are not found in any existing manuscripts. Throughout the book, I have presented the scriptural texts such that they include Jīva Goswāmī's purport. For the most part, the *anucchedas* have not been directly quoted. Doing so would have made the reading more cumbersome as well as a departure from the *bhāvānuvāda* format. All of the *anucchedas,* however, are fully explained. Interspersed throughout is my own inspiration derived from the study itself and twenty-five years of devotional practice within the tradition. The result of all of this is a guided tour of *Tattva-sandarbha* with explanatory notes incorporated into the text, making for a fairly comprehensive study.

I felt it appropriate to write a biographical sketch of Śrī Jīva Goswāmī to further introduce readers to him and thus help them to better enter into the spirit of his work. I have entitled this sketch Śrī Jīva Jīvanāmṛtam, the nectar of the life of Śrī Jīva. There is very little biographical data available to draw from. What I have written is not full of dates and details, rather I have tried to convey the tradition's feeling for Jīva Goswāmī. The sketch was written in sacred Vṛndāvana not far from the *samādhi mandira* of Jīva Goswāmī where his body is entombed. Thus it was written in a devotional atmosphere, with the intention of invoking the presence of Śrī Jīva that he might bless this effort. This sketch constitutes the first chapter.

In the second chapter, Śrī Jīva invokes the blessings of his own spiritual guides in the form of a *maṅgalācaraṇa*. This "auspicious invocation" is typical of classical works of this nature. The chapter informs the reader in brief as to that which will be discussed throughout the book.

The third chapter, which marks the beginning of the *pramāṇa khaṇḍa,* begins the search for valid evidence on the basis of which Śrī Jīva will establish his philosophy. Śrī Jīva dismisses various ways of knowing, all of which rely upon our instruments of perceiving, both senses and reason, which are inherently imperfect. He concludes his search resting with revealed sound represented in sacred literature. Without such revelation, Śrī Jīva contends, absolute knowing is not possible. Having accepted revealed sound, he refines his valid evidence. Śrī Jīva provides an excellent overview of the value of sacred literature, as well as a guide through the jungle of spiritual sounds known as the Upaniṣads and Purāṇas. The reader acquainted with the concepts of *śruti* and *smṛti* will be no doubt taken by the discussion regarding the significance of the *smṛti,* and the Purāṇas in particular, for Śrī Jīva's view is novel and his arguments persuasive.

The entire fourth chapter is dedicated to expounding the virtues of *Śrīmad-Bhāgavatam.* This book contains the philosophy of ecstasy, and out of all of the sacred Sanskrit texts, Jīva Goswāmī argues convincingly that it is the essence. Citing numerous quotations from a wide variety of sacred literature, as well as the opinions of many renowned scholars, Śrī Jīva floods us with his oceanic understanding of that literature which is sacred. After establishing his ultimate means of knowing, hearing from *Śrīmad-Bhāgavatam,* Śrī Jīva closes his *pramāṇa khaṇḍa* with an explanation of how he will proceed in the *prameya khaṇḍa.*

The fifth chapter is dedicated to explaining the key to understanding the entirety of India's sacred texts: examining the spiritual trance of Vyāsa. Vyāsa is considered the editor-in-chief of all of the Vedic literature. He entered into *samādhi* on the order of his guru, and it is this *samādhi* that gave rise to *Śrīmad-Bhāgavatam*. The *Bhāgavatam* is thus the *samādhi-bhāṣya*, or language of spiritual trance, spoken by Vyāsa in his mature realization. Through Śrī Jīva's analysis, the logic of and scriptural basis for the monistic conception of ultimate reality is brought under scrutiny. Śrī Jīva concludes that monism, exclusive nonduality, is fraught with inconsistencies, as is a metaphysic of exclusive duality. It is in this section that he presents his metaphysic of inconceivable simultaneous oneness and difference (*acintya-bhedābheda*) and asserts the superiority of love over knowledge, or more precisely, the view that love is the ultimate knowledge and means of knowing.

The final chapter explores the nature of nondual consciousness further, and draws our attention to what the *Bhāgavatam* calls the ultimate shelter. This chapter does so first by analyzing the individual atomic particle of consciousness, the soul. In this analysis, Śrī Jīva concludes that the ultimate shelter is Śrī Kṛṣṇa. Next Śrī Jīva reaches the same conclusion as to the nature of ultimate nondual consciousness through analyzing the *Bhāgavatam*'s discussion of universal influences, i.e., creation, annihilation, *karma*, etc. In the course of this twofold analysis, Buddhism's advocacy of voidism is discussed. Śrī Jīva offers us evidence based on our everyday experience as to the nature of our soul and its far reaching potential for love. In conclusion, the ultimate shelter in a Vedānta of aesthetics is revealed.

I hope that this study will be useful by way of further introducing Jīva Goswāmī to the world, as well as shedding light on the significance of the scriptural heritage of human society. *Tattva-sandarbha* may pleasantly surprise many only somewhat acquainted with Vedānta philosophy, for it presents the less-well-known inner heart of the head of Vedānta. It may also unsettle those who have settled themselves into the notion of *advaita-vedānta,* for *Tattva-sandarbha* is unsympathetic to this doctrine, as it is to its Buddhist counterpart. *Tattva-sandharba* reveals a divine doctrine of love grounded firmly in philosophy. Thus it serves to bridge the gap between the polar opposites of Eastern and Western religious tradition, the West largely represented by a doctrine of love and grace, the East by an ontology of consciousness.

Although in one sense an obscure text of interest to a sect of specialized practitioners and the few trained in the field of Indian philosophy, *Tattva-sandarbha* has a broader appeal as well. This is not to say that it is in any way easy reading for the general public. It is not. It is full of technical terms difficult to define in English, and it is at heart deeply philosophical. Yet it offers as a reward to those who pay close attention to its sermon a well reasoned metaphysic based upon revealed knowledge. It is a metaphysic that answers with new light the time-worn debate of our oneness with the absolute (non-dualism) versus our difference from it (dualism). Out of this metaphysic, realization of the ultimate pursuit of all living beings can logically arise.

All life pursues its own happiness, and in human life we can understand that it is love from which the greatest happiness is derived. *Tattva-sandarbha* offers a foundation upon which a life of love can be built such that it will never topple under the influence of time. It tells of the ultimate object of love, Śrī Kṛṣṇa, in the language of one who loves him. Hearing about Kṛṣṇa from Jīva Goswāmī in his *Tattva-sandarbha,* and ultimately his entire *Ṣaṭ-sandarbha,* many will conclude that they too have found, at least in theory, their loving propensity's repose in eternity.

List of Abbreviations:

Ag. P.	*Agni Purāṇa*
Bg.	*Bhagavad-gītā*
Brs.	*Bhakti-rasāmṛta-sindhu*
Bṛ. U.	*Bṛhad-āraṇyaka Upaniṣad*
CB.	*Caitanya Bhāgavata*
Cc. Ādi	*Caitanya-caritāmṛta Ādi-līlā*
Cc. Madhya	*Caitanya-caritāmṛta Madhya-līlā*
Cc. Antya	*Caitanya-caritāmṛta Antya-līlā*
Ch. U.	*Chāndogya Upaniṣad*
G. P.	*Garuḍa Purāṇa*
Ma. P.	*Matsya Purāṇa*
M. Bh.	*Mahābhārata*
N. P.	*Nārada Purāṇa*
Pa. P.	*Padma Purāṇa*
SB.	*Śrīmad-Bhāgavatam*
Śi. P.	*Śiva Purāṇa*
Sk. P.	*Skanda Purāṇa*
Tai. U.	*Taittirīya Upaniṣad*
Vā. P.	*Vāyu Purāṇa*
Vd. P.	*Viṣṇu-dharmottara Purāṇa*
Vi. P.	*Viṣṇu Purāṇa*
Vs.	*Vedānta-sūtra*

1

"That ground of being, while firm, is moving. Its movements, however, are not cause for concern for those who stand upon it. This is so because, to begin with, we are that ground. But in Śrī Jīva's eyes there is much more to tell that makes for a Vedānta of aesthetics."

Śrī Jīva Jīvanāmṛtam

The principal source materials from which to gather biographical information on Jīva Goswāmī are *Bhakti-ratnākara* and *Prema-vilāsa*. Both of these books chronicle events concerning the lives of Śrī Caitanya and his followers. *Prema-vilāsa* was written first, in the mid-16th century. *Bhakti-ratnākara* was written a century later. *Prema-vilāsa* was authored by Nityānanda dāsa, a resident of Bengal. Narahari Cakravartī, who spent the better part of his life in Vṛndāvana, wrote *Bhakti-ratnākara*.

Scholars have questioned the accuracy of *Prema-vilāsa*,[1] and although practitioners accept both as authoritative, they seem to favor the details of accounts found in *Bhakti-ratnākara*. Time and distance inevitably distort accounts of events. These two books were written a century apart, one in Bengal and the other most probably hundreds of miles away in Vṛndāvana. The details of events vary considerably in these two texts, yet they both accurately represent the *bhāva*, or ecstasy, of the events in question. Other than these two sources, the *Caitanya-caritāmṛta* also says a few words about Jīva Goswāmī, and Jīva Goswāmī sights his own geneology in his *Laghu-vaiṣṇava-toṣaṇī.*

From the tradition's point of view, Jīva Goswāmī's life history is the unfolding of his spirituality from an unmanifest state to a manifest state within human society. Śrī Jīva only appears

1. De, Sushil Kumar. *Early History of the Vaiṣṇava Faith and Movement in Bengal* (Calcutta: Firma K.L. Mukhopadhyay, 1961), p.66.

to "become" enlightened, and through a mystic arrangement, he actually feels as though at one time he was not. He is considered to be internally possessed of the transcendental emotions *(bhāva)* of a female lover (*gopī*) of the divine Kṛṣṇa. Internally, he experienced Kṛṣṇa's celestial realm. Externally, he appeared as a practioner of extreme renunciation and devotion. His life thus instructs us that the highest love of Kṛṣṇa, often portrayed as an unmarried girl's love for a young man, has little if anything in common with the affairs of unmarried young couples of this world. Whereas love of Kṛṣṇa is free from selfish desire, mundane love is based upon it.

We know that Jīva Goswāmī was the son of Vallabha. His ancestry was South Indian. Hailing from Karnataka, they were Sārasvata *brāhmaṇas.* He was born in Rāmakeli, West Bengal in 1513 C.E. Muslims ruled West Bengal at the time of Śrī Jīva's appearance, and it came to pass that his father and two uncles were employed by the governor, Nawab Hussain Shah. They held positions with influence similar to that of cabinet members of a president. Well-educated, cultured, pious, and wealthy, they led comfortable lives.

Although at that time there was relatively peaceful coexistence in Bengal between the Hindus and Muslims, when the three brothers accepted employment in the Muslim government, they became social outcasts of the Hindu religious society. They were accepted, however, and in no small measure, by Śrī Caitanya, an *avatāra* and God-intoxicated devotee at once, as well as a religious and social reformer. By that time, Śrī Caitanya had created quite a stir in West Bengal and Jagannātha Purī. Taking to the streets with cymbals and drums, he alienated both orthodox Muslims and Hindus, but collected a mass of followers from the ranks of each sect. His religion: passionate love of God. His method: chanting the names of God. While disturbing those entrenched in the formalities of a particular religious conceptual framework, he afforded those who followed him spiritual experience beyond religious formalities. Among the latter were Śrī Jīva's father and uncles, whom he would eventually follow.

Śrī Jīva's father and uncles had heard of Śrī Caitanya and corresponded with him. When Śrī Caitanya returned to Bengal from Puri, the news of his conversions there were rippling throughout India. He visited the home of these three Sārasvata *brāhmaṇas,* the home in which Śrī Jīva was a tender youth. What were the names of Śrī Jīva's uncles? We know only what names they received from Śrī Caitanya during this visit, and Jīva, having received this name subsequently from one of his uncles, is known only as such. Śrī Caitanya named Śrī Jīva's two uncles Sanātana and Rūpa and changed his father's name to Anupama. From this we can conclude that the three became Śrī Caitanya's disciples.

Shortly after being accepted by Śrī Caitanya, the brothers left family life and entered the life of devotion and renunciation, leaving Śrī Jīva behind. Yet they left with Śrī Jīva the spirit of their vision. The boy took note of how his elders left a life of material opulence for one ostensibly of begging. They left aristocratic status and wandered the breadth of India barefoot, clad only in loincloths, with water pots and rosaries as their only possessions. Sometimes they ate, more often they went without. Their renunciation, however, was merely a by-product of their love-intoxicated state. They fasted not so much as a conscious austerity, but as a result of their absorption in divine love—they *forgot* to eat and to sleep as well. Mendicants they appeared to be, but ordinary mendicants they were not.

Government employment may have ostracized them from the religious Hindu community, but it did not make them poor. They enjoyed considerable wealth in govenment service. Yet it was apparent to the young Jīva that they had not left religion for money, nor in joining Śrī Caitanya, money for mere religion. Theirs was a spiritual vision that transcended not only *dharma* (religion) and *artha* (wealth), but *kāma* (material enjoyment) and even *mokṣa* (liberation). This was the ideal of Śrī Caitanya: Kṛṣṇa *prema*, passionate love of God that belittles even salvation from the cycle birth and death (*saṁsāra*). Śrī Jīva glimpsed the effects of this love in Śrī Caitanya and its influence that overflowed onto his elders. They embraced the life of devotion after meeting merely once with Śrī Caitanya, his love-intoxicated state was so contagious. With a penetrating eye of introspection, Śrī Jīva analyzed the significance of his father and uncles' departure from home and chose to follow in their footsteps. Later, with the same penetrating vision, his eyes anointed with the salve of love (*prema*), he would write extensively on the philosophy of the love and ecstasy that Śrī Caitanya embodied.

Śrī Jīva was more than a handsome youth. His bodily features were those of a *mahā-puruṣa,* or great personality (by spiritual standards). According to the *Sāmudrika,* "There are thirty-two bodily symptoms of a great personality: five of his bodily parts are large, five fine, seven reddish, six raised, three small, three broad, and three grave."[2]

He was young when he left home. While still an adolescent, he questioned his mother about the life of renunciation and devotion. His mother dismissed his inquiry as no more than childhood infatuation with a life of material hardship and spiritual pursuit. Śrī Jīva surprised her by appearing before her in mendicant dress, having learned from her that such attire was requisite. More so she must have been astonished when

---

2. *pañca-dīrghaḥ pañca-sūkṣmaḥ/*
sapta-raktaḥ ṣaḍ-unnataḥ//
tri-hrasva-pṛthu-gambhiro/
dvātriṁśal-lakṣaṇo mahān// (Sāmudrika)

his apparent youthful infatuation for the dress of devotion, a mere monk's robe and shaven head, proved to be mature participation in spiritual emotion.

After leaving home, Śrī Jīva went to Navadwīp of West Bengal. It was here that Śrī Caitanya had appeared. In Navadwīp, then a seat of learning, Śrī Caitanya began his movement. Shortly after he had begun to manifest his ecstasy, he was joined by Prabhu Nityānanda, who is considered to be his "other self." Śrī Jīva met Nityānanda and was personally instructed by him in the esoteric doctrines of what would become known (chiefly through the writing of Jīva Goswāmī and his uncles) as Gauḍīya Vaiṣṇavism.

On the advice of Nityānanda, Śrī Jīva traveled from Navadwīp to Benares enroute to Vṛndāvana. There he studied under the tutelage of the famous Madhusūdana Vācaspati (not to be confused with Madhusūdana Sāraswatī, an Advaitin). Madhusūdana Vācaspati was related to the renowned Sārvabhauma Bhaṭṭācārya. He must have learned Vedānta from Sārvabhauma after the Bhaṭṭācārya himself learned Vedānta from Śrī Caitanya in the midst of the Bhaṭṭācārya's dramatic conversion.[3] Benares was immersed in an atmosphere of learning. There Śrī Jīva learned Vedānta and numerous other branches of knowledge in a very short time. It is apparent from his books that he was a good student, well versed in the philosophies of Vaiśeṣika, Nyāya, Sāṅkya, Yoga, Pūrva-mīmāṁsā, and Uttara-mīmāṁsā. This comprehensive knowledge is a characteristic of a *mahā-bhāgavata*, or superlative devotee.[4]

---

3. See *Caitanya-caritamṛtā, Madhya-līlā,* chapter six for an account of this event.

4. *śāstre yuktau ca nipuṇah sarvathā dṛdhaniścayah/*
prauḍhaśraddho 'dhikārī yah sa baktāvuttamo matah// (Brs. 2.17)

From Benares, he continued on to Vṛndāvana. By the time he arrived there his father had died prematurely. In Vṛndāvana, he took shelter of his uncles, Rūpa and Sanātana Goswāmīs, accepting spiritual initiation from Śrī Rūpa. Presumably it was from Śrī Rūpa that Jīva Goswāmī received the name Jīva, upon being initiated into the Kṛṣṇa *mantra*. The title Goswāmī is not hereditary, rather it is conferred upon one who has conquered over his mind and senses.

Śrī Rūpa, Sanātana, and Jīva were three of those known as the Six Goswāmīs. Together with these three lived Gopala Bhaṭṭa, Raghunātha Bhaṭṭa, and Raghunātha dāsa Goswāmīs. Amongst them, Śrī Jīva was the youngest and most prolific. He was a perfect disciple of Rūpa Goswāmī and certainly qualified to initiate others, yet it is questionable as to whether or not he personally initiated any disciples, although many considered themselves his disciples and he appears to have addressed some devotees as such.

Śrī Rūpa and Sanātana did not accept disciples, Śrī Jīva their nephew a lone exception. The reason for this was not their lack of qualification. It seems that the socioreligious climate of the times was respected by the Goswāmīs. They reformed the society yet remained within existing socioreligious parameters, having assessed that which they had to contend with in order to successfully establish an organized systematic school of thought (*sampradāya*) centered around the ecstasy of Śrī Caitanya. Thus for some time students desiring initiation were regularly referred to Gopala Bhaṭṭa Goswāmī, who hailed from a prestigious South Indian *brahmāṇa* family. If Śrī Jīva did not personally initiate, it was in pursuance of this strategy. The *sampradāya*'s next generation appears to have been less concerned with disturbing the socioreligious climate. By this time the *sampradāya* was better established, with a literary legacy of considerable size and temples built with the patronage of the

Rājās. Two of the *sampradāya*'s leading members, Narottama dāsa and Śyāmānanda, were not from *brāhmaṇa* families, and Śyāmānanda from the lowest caste *(śūdra)*, yet they did initiate widely while Śrī Jīva was still alive. Thus the policy of Śrī Rūpa and Sanātana, one probably followed by Śrī Jīva as well, was based not upon devotional conclusions of the *sampradāya*,[5] but upon consideration of the social climate of the day, as well as the humility of the three Goswāmīs.

Śrī Jīva devotedly served his seniors and continued to live in Vṛndāvana, eventually becoming the spiritual guide for all of the followers of Śrī Caitanya until the end of the sixteenth century. He was the ultimate authority in all esoteric and practical issues concerning the culture of spiritual love. After the departure of Śrī Rūpa and Sanātana, he served the community in this capacity even in the presence of others senior to himself.

His life in Vṛndāvana was that of extreme renunciation and devotion. He wore only the traditional loincloth and accepted many hardships in the service of the absolute. At the same time, he was intimately involved in excavating the places of Kṛṣṇa's pastimes and building temples for the deities of Rādhā-Kṛṣṇa and Śrī Caitanya. Fabulous temples of architectural wonder were arranged for the deities, yet Śrī Jīva himself slept beneath the trees. The Govindajī Mandir in particular is an extraordinary blend of architectural styles that reflects the prominent religious influences of the time, built as a monument to the deity that in Śrī Jīva's mind represented transcendence of religious convention. That Śrī Jīva was intimately involved in its fourteen

5. In Gauḍīya Vaiṣṇavism, qualification for acting as an initiating guru does not include birth in a *brahmāṇa* family. Although Rūpa and Sanātana were born in *brahmāṇa* families, their brahminical status was brought into question due to their association with the Muslim contingent.

years of construction is evidenced by his *Govinda mandir-aṣṭakam,* an eight verse tribute to this temple and its patrons.

At one point, the powerful emperor Akbar came to Vṛndāvana with the hope of meeting this extraordinary ascetic. Akbar was a man of enormous wealth and influence, yet he was humbled to hear of the spirituality of Śrī Jīva and his elders. He patronized Śrī Jīva to the extent of removing obstacles that impeded the development of Vṛndāvana by the Rājās, who subscribed to the religion of love explained by and embodied in Jīva Goswāmī.

More than twenty-five books are attributed to Śrī Jīva. The list of these twenty-five found in *Bhakti-ratnākara* ends with "etcetera." *Caitanya-caritāmṛtā* credits him with writing more than four hundred thousand verses. If this is accurate, it makes Śrī Jīva second only to Vyāsa in authoring Sanskrit verses concerning the nature of the absolute truth. The tradition holds that whatever he wrote was first fully manifest in his mind and once he committed a thought to writing he never changed it.

Of all of his books, *Ṣaṭ-sandarbha* is the most famous. In this sixfold treatise, he manifests his opulence of superhuman command over the enormous body of India's sacred Vedic and supplementary Vedic literature. From the Vedas, Upaniṣads, Purāṇas, Itihāsas, and the epic *Mahābhārata* to the Tantras and Āgamas, there seems not a page unturned by Śrī Jīva. His comprehension of their contents makes it appear almost as though he wrote them himself. Studying *Ṣaṭ-sandarbha,* one is held spellbound by this opulence alone, dumbfounded by Śrī Jīva's scriptural command, what to speak of the realization he so kindly shares therein. *Ṣaṭ-sandarbha* serves as the philosophical foundation for the ecstasy and love that Śrī Caitanya embodied and Śrī Jīva experienced so deeply.

In *Ṣaṭ-sandarbha,* Śrī Jīva argues persuasively that the ecstasy of Śrī Caitanya is that which the entirety of Vedic India's vast sacred literary heritage is pointing to. To his arguments and conclusions there are no doubt counterarguments, as all logic is inconclusive and scripture lends to innumerable interpretations. Yet it is the charm of his conclusions—Kṛṣṇa *līlā*—that is difficult to match. A more endearing conception of the absolute, reasonably and eloquently articulated and well supported by a sacred literary heritage is, if in existence, yet to express itself.

Śrī Jīva Goswāmī is one of the greatest religious philosophers in history. His spiritual lifestyle is instructive to us as well. It would be difficult to find a person as intelligent as Śrī Jīva, who at the same time thought so little of intelligence. He used his intellect to argue on behalf of the eternal soul, and more, its emotional potential in transcendence. While doing so, his life's example teaches us that there is indeed firm ground to stand on beneath the soft surface of the ground of our material experience. That ground of being, while firm, is moving. Its movements, however, are not cause for concern for those who stand upon it. This is so because, to begin with, we are that ground. But in Śrī Jīva's eyes there is more to tell, much more that makes for a Vedānta of aesthetics. Realizing ourselves to be consciousness is to stand at the door of transcendence. Śrī Jīva opens the door to a life in transcendence culminating in the circular love dance (*rasa*) of Śrī Śrī Rādhā-Kṛṣṇa, synonymous with the ecstatic chanting and dancing of Śrī Caitanya.

On the ground of consciousness, Śrī Jīva has crafted a deity out of the same material, his chisel the *Bhāgavata Purāṇa*. His deity is dark and handsome and never alone, standing eternally in the embrace of his feminine counterwhole. He rules over all by the force of affection and beauty. He is a deity more human than transcendent, more transcendent than human. Śrī Jīva has built a temple for this deity, and that too is made out of the ground of being, pure nondual consciousness. It is spacious and inviting in the most charming sense. Call this deity Kṛṣṇa, his feminine counterwhole Rādhā, and be done with a life of illusory happiness and empty promises of love. Calling their names, Śrī Jīva turned his back on this illusory world to tell us of another, which, as it turns out, is no more than this world when viewed through eyes anointed with divine love.

The world influenced by Western philosophy, to which this edition of his work is presented, will have to wrangle with what may appear to be foreign concepts and language (Sanskrit) to penetrate Śrī Jīva's mind and heart. Yet what modern readers will find is a vision not so foreign after all. In this vision lies the full potential of humanity—to turn from the senses' beastly call of the wild to the language of logic, and from the language of logic to the life of eternal love.

Maṅgalācaraṇa

2

"Existence need not be conscious, yet a conscious reality requires existence. Conscious existence need not be joyful, but if reality is joyful, it must exist and be conscious. Such is Kṛṣṇa: existence, consciousness, and joy—brahmeti paramātmeti bhagavān ity śabdyate."

Invoking Auspiciousness

Śrī Jīva Goswāmī begins his *Tattva-sandarbha* with the traditional *maṅgalācaraṇa,* invoking auspiciousness. A *maṅgalācaraṇa* generally consists of three elements: *namaskāra* (offering obeisances), *vastu-nirdeśa* (identifying the subject of the book), and *āśīrvāda* (offering or seeking blessings). *Maṅgalācaraṇa* traditionally also includes *anubandhas,* indispensable elements of Vedānta, that give the reader a brief acquaintance with the book. Jīva Goswāmī introduces three *anubandhas*: *sambandha* (knowledge of relationship), *abhidheya* (the means of attainment), and *prayojana* (the goal to be realized). Aside from this, Śrī Jīva also mentions the qualifications of the reader *(adhikāra).*

Śrī Jīva's *maṅgalācaraṇa* consists of the first eight *anucchedas* (sections) of his treatise. As *Tattva-sandarbha* begins with an introductory invocation in which the book's content is found in seed, similarly the entire *Tattva-sandarbha* is in one sense an introduction itself. It contains in seed Śrī Jīva's entire treatise consisting of six essays commonly known as *Ṣaṭ-sandarbha.*

In the first *anuccheda,* Śrī Jīva cites an important verse from *Śrīmad-Bhāgavatam,* which is considered to be the *vastu-nirdeśa* verse of his treatise. In this verse the subject of the treatise is identified. "In Kali-yuga, those who possess very fine theistic intelligence *(su-medhasaḥ)* worship Śrī Kṛṣṇa *(kṛṣṇa-varṇaṁ)* who has appeared in disguise *(tviṣākṛṣṇaṁ)* as Śrī Kṛṣṇa Caitanya. They do so through congregational chanting of the name of God *(yajñaiḥ saṅkīrtana-prāyaiḥ),* as Śrī Caitanya himself, with his arms raised in surrender as his only weapons (*sāṅgopāṅgāstra-pārṣadam*), has taught along with his eternal associates and expansions."[1]

By citing this verse at the outset, Jīva Goswāmī indicates that Śrī Caitanya is the subject of *Tattva-sandarbha (vastu-nirdeśa)*. Because *Tattva-sandarbha* is also a treatise that explains the *Śrīmad-Bhāgavatam*, it is indicated herein that the *Bhāgavatam* is ultimately about that which Śrī Caitanya embodies. This opening verse has been explained in various ways, thus Śrī Jīva has sought to define and thus fix its meaning in *anuccheda* two[2] wherein he offers his obeisances to his deity *(namaskāra)*.

Jīva Goswāmī follows the lead of Śrī Sanātana Goswāmī in explaining this verse. It was Sanātana Goswāmī, the eldest of the legendary Six Goswāmīs of Vṛndāvana, who first explained the verse as a reference to Śrī Caitanya. As we shall see, this explanation is pivotal to the entire Gauḍīya Vaiṣṇava theology. It identifies the deity of the Gauḍīyas (Śrī Caitanya) as God, a God who has come with his associates to teach the worship of himself (Śrī Kṛṣṇa), while at the same time hiding the fact that he is God. Thus although Sanātana Goswāmī's explanation is one that draws out a hidden meaning, it fits with the overall theory of the Gauḍīyas—that in the Kali-yuga God incarnates in a hidden manner, disguised as a devotee to teach the worship of himself.

The context in which this verse of the *Bhāgavatam* is found lends well to Sanātana Goswāmī's interpretation. In the eleventh canto of the *Bhāgavatam*, Karabhājana Muni is explaining

---

1. *kṛṣṇa-varṇaṁ tviṣākṛṣṇaṁ sāṅgopāṅgāstra-pārṣadam/*
yajñaiḥ saṅkīrtana-prāyair yajanti hi su-medhasaḥ// (SB. 11.5.32)

2. Baladeva Vidyābhūṣaṇa has explained this second *anuccheda* in this way in his commentary on *Tattva-sandarbha*. Kṛṣṇadāsa Kavirāja Goswāmī has also used it in Cc. Ādi 3.79–80 in the same way.

the *avatāras* of the four cosmic time cycles, or *yugas*, to King Nimi. Karabhājana Muni briefly describes the characteristics of the *yuga-avatāras*. He then explains the principal, and thus most efficacious, means of worship for each *yuga*, as taught by these millennia incarnations. After describing the first three *yugas*, Satya, Tretā, and Dvāpara, Karabhājana comes to the present *yuga* cycle, Kali-yuga. It is here that we find this verse.

As mentioned, other commentators have not revealed that this verse indicates Śrī Caitanya. Even Śrīdhara Swāmī's *Bhāgavatam* commentary, *Bhāvārtha-dīpikā,* which Śrī Caitanya so much respected,[3] does not point to Śrī Caitanya.[4] Yet in the eyes of the Gauḍīyas, this, rather than opposing their conclusions, indirectly lends support. This is so because the Gauḍīyas contend that the prerogative to reveal the *yuga-avatāra,* so special as he is in this particular Kali-yuga, lies with the *avatāra* himself and his subsequent followers. Thus even Vyāsadeva wrote about Śrī Caitanya in a covert way out of deference to Kṛṣṇa's own desire to remain hidden until his own direct followers proclaim his appearance to the world after his descent.

In the verse, the word *varṇam* has several meanings, all of which fit well with the contention that the verse describes Śrī Caitanya. *Varṇa* means syllable, class, and color. It can also

---

3. *śrīdharera anugata ye kare likhana/*
saba loka mānya kari' karibe grahaṇa//

"One who comments on *Śrīmad-Bhāgavatam* following Śrīdhara will be honored and accepted by all." (Cc. Antya 7.135)

4. Śrīdhara Swāmī states, *indranīla-maṇivad ujjvalam,* "[Kṛṣṇa is] dark like a sapphire, yet shines brightly." He thus explains the contradiction in this verse that the *avatāra* under discussion is black, yet not black. He also offers an alternative to *tviṣakṛṣṇaṁ* derived by not joining the *sandhi (tviṣākṛṣṇam):* "The wise worship Kṛṣṇa, who is blackish."

mean *varṇayati,* to describe.[5] "*Kṛṣṇa-varṇam*" therefore primarily indicates he whose name contains the syllables *kṛ* and *ṣṇa*. Śrī Caitanya's name after accepting the renounced order *(sannyāsa)* became Śrī Kṛṣṇa Caitanya, and he is known to have constantly uttered the holy name of Kṛṣṇa. He is, according to Jīva Goswāmī, in the category of God *(svāṁśa)* and not that of the living entities *(vibhinnāṁśa)*. Yet such is true of all *yuga-avatāras;* therefore, more precisely *kṛṣṇa varṇaṁ* indicates that this *avatāra* is of the class of Kṛṣṇa, that is, he is not an *avatāra* of Viṣṇu.[6] He is Kṛṣṇa (blackish), yet in this incarnation he does not appear blackish *(tviṣākṛṣṇa)* to the general public. Śrī Jīva notes, however, that Śrī Caitanya did appear in dark complexion on rare occasions such as when he revealed himself to Rāmānanda Rāya.[7] Thus the color of his soul within is black *(antaḥ kṛṣṇaṁ)*, yet he has accepted the disposition of his devotee to hide himself and is thus bearing an outward complexion that is golden *(bahir gauraṁ)*.[8]

Vital to this explanation is the well-known *Bhāgavatam* verse in which the four *yuga-avatāras* are discussed in terms of their complexions. "Your son appears in every *yuga* and has assumed

---

5. M. Monier-Williams, *Sanskrit English Dictionary* (New Delhi: Munshiram Manoharlal Publishers Pvt. Ltd., 1988), p. 1143.

6. Gauḍīya Vaiṣṇavas differentiate between Godhead and his expansions and incarnations (*svaṁsa)* and the *jīva* souls *(vibhinnāṁśa)* and further differentiate Kṛṣṇa from all other *avatāras* (*kṛṣṇas tu bhagavān svayam).*

7. *pahile dekhiluṅ tomāra sannyāsi-svarūpa/*
ebe tomā dekhi muñi śyāma-gopa-rūpa//

"At first I (Ramānanda) saw you in the form of a *sannyāsi,* but now I see you in a dark form (Śyāmasundara) as the cowherd boy." (Cc. Madhya 8.268)

8. Gauḍīya Vaiṣṇavas consider Kṛṣṇa's blackish color and Śrī Rādhā's golden color to correspond with their dispositions *(bhāvas)*. Śrī Caitanya being Kṛṣṇa with the disposition of Rādhā is thus of golden complexion.

previously three different colors—white, red, and golden. Now he is appearing in a blackish color."[9] In this verse, Gargamuni, Kṛṣṇa's family priest, is conducting the traditional name-giving ceremony. He mentions that Kṛṣṇa appeared in other millennia (other than the Dvāpara-yuga), and that he bore white, red, and golden complexions. Because he now had a blackish complexion, he was to be called Kṛṣṇa (black). As the *avatāras* of the Satya and Tretā *yugas* are white and red respectively, this verse confirms that the Kali-yuga-*avatāra* is golden. Although he is the *yuga-avatāra* of the Kali-yuga, he is not merely a *yuga-avatāra* of golden *(pīta)* complexion, but he is that same black Kṛṣṇa *(avatārī)* appearing in a golden complexion.

The Gauḍīyas maintain that Kṛṣṇa is the very source of all *avatāras*[10] yet occasionally appears in the place of the *yuga-avatāra* for a special purpose. This special purpose is relative to his own inner pleasure, more so than to the plight of the bound souls whose benefit is the direct concern of the *yuga-avatāra.* Through Śrī Caitanya, Kṛṣṇa himself, the bound souls are doubly blessed. Not only do they learn the *yuga-dharma,* they are benedicted with the special compensation of Kṛṣṇa *prema.* Through the recommended *dharma* of the *yuga,* they are afforded the special opportunity to attain the highest spiritual love of Kṛṣṇa (Kṛṣṇa *prema)* and enter into the inner realm of Kṛṣṇa.[11]

---

9. *āsan varṇās trayo hy asya gṛhṇato 'nuyugaṁ tanuḥ/*
śuklo raktas tathā pīta idānīṁ kṛṣṇatāṁ gataḥ// (SB. 10.8.13)

10. See Cc. Ādi 2 for a detailed discussion as to how the Gauḍīyas understand that Śrī Kṛṣṇa is *svayam bhagavān* and that Śrī Caitanya is not merely an *avatāra* of Śrī Kṛṣṇa but *svayam bhagavān* himself. The rarity of this appearance is further discussed in Cc. Ādi 3.6–10. That Śrī Kṛṣṇa is *svayam bhagavān* is also dealt with exhaustively in Jīva Goswāmī's *Kṛṣṇa-sandarbha.*

11. See Cc. Ādi 3 for an explanation of the inner (to bestow *mādhurya-prema*) and outer (to promote the *yuga-dharma)* reasons for Śrī Caitanya's descent.

In the Gauḍīya understanding we find a God who takes the role of searching himself out. As it is particular to the human species to search out its origins, so the supreme deity as Śrī Caitanya searches himself out in the guise of a human being. Thus the absolute teaches and experiences the self-exploration that is crucial to human existence. The search of Śrī Caitanya is *bhakti,* devotion, within which self-introspection finds its deepest expression. *Bhakti* churned into *prema,* transcendental love, reveals the optimum about the nature of the absolute. Thus love itself is the goal of life, even more so than is Kṛṣṇa—love's ultimate object. Since that love is personified as Śrī Rādhā, devotion to her is the zenith of transcendental achievement for the Gauḍīyas. This is the hidden message of the *Bhāgavatam.* It is this message that the combined form of Rādhā-Kṛṣṇa appearing as Śrī Caitanya has come to relish and distribute to all souls.

More so than Śrī Kṛṣṇa's humanlike appearance, or *nara-līlā,* Śrī Caitanya's teaching pastime, *ācārya-līlā,* comes close to humanity. Śrī Caitanya teaches us in the garb of a devotee, while Kṛṣṇa's descent, although humanlike, is difficult to understand and filled with uncommon acts. Yet although Śrī Caitanya in this sense comes closer to humanity, helping us in our plight, his inner purpose is more removed from humanity. This is so because he is in actuality Kṛṣṇa in his most introspective mood: Kṛṣṇa in search of his own significance. Thus Śrī Caitanya's teaching both makes Kṛṣṇa *līlā* accessible and allows the devoted to explore the most introspective moments of the absolute.[12] Śrī Caitanya is Kṛṣṇa giving himself most completely.

It has become fashionable for disciples to proclaim their gurus to be Kṛṣṇa. Most frequently this occurs in monistic tra-

---

12. See Cc. Ādi 4 for an detailed explanation of Kṛṣṇa's introspection and the threefold inner cause of his descent as Śrī Caitanya.

ditions, wherein it is thought that the infinitesimal *jīva* soul is itself Godhead. According to this tradition, the *jīva,* or individual soul, is Brahman, undifferentiated consciousness, but has yet to realize it. When the *jīvas* are enlightened, they realize that the concepts of the *jīva* and the world are false. This tradition therefore lends to identifying one's guru, the realized soul, with Godhead in every respect.

The Gauḍīyas have proclaimed in a different way that their *sampradāya guru* is God.[13] The extent to which the Gauḍīyas have gone to support their contention far exceeds that of others who have in one way or another sought to identify their *ācārya* with Kṛṣṇa. Logic and scripture, over which the Gauḍīya *ācāryas* demonstrate remarkable command, along with the high states of devotion they themselves have attained, compels one to take their proclamation seriously.[14]

For Jīva Goswāmī, the truth of Śrī Caitanya's descent is the essence of *Śrīmad-Bhāgavatam*. Thus most appropriately Śrī Jīva has opened his treatise on the nature of truth as revealed in *Śrīmad-Bhāgavatam* with a verse from the *Bhāgavatam* in which Śrī Caitanya's glory is heralded, following it in his second *anuccheda* with his own verse, which explains the meaning of the first while offering obeisances unto his deity.

In *anuccheda* three, Śrī Jīva seeks the blessings *(āśīrvāda)* of Śrīla Rūpa and Sanātana Goswāmīs, the two leaders of the leg-

---

13. In the opening remarks of *Ṣaṭ Sandarbha,* Śrī Jīva has described Śrī Caitanya thus, "the presiding deity of the thousands of his *sampradāya.*"

14. The *Gaura-gaṇoddeśa-dīpikā* of Kavikarṇapūra is noteworthy in this connection. It describes all of the eternal associates of Śrī Kṛṣṇa in terms of their appearances in the *līlās* of Śrī Caitanya. Also in both CB. and Cc. many striking parallels are brought out in terms of the behavior and temperament of individuals in Caitanya *līlā* and their postulated counterroles in Kṛṣṇa *līlā*. Moreover, the *līlās* themselves often show a striking correspondence.

endary Six Goswāmīs, *jayatāṁ mathurā bhūmau śrīla-rūpa-sanātanau.* These two were the uncles of Jīva Goswāmī, and Rūpa Goswāmī his initiating spiritual master as well. Under their direction, Jīva Goswāmī cultivated Kṛṣṇa *bhakti* in Mathurā-maṇḍala. The significance of Jīva's mention of Mathurā is considerable. To be great is one thing, but if one's greatness is known in a place which is itself glorious, so much greater is one's glory. Mathurā is the "place," or state of consciousness, that gives birth to the absolute truth. It is said that a self-realized soul's acting in his transcendental position is called Mathurā.[15] Mathurā is not an earthly location, yet it appears on earth to facilitate the transcendental sport of Śrī Kṛṣṇa.

More than five hundred years ago, the glory of Mathurā was intertwined with the glory of Rūpa and Sanātana. Under the direction of Śrī Caitanya, they established Mathurā as an important place of worship and identified many of the places where thousands of years ago Śrī Kṛṣṇa performed his pastimes. This is mentioned in *Caitanya-caritāmṛta* thus: "O Sanātana, you should preach the *bhakti-śāstras* and uncover the lost places of pilgrimage *(lupta-tīrthera)* in Mathurā."[16]

To this day Mathurā-maṇḍala is experiencing world acclaim, and it is regularly frequented by patrons of all nations. What is the cause of this attention to what otherwise might seem a dusty and backward village of rural India? Śrīla Rūpa and Sanātana Goswāmīs and their followers in the Gauḍīya Vaiṣṇava *guru-paramparā.*

---

15. *mathyate tu jagat sarvaṁ brahma-jñānena yena vā/*
tat-sāra-bhūtaṁ yad yasyāṁ mathurā sā nigadyate//

A. C. Bhaktivedanta Swami Prabhupāda, *Śrīmad-Bhāgavatam* (Los Angeles: Bhaktivedanta Book Trust, 1977), p. 111 (purport).

16. *tumiha kariha bhakti-śāstrera pracāra/*
mathurāya lupta-tīrthera kariha uddhāra// (Cc. Madhya 23.103)

While all of Europe and, under European influence, much of India, either condemned or turned a blind eye to the love sports of Vṛndāvana Kṛṣṇa of Mathurā-maṇḍala,[17] the Gauḍīya *ācāryas* held fast to their convictions as to the divinity of Vraja Kṛṣṇa and his encore appearance in the Kali-yuga as Śrī Caitanya. It is this conviction and commitment to cast this vision worldwide, fulfilling Śrī Caitanya's own prediction,[18] to which the modern world is indebted. Because of them, Mathurā Vṛndāvana is now a well-known place of refuge for the devoted and a precious mine of religious gems for the devoted and the scholarly alike to excavate.

Thus Śrī Jīva proclaims, "May Rūpa and Sanātana, the two preceptors of the paramount truth, under whose direction this book is being written, be ever glorified in the land of Mathurā."

Amongst the Six Goswāmīs, Śrī Gopāla Bhaṭṭa also figures prominently, particularly with regard to *Ṣaṭ-sandarbha.* In *anuccheda* four, Śrī Jīva indirectly mentions him as he does at the outset of each of his six *sandarbhas*. The reason for this indirect reference may be traced to Gopāla Bhaṭṭa Goswāmī's temperament, which is revealed through the *paramparā* tradition. Kavirāja Goswāmī[19] has also mentioned Gopāla Bhaṭṭa sparingly in his most famous work, *Caitanya-Caritamṛta,* because

---

17. L. David Haberman, "Divine Betrayal; Krishna-Gopal of Braja in the Eyes of Outsiders," *Journal of Vaishnava Studies,* Vol. 3 No. 1 (1994) pp. 93–103.

18. *pṛthivīte āche yata nagarādi grāma/*
sarvatra pracāra haibe mora nāma//

"My (Śrī Caitanya's) name will be chanted in every town and village." (CB. Antya 4.126)

19. Kavirāja Goswāmī is from the second generation of the disciplic succession of Śrī Caitanya and is considered along with Vṛndāvana dāsa Ṭhākura to be the authorized biographer of Śrī Caitanya.

Gopāla Bhaṭṭa asked that his name be deleted from the text.[20] Yet Gopāla Bhaṭṭa in particular had much to be proud of, hailing as he did from a highly respectable South Indian *brāhmaṇa* family. He was the son of the head priest of the Śrī Raṅgam temple, which is the principal center of the Śrī Vaiṣṇava lineage.

Converted at an early age along with his father and uncle from Śrī Vaiṣṇavism to Gauḍīya Vaiṣṇavism by Śrī Caitanya himself, Gopāla Bhaṭṭa Goswāmī came to Mathurā Vṛndāvana after his parents left the world. There he eventually founded the Rādhā-Ramaṇa temple. According to Śrī Jīva Goswāmī's fourth *anuccheda,* "A certain Bhaṭṭa, who was a friend of Rūpa and Sanātana, born in a South Indian *brāhmaṇa* lineage, wrote a book after studying the writings of other prominent Vaiṣṇavas." This Bhaṭṭa is Gopāla Bhaṭṭa Goswāmī. The other prominent Vaiṣṇavas are Rāmānujācārya, Madhvācārya, Śrīdhara Swāmī, and others. The book he wrote is the one under discussion, *Ṣaṭ-sandarbha.*

Although Śrī Jīva gives the credit of authorship to Śrī Gopāla Bhaṭṭa, he states in *anuccheda* five that the book as composed by Gopāla Bhaṭṭa consisted primarily of notes not arranged in any particular order with entire sections missing. Śrī Jīva then humbly states, "Now *jīvakaḥ* (one small soul) will write it out in proper sequence." In response to Jīva Goswāmī's humility, his followers are fond of citing a line from the *Bhāgavatam* and attaching to it a novel meaning. *Jīvo jīvasya jīvanam* (lit. one living being, or *jīva,* is food for another), for Śrī Jīva's devout followers has become "One *jīva* (Śrī Jīva Goswāmī) sustains all *jīvas.*"

---

20. A. C. Bhaktivedanta Swami Prabhupāda, *Caitanya-caritāmṛta* (Los Angeles: Bhaktivedanta Book Trust, 1973), p. 319 (purport).

In *anuccheda* six, Jīva Goswāmī throws a curse and describes the qualification of the reader *(adhikāra)*. "May they alone whose principal desire it is to worship the lotus feet of Śrī Kṛṣṇa see this book." From this it is clear that only the devoted will "see," or have capacity to understand, its significance. Others, *śapatho 'rpitaḥ*, are cursed and thus barred from reading, i.e. understanding, *Tattva-sandarbha*'s significance. This "curse" is not particular to this treatise. Similar statements are found throughout the sacred texts. At the outset of the *Bhāgavatam* in the *vastu nirdeśa-śloka*, for example, we find *nirmatsarāṇāṁ satāṁ*,[21] this book is not for those who are envious (not devoted to Kṛṣṇa), rather only those who are *satāṁ*, truthful, and nonenvious can enter into the mystery of its understanding. In the *Bhagavad-gītā*, Kṛṣṇa says the same, *vācyaṁ na ca māṁ yo 'bhyasūyati*," [this text] should never be spoken to those who are envious of me."[22]

In *anuccheda* seven, after paying homage to the community of initiating and instructing gurus, Śrī Jīva states his intention to write the *Bhāgavata-sandarbha*.[23] He also mentions the *sambandha* of his book—the relationship between *Ṣaṭ-sandarbha* and *Śrīmad-Bhāgavatam*. The relationship is that *Ṣaṭ-sandarbha* explains the *Śrīmad-Bhāgavatam*.

Anuccheda eight states the subject of *Śrīmad-Bhāgavatam*. The subject of the *Bhāgavatam* is Kṛṣṇa, the nondual absolute appearing in three features: Brahman, Paramātmā, and Bhagavān. The Bhagavān feature of the absolute is Kṛṣṇa. He is joy himself. Because he is so, he also exists and is conscious. For one to exist, one need not be cognizant. If, however, one is cognizant, one

---

21. SB. 1.1.2

22. Bg. 18.67

23. What is now commonly known as *Ṣaṭ-sandarbha* was originally called *Bhāgavata-sandarbha*.

must exist as well. One can exist and be cognizant without being joyful. But if one is joyful by nature, one must exist and be cognizant. Because Kṛṣṇa is nothing short of joy itself, out of necessity this nondual absolute person is also known in two other features. Relative to existence, he manifests as Paramātmā, in terms of cognizance, as Brahman. In his Paramātmā feature, he expands the world of matter, existence without cognizance or joy. In his Brahman feature, he brings cognizance to the world of matter. As Bhagavān, he turns it into an abode of joy.

Anuccheda eight also states the subject of the *Bhāgavatam*'s relationship with the *Bhāgavatam* itself. The relationship between the subject of the *Bhāgavatam*, Śrī Kṛṣṇa, and the *Bhāgavatam* is that the *Bhāgavatam* reveals the truth about Śrī Kṛṣṇa, the ultimate reality. This eighth *anuccheda* states as well the purpose of the *Bhāgavatam*, the fruit of its study *(prayojana)*—love of Kṛṣṇa. It states also that the means by which the purpose of the *Bhāgavatam* will be fulfilled *(abhidheya)* is devotional culture, *bhakti*. Jīva Goswāmī will demonstrate this in brief in the *prameya khaṇḍa* of *Tattva-sandarbha*.

These three *anubandhas—sambandha, abhidheya, and prayojana*—also form the basis of the entire *Ṣaṭ-sandarbha*. *Tattva, Bhagavat, Paramātmā,* and *Kṛṣṇa-sandarbhas* all deal with the nondual absolute appearing in three manifestations, Brahman, Paramātmā, and Bhagavān. These *sandarbhas* describe this nondual reality from different angles of vision. They deal with the knowledge of how, for example, God is related to the world and the *jīva* souls, how the *jīva* souls are related to the world, and so on. This all falls in the category of *sambandha,* or the knowledge of relationship. *Bhakti-sandarbha* addresses the means *(abhidheya)* of attaining the goal, such as hearing and chanting about the Lord. The final *sandarbha, Prīti,* addresses the entire treatise's goal *(prayojana)*, which is the attainment of *prema,* or love of Kṛṣṇa.

This eighth *anuccheda* is the final and perhaps the most significant of Śrī Jīva's opening statements. "May Śrī Kṛṣṇa the original Personality of Godhead, *svayam bhāgavan,* who is known as Brahman, pure consciousness, and described thus in the Upaniṣads, whose partial manifestation is the Paramātmā presiding over his material energy, and who in his principal form is known as Nārāyaṇa sporting in Vaikuṇṭha, give *prema* to those who worship his feet." This statement consists of a condensed description of what the entire *Ṣaṭ-sandarbha* discusses in detail. It is based on two important verses of the *Bhāgavatam.* "Learned transcendentalists who know the absolute truth describe this nondual reality as Brahman, Paramātmā, and Bhagavān."[24] "All these previously described incarnations are plenary portions or portions of plenary portions of the *puruṣa avatāra,* but Kṛṣṇa is the original Godhead, the source of all *avatāras.* When these *avatāras* come to the world they relieve it of its burden."[25] Both of these verses appear later in the main text. The first is discussed considerably in *Tattva-sandarbha* and more thoroughly in the *Bhagavat-sandarbha* and *Paramātmā-sandarbha,* while the second, although directly cited in *Tattva-sandarbha*'s main text, is thoroughly discussed in *Kṛṣṇa-sandarbha.*

The *advaya-jñāna,* or nondual reality, of the *Bhāgavatam* is Śrī Kṛṣṇa, who manifests as Brahman, Paramātmā, and Bhagavān. According to Śrī Jīva, Kṛṣṇa is the source of Bhagavān, and is thus addressed in the *Bhāgavatam* as *svayam bhagavān (kṛṣṇas tu bhagavān svayam).* Bhagavān is Kṛṣṇa, not that Kṛṣṇa is Bhagavān. Again, Kṛṣṇa is "*svayam bhagavān.*" He is that form of Godhead that depends upon no other for his support. The Upaniṣadic

24. *vadanti tat tattva-vidas tattvaṁ yaj jñānam advayam/*
brahmeti paramātmeti bhagavān iti śabdyate// (SB. 1.2.11)

25. *ete cāṁśa-kalāḥ puṁsaḥ kṛṣṇas tu bhagavān svayam/*
indrāri-vyākulaṁ lokaṁ mṛḍayanti yuge yuge// (SB. 1.3.28)

texts that describe the absolute as Brahman are speaking about Śrī Kṛṣṇa indirectly. Equating as they do the *jīva* soul with Brahman in essence and describing that Brahman as formless, without qualities, and so on, they describe Śrī Kṛṣṇa partially as he is realized by those who tread the path of knowledge *(jñāna-mārga).* The *yogīs* realize Śrī Kṛṣṇa's Paramātmā feature, who presides over the cosmic manifestation and resides within every universe and every *jīva*'s heart. It is Śrī Kṛṣṇa who is known as Nārāyaṇa in the spiritual world, and it is he alone in his original form who bestows the highest goal of life, *prema,* upon those who engage in *bhakti.*

This final *anuccheda* of the invocation is tied to Śrī Jīva's first *anuccheda.* Together they introduce the *vastu-nirdeśa,* or essential subject matter of the entire *Ṣaṭ-sandarbha.* An explanation of these two *anucchedas* is found in Kṛṣṇadāsa Kavirāja Goswāmī's *Caitanya-caritāmṛta.* Kṛṣṇadāsa Kavirāja Goswāmī's *vastu-nirdeśa* verse explains that which Śrī Jīva has divided into these two *anucchedas.* This parallel verse of *Caitanya-caritāmṛta* runs thus: "What the Upaniṣads describe as the nondifferentiated absolute, Brahman, is but the effulgence of his form, and the indwelling Paramātmā is but his plenary portion. He, Śrī Caitanya, is Śrī Kṛṣṇa himself (Bhagavān) full in all six opulences, whom no truth is equal to or greater than."[26]

Thus it is the opinion of Jīva Goswāmī and the Gauḍīya Vaiṣṇava *sampradāya* that Śrī Kṛṣṇa Caitanya is *svayam bhagavān* Śrī Kṛṣṇa himself, and that his appearance exemplifies and reveals the essence of *Śrīmad-Bhāgavatam.*

---

26. *yad advaitaṁ brahmopaniṣadi tad apy asya tanu-bhā/*
ya ātmāntaryāmī puruṣa iti so 'syāṁśa-vibhavaḥ//
ṣaḍ aiśvaryaiḥ pūrṇo ya iha bhagavān sa svayam ayaṁ/
na caitanyāt kṛṣṇāj jagati para-tattvaṁ param iha// (Cc. Ādi 1.3)

PRAMĀṆA KHAṆḌA

3

"Śāstra, like the deity, is an instance of that which is eternal meeting with the temporal. At the junction where eternity meets time, we find the śāstra. There, the eternal appears temporal, yet it speaks to us only about eternity, and through it we glimpse that which is eternal."

In Search of Valid Evidence

To establish the truth, the means of establishing truth must be considered. If an atheist asks a theist to prove the existence of God, the theist must then ask, "What will you consider valid proof?" In a court of law, each attorney attempts to prove that the defendant is either guilty or not guilty. To do so, each attorney must present valid evidence.

In the *pramāṇa khaṇḍa* division of *Tattva-sandarbha,* Jīva Goswāmī establishes his *pramāṇa*—that which will serve as final and conclusive proof of his statements. Throughout the *Ṣaṭ-sandarbha,* Śrī Jīva puts forward many postulates (*viṣaya*) and many doubts (*saṁśaya*) that arise as to the validity of those postulates. He also strengthens those doubts by arguing strongly (*pūrvapakṣa*) against his own postulate. Then he gives the proper conclusion validating his original postulate (*siddhānta*) and demonstrating as well that his conclusion has been arrived at in due consideration of context (*saṅgati*).[1] In doing so, he cites his established *pramāṇa.*

This section of *Tattva-sandarbha* is vital to the entire *Ṣaṭ-sandarbha,* for without understanding it, one will not be able to appreciate the conclusive knowledge (*prameya*) which follows. Śrī

1. This refers to *adhikaraṇa,* the fivefold system of argument for arriving at conclusive knowledge that is used in *Vedānta-sūtra.* In *Tattva-sandarbha,* Śrī Jīva applies an approximation of this system.

Jīva states, "To establish that which has just been mentioned…the standard of valid knowledge will be judiciously decided."

Ordinary people, who have misidentified themselves with the material body, are subject to four defects: confusion (*bhrama*), inattention (*pramāda*), deception (*vipralipsā*), and imperfect senses (*karaṇāpāṭava*). As a result of this, Jīva Goswāmī concludes that their experience in and of itself is not acceptable as valid and conclusive knowledge.

That humanity is crippled by these defects should be apparent to any objective observer. *Bhrama*, or confusion, begins with the *jīva* soul's misidentification with the material body. We want to make our bodies perfectly healthy, beautiful, and so on, only because these are qualities of the soul, which is now identifying erroneously with the body. Because the soul is a unit of perfection, it wants to make the body as perfect as itself, while unaware that the body is different from the self. One might question just what kind of perfection the soul has when it is capable of being deluded into misidentifying with the material body. This query is answered in the *prameya* section of *Tattva-sandarbha.* At this point, Jīva Goswāmī merely wants to shed light on the imperfections of the materially conditioned state of consciousness, a state of confusion. Not only do we confuse ourselves with our bodies, we also sometimes mistake one material object for another, as in the classic example in which one misidentifies a rope to be a snake. Thus *bhrama,* or the tendency to be illusioned, extends from our illusion about our own self to illusion about other material objects as well.

Pramāda, or inattentiveness, occurs when the mind and senses are not focused on the same sense object at the same time. For example, if our eyes are focused on a form but our mind is not, we do not experience everything that we could about that form. This inattentiveness results in our making mistakes. Because we are not attentive in school, we make mistakes when tested. This inattentiveness, or the tendency to make mistakes, is a natural condition of our material life. *Vipralipsā*, or cheating, occurs to the extent that we are in material consciousness, for material consciousness amounts to not acknowledging the proprietorship of God.

Karaṇāpāṭava, or imperfect senses, means that every sense is limited. With our eyes we cannot hear. With our ears we cannot see. Describing these limitations of the senses implies that there are senses that are not defective. This is so in the case of Kṛṣṇa's senses, which are said to be interchangeable. Senses are also defective in terms of the particular function they are designed to perform. Eyes are designed for seeing, yet even when functioning in this capacity they often give us imperfect information. Sometimes their capacity is impaired by circumstances, such as the amount of light provided or the distance of the object from the viewer. Even under ideal circumstances, however, they can provide imperfect information. The senses also fail us when we attempt on their strength to understand spiritual subject matter, which lies beyond their jurisdiction. Thus one crippled by the senses cannot provide valid testimony as to the nature of truth. Therefore Jīva Goswāmī summarily rejects those who are handicapped by these defects and labels them as unreliable. He finds reason, thereby, to conclude that sense perception (*pratyakṣa*), the most common means of knowing, is not capable in and of itself to serve as valid and conclusive evidence.

While animals are equipped with senses and little if any reason, humans are said to be rational animals. Dogs howl and jump up at the moon, assuming it is within reach. Lacking sufficient reasoning, they cannot understand that although the full moon appears within reach it is actually far, far away. The sun appears to our eyes as a glowing mass about the size of a basketball. With the help of reasoning, however, we can understand that the sun is larger than the earth on which we are standing, yet millions of miles away. The power of reasoning is great, greater than the power of the senses. Brain is more powerful than brawn, and mind mightier than matter. Logic comes to our aid where the senses fail us.

In the Vedic tradition, logic (*nyāya*) is five-sided as opposed to three-sided logic most common in Western culture. In Western logic, an argument is supported by a major and minor premise. The major premise contains the major term that is the predicate of the conclusion, and the minor premise contains the minor term that is the subject of the conclusion. Common to both premises is the middle term that is excluded from the conclusion. A typical example is: "Every virtue is laudable; kindness is a virtue; therefore, kindness is laudable." The Vedic tradition's five-sided logic begins with a statement followed by a reason. This is followed by a major premise in the form of a rule, which is followed by an example. Lastly the conclusion is reached. For example, one can state that "behind the mountain there is fire." The reason in support of this is "because there is smoke." The rule is "wherever there is smoke, there is fire." This is followed by an example, from which the conclusion is drawn.

In either case, Western or Eastern, Śrī Jīva contends that logic is not capable of delivering conclusive evidence as to the nature of truth. In the example of smoke and fire, as in all cases, universal application is lacking. One's premise may not be true in all instances, and no one can experiment in all circumstances to find out if this is so. Smoke can exist where there is not fire. Should rain put out a fire behind the mountain moments before the smoke comes into our view, we would be mistaken to conclude that there is fire behind the mountain merely because we can see the smoke. If we consider universal application imperative, inference is inconclusive. Thus Śrī Jīva also rejects *anumāna* (inference) in his search for a perfect *pramāṇa*.

Altogether Jīva Goswāmī discusses ten *pramāṇas* in his *Sarvasaṁvādinī*, a commentary on *Tattva-sandarbha*. Seven of the *pramāṇas* discussed therein, however,[2] are all dependent upon *pratyakṣa* and *anumāna*. In *Tattva-sandarbha*, Jīva Goswāmī exposes the shortcomings of relying on either of these two *pramāṇas* and thus disqualifies the other seven as well.

After finding the other *pramāṇas* imperfect, Jīva Goswāmī introduces the reader to *śabda pramāṇa*, or revealed sound appearing in the world. Words of those handicapped by the above-mentioned four defects are not reliable, but words that come from a plane free from those defects are most reliable.

Here begins an explanation of the significance of the *śabda pramāṇa*. It is important to note that Indian theological systems rely heavily upon scripture. Śrī Jīva's acceptance of *śabda* is hardly a lone voice. All six *darśanas* of Indian philosophy[3] accept the *śabda* as a valid means of knowing. Reliance upon *śabda* is fundamental to Vedānta. Vedānta tells us that without scripture, the written manifestation of *śabda* known as *śāstra pramāṇa*, Brahman can never be realized, *śāstra-yonitvāt*.[4] That which can be known by other means is not the subject matter of the *śāstra*. The subject of the *śāstra* is categorically different from that which can be understood through reasoning and sense perception, as the *śāstra* is categorically different from the senses and the intellect.

---

2. *Upamāna* (knowledge derived through understanding similarities), *arthāpatti* (ascertaining the cause by seeing the effect), *anupalabdhi* (knowledge through understanding nonexistence or nonperceptability of a particular object), *ārṣa* (the words of *devās*), *aitihya* (knowledge through tradition), *ceṣṭā* (knowledge through *mudrā*, or symbols), *sambhava* (knowledge through probability).

3. The six *darśanas* are Vaiśeṣika, Nyāya, Sāṅkhya, Yoga, Pūrva Mīmāṁsā, and Uttara Mīmāṁsā (Vedānta).

4. Vs. 1.1.3

Often Hindu spirituality is thought of in the West as a "mystical" tradition, as opposed to the scripturally based "rational" tradition of the West. Nothing could be further from the truth.[5] This misconception is perhaps the greatest distortion of the Hindu tradition found in popular "Eastern mysticism." Just what scripture is, however, is often explained more rationally by Eastern practitioners than by popular Biblical advocates. For the most part, there is also greater emphasis on, and in-depth explanation of, the mystical experience of transcendent life in the Hindu scriptures than the explanation found in the scriptural tradition of the West. Furthermore, the West's Bible is not considered sacred sound in the same way as the *śāstra* is. The Bible, although divinely inspired, has human origins. It is not, therefore, considered *śabda.*

Śāstra is independent of both *pratyakṣa* and *anumāna*. *Śāstra pramāṇa* alone is independent of all others, and it alone is reliable in all circumstances. Other *pramāṇas* when viewed as subordinate to *śāstra* also become reliable. *Pratyakṣa* and *anumāna* that are in concord with *śāstra* are reliable. Only unaided by *śāstra* are they rejected. If that which we perceive with our senses does not contradict the *śāstra,* that perception is valid. Reason directed and illumined by *śāstra* plays an important role in the systematic inquiry into Brahman.

The important principle here is that those now experiencing imperfection, materially conditioned *jīvas,* require help from the plane of perfection to know perfection. Everyone wants perfect knowledge. The only variable remaining is how one goes about achieving it. According to Śrī Jīva, imperfect means of knowing will not produce perfect knowledge. Perfect knowledge is just that—perfect. Its perfection necessitates that

---

5. George C. Adams, Jr., *The Structure and Meaning of Bādarāyaṇa's Brahmasūtras,* (New Delhi: Motilal Banarsidass Publishers Pvt. Ltd., 1993), p. 44.

in the least it is conscious as are we, this being our essential and higher nature. Perfect knowledge is not something inanimate over which we conscious beings can rule. If we approach perfect knowledge with the imperfect idea of subordinating it to ourselves, we will never know perfection. Rather such perfect knowledge, being superconscious, is venerable by us. If it so chooses to reveal itself to us, then only can we know it. *Śāstra* represents the plane of perfect knowledge exercising itself in relation to the plane of imperfection, within which we units of relative perfection at present dwell.

Śāstra pramāṇa has no human origin. It is *apauruṣeya,* not created by any human being. *Apauruṣeya* also means that which is eternally existing without beginning. To help us conceive of the eternal nature of the Vedas (the prime example of *śāstra*), they are sometimes described metaphorically as the breath of God. Just as one breathes for the entire duration of one's life, similarly the Vedas are eternally existing along with the Godhead. They manifest from time to time, and therefore at times they are unmanifest to human society. In its cruder form, *śāstra* is constituted of codes of working direction for humanity. In its subtle expression, it directly reveals the nature of the self unfettered by material nature. Its sole subject is Brahman, the absolute, about which the *śāstra* speaks both indirectly and directly. The *apauruṣeya* nature of the *śāstra* does not preclude it from being written down and disseminated through humanity; rather, it implies that its meaning merely manifests in written form at a certain point in human history.

Śāstra is the Veda, whose nature is eternal and from which the world has come. Through Vedic revelation, Brahmā, the creator, is said to have created. It is that sound revelation that purifies the senses of those who repeatedly hear it. Only through knowledge derived from *śāstra* can we rise above the limits of our own logic and enter the land of the soul, which is ever superior to intellect, even as intellect is superior to mind, mind superior to senses, and senses superior to gross matter consisting of sense objects.

Inferior means cannot reveal superior ends. Mind can understand senses, but senses can never know the mind. Intellect, being inferior to the soul, does not have sufficient power to reveal the soul. Intellect's power is itself derived from consciousness. How then can it shed light upon the soul anymore than a candle can shed light upon the sun? This is the argument that leads us to *śāstra*. *Śāstra* is the infallible *pramāṇa* because it is handed to us through an unbroken chain of disciplic succession *(guru-paramparā)* consisting of reliable persons.

Śāstra is the experience of eternal knowledge heard by realized souls and subsequently voiced by them. It was manifest in the heart of the creator Brahmā,[6] spoken by him to form the world, and later compiled and edited by God incarnate, Kṛṣṇa-dvaipāyana Vyāsa, and his disciples.[7] *Śāstra* comes to us as the voice of one who has seen something wonderful and is pressed to tell us about it. Hearing such may indeed afford the greatest impetus for one who has not yet seen reality. *Śāstra* shows the way, upon which following one sees for oneself. It is in-depth speech about that which one can never say enough, *īkṣater naśabdam*.[8]

The *śāstra* implores us not to do away with language and logic, but to use them to their fullest potential. Study of the *śāstra* reveals the necessity for adopting transrational means of knowing. The Vedas inspire their reader, theoretically as to the goal and practically as to the means of reaching that goal. In this

---

6. *tene brahmā hṛdā ya ādi-kavaye* (SB. 1.1.1)

7. *mahā-muni kṛte* (SB. 1.1.2)

8. Vs. 1.1.5

way, through the medium of pen and paper, reality informs us about itself. *Śāstra* thus directs us beyond its outer representation in words to embrace the spiritual reality its sound corresponds with. In doing so, it taxes the limit of our reasoning power.

A doubt may arise as to how a mere book can be held so high. Books are usually products of human thought and language, inadequate in so many ways. Are not the *śāstras* also the products of human minds? Why should the *śāstras* be considered differently? However divine their origin may be, even if we grant for the sake of argument that they are from God himself, books still have not arrested divinity and held it prisoner in human language. How can the *śāstra*, while using thought and language, be used to prove that which is beyond the reach of both mind and speech?

These are pressing questions. Their answers lie in proper acquaintance with the nature of consciousness. In short, the pure consciousness of the absolute is not restricted as matter is. It is beyond the jurisdiction of matter. It can do what matter cannot. It can take the form of that which is material and remain spiritual at the same time, appearing as the deity, the *śāstra*, and so forth. *Śāstra*, like the deity, is an instance of that which is eternal meeting with the temporal. At the junction where eternity meets time, we find the *śāstra*. There, the eternal appears temporal, yet it speaks to us only about eternity, and through it we glimpse that which is eternal.

The divine word for Śrī Jīva is itself Brahman. He advocates the doctrine of Varṇavāda, originally developed in the Mīmāṁsā school. Although Śrī Jīva differs significantly from the Mīmāṁsā school as to the import of the *śāstra*, he concurs with them as to the eternal nature of the Veda. How is the *śāstra* eternal? How does it differ from ordinary speech? It differs in two ways. Although its words are the same as those of ordinary speech, its word order is different. The word order of the *śāstra* is not dependent on the determination of any individual. As the sequence of the Vedic words is eternally fixed, so is the relationship between Vedic words and the objects they seek to describe. There is an innate relationship between the Vedic words and their objects. This relationship is not something determined by convention in human society. *Śāstra,* the written form of the eternal *śabda,* is the faithful reproduction in a physical medium of that which has always existed. It is an empirical yet spiritual manifestation that occurs repeatedly. *Śāstra* appears and disappears in time and space as the world of time and space itself appears and disappears in an endless cycle.

Martin Heidegger's modern notion that "language speaks" may help us to understand the nature of Vedic injunctions. Vedic *mantras* have an intention of their own. They are not the directives of speakers voided in language. Because of *śāstra*'s particular arrangement of words and the innate relationship between those words and their objects, if one regularly recites the *śāstra* and follows its injunctions, one can realize Brahman.

Yet *śāstra* does not tell us that by reading or understanding its conclusions with our intellect the absolute will thus be realized. This is not its claim. It does not seek to prove by its argument and reasoning that which itself is beyond proof, being eternally self-established. Proof lies in our experience alone of that which is, of that which we are in essence—units of experience, consciousness. Proof of the validity of *śāstra* itself as a valid means of knowing lies in those who have realized its subject through the means recommended therein. And they have not hidden themselves from us.

The *śāstra* reasons with us to take up the means of experiencing its subject and thereby to experience our true self. Those who have realized such descend again to our human reality and speak to us in the common language of humanity, that of reasoning, as well as in joyful exclamations about that which they have seen. They are the firsthand witnesses whose testimony is the final word. Printed, their words become *śāstra,* revealed knowledge, free from human defects.

Having established his *pramāṇa* in a general sense and resting with *śabda,* Jīva Goswāmī begins to reveal the extent of his scriptural knowledge and the depth of his understanding of the *śāstra*. His knowledge is as vast as the Vedas themselves. Śrī Jīva quotes from the *śabda* to further establish its infallibility and the faulty nature of reasoning unaided by scripture. By quoting such, Śrī Jīva is showing that his opinion is based on *śāstra*. First he cites the *Vedānta-sūtra,* "Logic affords no standing."[9] The idea here is that by logical conjecture alone one will never reach conclusive truth, for any logical argument can be defeated by another *ad infinitum*. It is worth noting that this statement is quoted from the scripture that gives the logic of the Vedic conclusions, *Vedānta-sūtra (nyāya śāstra)*. In the *Vedānta-sūtra,* Vyāsa demonstrates how all the revealed scripture is speaking about the same thing, the shared experience of those who have realized transcendence.

Next Śrī Jīva quotes from the *Mahābhārata,* "Reason fails to understand the inconceivable, which is forever distinct from material nature."[10] That which is superior to intellect—consciousness—is inconceivable by intellectual exercise, yet it becomes conceivable when means that are transrational are invoked. As the *Vedānta-sūtra* says, "The absolute is known from *śāstra,*" and "That which appears contradictory is not so. So states the scripture, from which we can know the absolute."[11]

---

9. *tarko 'pratiṣṭhānāt* (Vs. 2.1.11)

10. *acintyāḥ khalu ye bhāvā na tāms tarkeṇa yojayet//*
(M. Bh. Bhīṣmaparvan 5.12)

11. *śāstra-yonitvāt, śrutes tu śabda-mūlatvāt* (Vs. 1.1.3, 2.1.27)

Śrīmad-Bhāgavatam says something more on the subject: "O Lord, the Vedas are the supreme eye through which the demigods, ancestors, and humans can understand that which is otherwise inconceivable, such as the ultimate goal of life and the means of attaining it. The Vedas can make the inconceivable conceivable because they lie beyond the range of the senses."[12]

Yet acquiring Vedic knowledge is not a simple task. Even sages such as Kaṇāda, Gautama, Kapila, Patañjali, Jaimini, and Vyāsa appear to differ in their interpretation of *śāstra*. The Vedas are also vast, yet that which is available to us today represents only a fraction of the entirety of Vedic literature. Furthermore, to understand the Vedas not only is a teacher required, but the students themselves must have certain qualifications to be accepted as pupils of the Vedas. To meet these qualifications is practically impossible in the present age, for "in Kali-yuga people are short-lived, forgetful, unfortunate, and misguided."[13] Therefore, Jīva Goswāmī concludes that in search of the perfect *pramāṇa* within the *śabda* we should begin with the Purāṇas and Itihāsas.

While the Vedas are called *śruti*, the supplementary Purāṇas and Itihāsas are called *smṛti*, as are the six Vedāṅgas. There is a controversy as to what constitutes *śabda*. Some scholars accept only the *śruti*, while others both *śruti* and *smṛti*. Those who argue in favor of accepting the *śruti* alone do so without comprehensive knowledge of all that the *śruti* proclaims. Śrī Jīva Goswāmī is quick to refer them to the *śruti* itself in establishing his claim that the Purāṇas and Itihāsas should be turned to for conclusive evidence: "...in the same way, dear one, the

12. *pitṛ-deva-manuṣyāṇāṁ vedaś cakṣus taveśvara/*
śreyas tv anupalabdhe 'rthe sādhya-sādhanayor api// (SB. 11.20.4)

13. *prāyeṇālpāyuṣaḥ sabhyāḥ kalāv asmin yuge janāḥ/*
mandāḥ sumanda-matayo manda-bhāgyā hy upadrutāḥ// (SB. 1.1.10)

Ṛg Veda, Yajur Veda, Sāma Veda, Atharva Veda, Itihāsas, Purāṇas...have been breathed forth from that great being."[14] Indeed, the Purāṇas are said to *"pūrana,"* complete, the Vedas,[15] and are thus named such. Furthermore, certain portions of the Vedas can only be understood by referring to the Purāṇas and Itihāsas, "The Vedas should be supplemented with the Itihāsas and Purāṇas."[16] To stress that the Vedas of divine origin cannot be supplemented by anything less than literature that is of the same divine origin, Śrī Jīva gives the example that a broken golden bracelet cannot be repaired with lead.

The Purāṇas are different from the Vedas only in terms of the technical nature of their respective composition. Otherwise they are one, in that both are of divine origin. The composition of the Vedas is lofty and difficult to study and recite. Vedic Sanskrit is also different from the *laukika* Sanskrit found in the Purāṇas. If one is to study the *śruti*, the Vedic accent *(krama)* and word order *(pada)* are very important to master. It is for this reason, not out of a spirit of oppression, that unqualified persons are barred from studying the Vedas. Just as only qualified people can enter postgraduate studies, similarly only qualified people can study the Vedas. If unqualified persons ignore this prohibition, they will undoubtedly misrepresent the Vedas to the masses. This was done by many European scholars who attempted to understand the Vedas without undergoing the proper training. Thus if it is argued that because the Vedas are not acceptable as a perfect *pramāṇa*, the same would apply to the so-called fifth Veda (the Purāṇas) the above makes clear

---

14. *evaṁ vā are 'sya mahato bhūtasya niḥśvāsitam etad yad ṛg-veda yajur-vedaḥ sāma-vedo 'tharvāṅgirasa itihāsaḥ purāṇam//* (Br. U. 2.4.10)

15. Both *pūraṇa* and Purāṇa are derived from the root *pṝ*, to make full, complete, supplement.

16. *itihāsa-purāṇābhyāṁ vedaṁ samupabṛmhayed//* (M.Bh. *Ādiparvan* 1.267)

both a unity and distinction between the two thereby refuting this point.

The *Skanda Purāṇa* describes how the Purāṇas were manifest: "In ancient times the grandfather of the demigods, Brahmā, performed severe austerities, and thus the Vedas and six Vedāṅgas became manifest through him. Then the complete Purāṇa, which embodies all scripture and is unchanging, came from Brahmā's mouth in a million verses. Listen to the divisions of that Purāṇa: the Brahmā Purāṇa is first..."[17]

Jīva Goswāmī quotes this important verse for two reasons. The obvious one is to further establish the Vedic and eternal nature of the Purāṇas. Regarding this he notes that "consisting of millions of verses" refers to the well-known fact that the Purāṇas' earthly manifestation of four hundred thousand verses is a condensed form of the original Purāṇas.[18] Śrī Jīva also cites statements from *Śrīmad-Bhāgavatam, Bhaviṣya Purāṇa,* and *Chāndogya Upaniṣad* to further establish this first point and lead into the second. "He breathed forth the four Vedas from his four mouths beginning with the one facing east."[19] "Then the Lord who knows all breathed forth the Itihāsas and Purāṇas, the fifth Veda, from all of his mouths."[20] Here the Itihāsas and Purāṇas are directly called "Veda," and signifi-

---

17. *purā tapaś cacārogam amarāṇāṁ pitāmahaḥ/*
āvirbhūtas tato vedaḥ sa-ṣaḍ-anga-pada-kramaḥ//
tataḥ purāṇam akhilaṁ sarva-śāstra-mayam dhruvam/
nitya-śabda-mayaṁ puṇyaṁ śata-koṭi-pravistaram //
(Sk. P. Prabhasa Khaṇda 2.3–5)

18. Evidence for this is found in *Matsya Purāṇa* 53.9–11 cited later in *anuccheda* fourteen.

19. *ṛg-yajuḥ- sāmātharvākhyān vedān pūrvādibhir mukhaiḥ* (SB. 3.12.37)

20. *itihāsa-purāṇāni pañcamaṁ vedam īśvaraḥ/*
sarvebhya eva vaktrebhyaḥ sasṛje sarva-darśanaḥ// (SB. 3.12.39)

cantly, this fifth Veda came from all of Brahmā's mouths simultaneously. "Itihāsas and Purāṇas are the fifth Veda."[21] "Vyāsa taught the Vedas, with the *Mahābhārata* as the fifth. The Purāṇas and Itihāsas are thus the fifth Veda."[22] " I have learned from the *Ṛg Veda*, the *Yajur Veda*, the *Sāma Veda*, and the fourth, the *Atharva Veda*, as well as Itihāsas and Purāṇas, the fifth Veda."[23]

The second reason for citing the verse of the *Skanda Purāṇa* is that it mentions that the first Purāṇa was the *Brahmā Purāṇa*, which is well known as one of the eighteen Mahā Purāṇas. Thus this reference stands as scriptural evidence to refute the contention that the Itihāsas and Purāṇas referred to as the fifth Veda are not the Purāṇas and Itihāsa per se, rather the sections of the Vedas themselves that are historical *(itihāsa)* and mythological *(purāṇa)*.[24] Scholars have contended, Śaṅkara among them, that the Purāṇas are less authoritative than the Vedas. It is much more difficult to support Śaṅkara's monistic doctrine of illusion *(māyāvāda)* if one takes the entirety of revealed scripture into consideration. Therefore Śaṅkara stressed the Upaniṣads, and certain Upaniṣads in particular. He stressed the Upaniṣads that contain mythological and historical sections.

Apparently, at the time Śrī Jīva compiled *Tattva-sandarbha* there was considerable emphasis on the importance of the Vedas, but it was not emphasized that the Itihāsas and Purāṇas

---

21. *purāṇaṁ pañcamo vedaḥ //* (SB. 1.4.20)

22. *itihāsaḥ purāṇaṁ ca pañcamo veda ucyate/*
vedān adhyāpayām āsa mahābhārata-pañcamān//
(M. Bh. Mokṣadharma 340.11)

23. *ṛg-vedaṁ bhagavo 'dhyemi yajur-vedaṁ sāma-vedam*
ātharvaṇaṁ caturtham itihāsaṁ purāṇaṁ pañcamaṁ vedānāṁ vedam//
(Ch. U. 7.1.2)

24. Br. U. 2.4.10

are equal expressions of the *śabda*. The Vedas are considered *śruti*, or that which is directly uttered by the Lord. The Purāṇas and Itihāsas are generally considered *smṛti*, or that which is recollected (after hearing the *śruti*, thus serving as a reiteration of the original *śruti)*. Śrī Jīva ends the debate as to the relative importance of *śruti* over *smṛti* by proclaiming the Itihāsas and Purāṇas themselves to be *śruti*. As per the standard, he demonstrates his conviction with numerable scriptural references. From *anuccheda* fourteen to *anuccheda* seventeen, making use of strong logic, he cites verses which serve to make clear the Purāṇas' glory.

Sūta Goswāmī, who was given charge of the Purāṇas on the order of Vyāsa, explains why the Purāṇas and Itihāsas are considered the fifth Veda: "Vyāsadeva, the Lord himself, gave the charge of the Itihāsas and Purāṇas to me. First there was only the *Yajur Veda*, which he divided into four: *Ṛg*, *Sāma*, *Atharva*, and *Yajur*. With this division came the four priests, the *hotṛ*, *udgātṛ*, *brāhmaṇa*, and *adhvaryu*, respectively, along with sacrifice. Then, O best of the twice born, after compiling the four Vedas, Vyāsa, who understood the meaning of the Purāṇas, compiled them by gathering together that which he himself witnessed *(ākhyānas)*, that which he heard from others *(upākhyānas)*, and various songs *(gāthās)*, all of which were part of the original *Yajur Veda*."[25] The fact that the Purāṇas were originally part of the *Yajur Veda* makes it clear that they are not separate writings, but are indeed part of the Vedas themselves. Śrī Jīva further reasons that because during Vedic sacrifices scriptures are read, and among those recommended

---

25. *itihāsa-purāṇanāṁ vaktāraṁ samyag eva hi/*
māṁ caiva pratijagrāha bhagavān īśvaraḥ prabhuḥ//
eka āsīd yajur vedas taṁ caturdhā vyakālpayat/
catur hotram abhūt tasmiṁs tena yajñam akālpayat// (Vā. P. 60.16–17)

for reading are the Purāṇas, the Purāṇas are certainly Vedic in nature.

The necessity of the Purāṇas and the nature of their arrangement are mentioned further in the *Matsya Purāṇa* wherein the Lord says, "O best of the twice born, seeing that man's capacity to understand the Purāṇa diminishes in time, I myself take the post of Vyāsa (compiler) in every age and summarize it."[26] More clearly, "To secure the well-being of people in general, I present the original Purāṇa in a more concise form. In every Dvāpara-yuga, the condensed Purāṇa of four hundred thousand verses is divided into eighteen divisions and made manifest in the world, while the original Purāṇa consisting of millions of verses continues to exist in the heavenly planets."[27] Here it is noteworthy that from time to time the Lord himself incarnates as a "Vyāsa," or compiler of the Vedic knowledge. The particular Vyāsa for the present age is Kṛṣṇa-dvaipāyana Vyāsa, who is an empowered *avātara.*

The *Śiva Purāṇa* speaks along the same lines, "The Lord Vyāsa divided the Vedas into four sections, and thus he is known as Veda-Vyāsa, or one who divides the Vedas. He also condensed the Purāṇas into four hundred thousand verses from its original form of millions of verses found in the heavens."[28]

---

26. *kālenāgrahaṇaṁ matvā purāṇasya dvijottamāḥ/*
vyāsa-rūpam ahaṁ kṛtvā saṁharāmi yuge yuge// (Ma. P. 53.9)

27. *catur-lakṣa-pramāṇena dvāpare dvāpare sadā/*
tad aṣṭādaśadhā kṛtvā bhūrloke 'smin prabhāṣyate//
adyāpy amartya-loke tu śata-koṭi-pravistaram/
tad-artho 'tra catur-lakṣaḥ saṅkṣepeṇa niveśitaḥ// (Ma. P. 53.10–11)

28. *saṁkṣipya caturo vedāṁś caturdhā vyabhajat prabhuḥ/*
vyasta-vedatayā khyāto veda-vyāsa iti smṛtaḥ//
purāṇam api saṅkṣiptaṁ catur-lakṣaḥ-pramāṇataḥ/
adyāpy amartya-loke tu śata-koṭi-pravistaram// (Śi. P. 1.33–34)

Someone may argue that the Purāṇas are identified with different sages and demigods and as such have them as their origin. For example, *Skanda, Agni,* and other such Purāṇas are identified with the devotees Skanda, Agni, and so on. Are they not then of worldly origin as opposed the *apauruṣeya* Veda? To this Śrī Jīva replies that the names connected with such Purāṇas are the names of those who principally made their knowledge available in the world. Furthermore, such is the standard for the *śruti* as well. For example, "Kaṭha" is the name of the sage most known for disseminating the knowledge of that *śruti (Kaṭha Upaniṣad).*

In *anuccheda* fifteen Śrī Jīva answers the argument of those who attribute divine origin only to the Vedas but not the Purāṇas. Most modern-day scholars, however, do not accept that the Vedas, what to speak of the Purāṇas, are anything but the writings of various people over several centuries. They make a similar argument to the one just addressed by Śrī Jīva. Further, they date various Purāṇas according to the time period in which a prominent person of the same name lived. They also try to connect names and descriptions of places described in the *śāstras* to names and description of places of which they know the time period. In this way, scholars conclude that a particular Purāṇa was written during that time period. The difference in the style of Sanskrit composition between various literatures also leads them to conclude that particular literatures were written at times during which a particular style of Sanskrit was, as far as they can tell, in vogue. These are all good guesses, yet hardly conclusive. Nor do such conjectures in anyway disprove the opinion of those who venerate the *śāstra,* attributing to it divine origin. Such persons, among whom Jīva Goswāmī is very prominent, are also scholars—devotee scholars.

The spirit of Jīva Goswāmī's reply to those who doubt the divine origin of the Purāṇas, having identified the Purāṇas with the names of those of worldly origin, is worth discussing. Just as Newton made the law of gravity well-known and thus the principle of gravity is often referred to as Newton's Law, so similarly various sages and demigods are identified with particular branches of eternal knowledge found in the Purāṇas. The law of gravity and other such discoveries of science are principles of nature that have little to do with those who have "discovered" them. This is even more so with the kind of knowledge contained within the Vedas and Purāṇas. They are not filled with the speculative opinions of ordinary or even highly intelligent humans. In Śrī Jīva's opinion, they are eternal knowledge manifest in written form, in order that humanity might take advantage of the knowledge of how our world and the world beyond our present purview works from the perspective of the originator of both realms.

There should be no doubt that all knowledge is existing at all times. It is not something that is manufactured in the laboratory of our mental system. It is forever self-existing. What is not ever existing is our comprehension of that knowledge. Do we the unenlightened *discover* it, whether transcendent or mundane? This manner of speech carries with it the notion that the credit is ours; that we are the subject, knowledge being the object of our discovery. It might be more accurate to consider knowledge the subject and ourselves, although conscious, nonetheless subordinate to the knowledge itself. We after all are the unenlightened, and revealed knowledge is the cause of our eventual enlightenment. Transcendental knowledge is thus at least as conscious as are we, and hardly an inanimate object of our investigation. As it reveals itself, so it shall be known. We may position ourselves such that the likelihood that knowledge will reveal itself is increased or decreased. The prerogative to reveal or conceal, however, lies with the potent knowledge itself. This knowledge, manifest in written form for human society, is what Śrī Jīva is speaking of when he discusses his *pramāṇa*, refining it as he has thus far from the Vedas themselves to the Purāṇas and Itihāsas.

The glory of the Purāṇas is greater still on account of the Purāṇas' accessibility. As mentioned earlier, they were assigned to Sūta, Romaharṣaṇa-sūta. The term *"sūta"* refers to one born of a mixed caste. By giving the charge of the Purāṇas and Itihāsas to Śrī Sūta, Vyāsadeva made the Vedic knowledge available to those of lesser qualification. Jīva Goswāmī compares the Purāṇas to the holy name of Kṛṣṇa, the very essence of the Vedas, through which Śrī Kṛṣṇa makes himself available to all, regardless of caste distinction. The Purāṇas are "the choicest fruits of the vine of the Vedas." Regarding the name of Kṛṣṇa, *Skanda Purāṇa* states: "The holy name of Kṛṣṇa is the sweetest of the sweet. It is the auspiciousness of that which is auspicious; the choicest fruit of the vine of Vedic literature. If anyone chants this name even once, either with devotion or contempt, the holy name will take that chanter beyond the world of birth and death."[29] *Viṣṇu-dharmottara Purāṇa* also mentions, "A person who has uttered the two syllables *ha* and *ri* has already studied all of the Vedas."[30] As Kṛṣṇa's name has not become less important or potent through accessibility, so the Purāṇas, as opposed to the Vedas, are not less important and potent on account of their being accessible to the masses. Indeed, they are the essence of the Vedas.

---

29. *madhuram-madhuram etan maṅgalaṁ-maṅgalānāṁ/*
sakala-nigama-vallī-satphalaṁ cit-svarūpam/
sakṛd api parigītaṁ śraddhayā helayā vā/
bhṛguvara nara-mātraṁ tārayet kṛṣṇa-nāma// (Sk. P.)

30. *ṛg-vedo 'tha yajur-vedaḥ sāma-vedo 'py atharvaṇaḥ/*
adhītās tena yenoktaṁ harir ity akṣara-dvayam// (Vd. P.)

The Itihāsas and Purāṇas determine the meaning of the Vedas. As mentioned in the *Viṣṇu Purāṇa,* "While narrating historical events in the *Mahābhārata,* Vyāsa in actuality is illustrating the meaning of the Vedas. Without a doubt, all the Vedas are found in the Purāṇas."[31] In other words, through the descriptions found in the *Mahābhārata* of political intrigue, romance, war, religious life, and so on, Vyāsa, in a most captivating manner, has explained the essence of the Vedas for common people. Those who have studied the *Mahābhārata* through the *guru paramparā* can trace the narrations in the text to their source found in the Vedas.

Still some people insist that the Itihāsas and Purāṇas are merely commentaries on the Vedas, and not Vedic themselves. Śrī Jīva granting them this for the sake of argument answers that even if that is so, they are the best of commentaries, having been expounded by Vyāsa himself. If we are to consider the value of any book, we will have to first consider who wrote it. This is the argument that Śrī Jīva makes in favor of the Purāṇas. Based on the fact that they were written by Vyāsa, they must be given serious consideration. Who is the Vyāsa that wrote the Purāṇas? Jīva Goswāmī lets the Purāṇas speak for themselves. The glory of Vyāsa is found in the *Padma Purāṇa,* "Vyāsa knows more than all others including Brahmā. He knows all that can be known, and his knowledge is not attainable by others."[32]

It has been said that Vyāsa's mind is like the sky itself. As all sound is contained in the sky (ether), so all knowledge is contained within the mind of Vyāsa. The *Skanda Purāṇa* states,

---

31. *bhārata-vyāpadeśena hy āmnāyārthaḥ pradarśitaḥ/
vedāḥ pratiṣṭhitāḥ sarve purāṇe nātra saṁśayaḥ//* (Vi. P.)

32. *dvaipāyanena yad buddhaṁ brahmādyais tan na budhyate/
sarva-buddhaṁ sa vai veda tad buddhaṁ nānya-gocaram//* (Pa. P.)

"From the sky of Vyāsa's mind others have taken pieces of knowledge for themselves in the same way one might take something from another's house."[33] The significance of this statement is that as the sky is unlimited, so is Vyāsa's mind, and thus he can enter into anything and know it. Sound also travels in the sky, and to hear sound one therefore needs the sky in which it is contained. No sound can exist outside of the sky. Similarly, no knowledge, no *śabda*, can be experienced outside of that which manifest in the mind of Vyāsa, the Veda. To appreciate this, one must study the Vedas, wherein one will find that even the modern conveniences of our high-tech times are discussed therein, albeit in different terms and brought about by different means. The language itself in which the Vedas were written is a good example. Sanskrit has been termed a perfect computer language.[34]

In *Viṣṇu Purāṇa,* Vyāsa's father Parāśara states: "During the twenty-eighth *manvantara,* the Lord himself appearing as my son took the original Veda and divided it into four distinct Vedas. Since that time all others holding the post of Vyāsa including myself have followed this example. The way in which Veda-Vyāsa arranged the Vedas is accepted by all. O Maitreya, Kṛṣṇa-dvaipāyana Vyāsa is God himself, Nārāyaṇa, for who but him could have written the *Mahābhārata*?"[35]

---

33. *vyāsa-citta-sthitākāśād avacchinnāni kānicit//*
anye vyavaharanty etāny urīkṛtya gṛhād iva// (Sk. P.)

34. Vyāsa Houston, "Language of Enlightenment," *Clarion Call,* Vol. 2 No. 3 (1989), p. 43.

35. *tato 'tra mat-suto vyāsaḥ aṣṭa-viṁśatime 'ntare/*
vedam ekaṁ catuṣ-pādaṁ caturdhā vyabhajat prabhuḥ//
yathātra tena vai vyastā veda-vyāsena dhīmatā/
vedas tathā samastais tair vyāsair anyais tathā mayā//
tad anenaiva vyāsānāṁ śākhā-bhedān dvijottama/

In the *Skanda Purāṇa* it is stated: "In the Satya-yuga, knowledge emanating from Nārāyaṇa was protected. Then in the Tretā-yuga it became distorted to some extent, and more so in the Dvāpara-yuga. Then when knowledge turned into ignorance as a result of the curse of Gautama, the demigods headed by Brahmā and Śiva took shelter of Nārāyaṇa, informing the Lord of the situation. Then the great sage, the Lord himself, descended as the son of Parāśara and Satyavatī to rescue the Vedas."[36] Here Śrī Jīva says the Vedas saved by Vyāsa include the Purāṇas and Itihāsas, which alone afford the highest welfare. The Purāṅas and Itihāsas are superior to the Vedas. As the *Nārada Purāṇa* states: "O Pārvatī, the Purāṇas are more important than the Vedas. Without a doubt all the Vedas are sheltered in the Purāṇas. One who disregards the Purāṇas, even if he has good qualities, such as good behavior and peaceful demeanor, will not get shelter anywhere and will have to take birth as an animal."[37] *Skanda Purāṇa* states: "O best of the twice born, the meaning of the Purāṇas is unchanging just like

---

catur-yugeṣu racitān samasteṣv avadhāraya//
kṛṣṇa-dvaipāyanaṁ vyāsaṁ viddhi nārāyaṇaṁ prabhum/
ko 'nyo hi bhuvi maitreya mahābhārata-kṛd bhavet// (Vi. P. 3.4.2–5)

36. *nārāyaṇād viniṣpaṇṇaṁ jñānaṁ kṛta-yuge sthitam/*
kiñcid tad anyathā jātaṁ tretāyaṁ dvāpare 'khilam//
gautamasya ṛṣeḥ śāpāj jñāne tv ajñānatāṁ gate/
saṇkīrṇa-buddhayo devā brahma-rudra-puraḥ-sarāḥ//
śaraṇyaṁ śaraṇaṁ jagmur nārāyaṇam anāmayam/
tair vijñāpita-kāryas tu bhagavān puruṣottamāḥ//
avatīrṇo mahā-yogī satyavatyāṁ parāśarāt/
utsannān bhagavān vedān ujjahāra hariḥ svayam// (Sk. P.)

37. *vedārthād adhikaṁ manye purāṇārthaṁ varānane/*
vedāḥ pratiṣṭhitāḥ sarve purāṇe nātra saṁśayaḥ//
purāṇam anyathā kṛtvā tiryag-yonim avāpnuyāt/
su-dānto 'pi su-śānto 'pi na gatiṁ kvacid āpnuyāt// (N. P.)

that of the Vedas. The Vedas are all sheltered in the Purāṇas without a doubt. The Veda has a fear that unqualified people will read her and then distort her meaning. Thus the significance of the Veda was fixed in the Purāṇas and Itihāsas. That which is not found in the Vedas is found in the *smṛti*. [Here referring to the Vedāṅgas.] That which is not found there is found in the Purāṇas. Those who know even the Vedas, Vedāṅga, and Upaniṣads are not learned if they do not know the Purāṇas."[38]

In *Tattva-sandarbha,* Jīva Goswāmī has removed the clouds of imaginary notions that stress the Vedas over the Purāṇas with the sun-like rays of the *śāstra*. Jīva Goswāmī's *śāstric* knowledge is overwhelmingly comprehensive. He has established that within the *śabda,* the Purāṇas are more important than the Vedas, more accessible, and more readily available as well. Yet while we catch our breath here, Śrī Jīva is not yet finished. He continues to refine his *pramāṇa* from here.

Although the Purāṇas are more important than the Vedas, more accessible, and more readily available, they, like the Vedas, are not available in their entirety. Moreover, they advocate the supremacy of not one but a variety of deities. One Purāṇa says that Brahmā is supreme, another Viṣṇu, still another Śiva, and so on. Thus they are difficult to understand, if not confusing. To support his argument, Jīva Goswāmī quotes

---

38. *vedavān niścalaṁ manye purāṇārthaṁ dvijottamāḥ/*
vedāḥ pratiṣṭhitāḥ sarve purāṇe nātra saṁśayaḥ//
bibhety alpa-śrutād vedo mām ayaṁ cālayiṣyati/
itihāsa-purāṇais tu niścalo 'yaṁ kṛtaḥ purā//
yan na dṛṣṭaṁ hi vedeṣu tad dṛṣṭaṁ smṛtiṣu dvijāḥ/
ubhayor yan na dṛṣṭaṁ hi tat purāṇaiḥ pragīyate//
yo veda caturo vedān sāṅgopaniṣado dvijāḥ/
purāṇaṁ naiva jānāti na ca sa syād vicakṣaṇaḥ// (Sk. P. 2.90–93)

from the *Matsya Purāṇa*: "A Purāṇa consists of five elements,[39] as opposed to an Ākhyāna.[40] The *sāttvika* Purāṇas glorify Hari; the *rājasika* Purāṇas glorify Brahmā, and the *tāmasika* Purāṇas glorify Agni and Śiva. Purāṇas dealing with mixed modes of nature glorify Saraswatī and the *pitṛs*."[41] Jīva Goswāmī explains this verse thus: Agni refers to the various sacrifices offered in the three different fires; *śivasya ca* refers to Śiva and his consort; "mixed *kalpas*" refers to those Purāṇas composed of all three modes of nature. Sarasvatī refers to the goddess Sarasvatī and various other demigods and goddesses. *Pitṛs* refers to those sacrifices by which one can attain the *pitṛloka*.

The same *Matsya Purāṇa* tells us which Purāṇas deal with which modes of nature. But the question remains as to which Purāṇas, if any, are actually the best. How can one determine the relative importance of each grouping of Purāṇas? Here Jīva Goswāmī has concluded that because all the Purāṇas are advocating different deities as supreme, they cannot all be correct. Yet, because they are Purāṇas, they cannot be wrong either.

Monistic followers of Śaṅkara attempt to solve the problem of the multitude of gods and goddesses glorified throughout Vedic literature with the simplistic explanation that it is *nirviśeṣa*

---

39. The five elements that make up a Purāṇa are *sarga* (creation), *visarga* (secondary creation), *vaṁśa* (list of the dynasties), *vaṁśānucarita* (the activities of the various people of the dynasties), and *manvantara* (description of the Manus).

40. Ākhyānas are similar to Purāṇas and are found in the Vedas. They do not, however, contain the five essential elements of a Purāṇa.

41. *pañcāṅgaṁ ca purānaṁ syād ākhyānam itarat smṛtam/*
sattvikeṣu ca kalpeṣu māhātmyam adhikaṁ hareḥ//
rājaseṣu ca māhātmyam adhikaṁ brahmaṇo viduḥ/
tadvad agneś ca māhātmyaṁ tāmaseṣu śivasya ca/
saṅkīrṇesu sarasvatyāḥ pitṛṇāṁ ca nigadyate// (Ma. P. 190.13–14)

Brahman that is represented by innumerable gods and goddesses, suited as they are to different psychological types of practitioners. Thus for Śaṅkara, all of the Hindu pantheon represents an absolute that is ultimately without form. Worship of any of these forms leads to the one formless absolute. Form worship is considered worship of *saguna* Brahman, or Brahman manifesting in the material mode of *sattva* (goodness). By propitiating this so-called Brahman with material qualities and form, one is thought to eventually come to knowledge and realize that which is formless, *nirviśeṣa* Brahman. There are, however, more than a few problems with this approach. The least of these problems is the fact that nowhere in the *Vedānta-sūtra,* upon which Vedāntic doctrines must be based, is there any mention of anything remotely resembling Śaṅkara's imaginary *saguna* Brahman, or a relative absolute.[42] There is on the other hand much about an absolute with qualities and form that is constituted of Brahman rather than matter. Brahman is, according to *Vedānta-sūtra,* that about which there is much to say.[43] "The Lord has his own *parā śakti* which is herself the truth, and he has attributes as well." [44]

Śrī Jīva Goswāmī offers another, more plausible and scripturally supportable solution to the dilemma of many gods found in his now refined *śabda-pramāṇa,* the Purāṇas. All of the Purāṇas are correct, yet they are written for different groups of people, who are not all ready to hear the entire truth. As *Vedānta-sūtra* informs, *tat tu samanvayāt,*[45] proper understand-

42. George C. Adams, Jr., *The Structure and Meaning of Bādarāyaṇa's Brahma-sūtras,* p.129.

43. *īkṣater nāśabdam* (Vs. 1.1.6)

44. *sāeva hi satya-ādayaḥ* (Vs. 3.3.39)

45. Vs.1.1.4

ing of the unified message of the *śāstra* requires that we understand the context in which each text appears. Brahman, the subject of the Vedas, is spoken of directly and indirectly throughout the *śāstra*. With regard to the groupings of the various Purāṇas, categorized as they are in terms of the three modes of material nature, it should be apparent that some are written for those in the mode of ignorance, some for those in passion, and some for those in goodness. Those primarily influenced by the mode of ignorance *(tamas)* are encouraged to worship in one way; those influenced by passion *(rajas)* another. Those influenced by the mode of goodness *(sattva)* are taught to worship in yet another fashion. The purpose behind this threefold advocacy, however, is one. Gradually those in the mode of ignorance are elevated to passion through the *tāmasika* Purāṇas, and those in passion to goodness through the *rājasika* Purāṇas. Of the three material modes, *sattva,* or goodness, is best. Śrī Jīva cites *Bhagavad-gītā* and *Śrīmad-Bhāgavatam* as evidence: "From *sattva* knowledge arises,"[46] and "Goodness *(sattva)* is best, because by goodness one can come to realize the absolute truth (Brahman)."[47] Thus Śrī Jīva concludes that it is the *sāttvika* Purāṇas that lead us directly to the highest truth. From them we can learn who is the supreme Godhead and the supreme means of attainment. The other Purāṇas must be understood in relation to the *sāttvika* Purāṇas. This is the proper context.

The *sāttvika* Purāṇas, however, while emphasizing the supreme Godhead seem to differ. For example, the *Viṣṇu Purāṇa* advocates Viṣṇu, the *Varāha Purāṇa* praises Varāha *avatāra,* and the *Bhāgavata Purāṇa* emphasizes Kṛṣṇa. Although in a sense these deities are all the same *(viṣṇu tattva),* as opposed to Śiva,

---

46. *sattvāt sañjāyate jñānaṁ* (Bg. 14.17)

47. *sattvaṁ yad brahma-darśanam* (SB. 1.2.24)

Brahmā, Indra, and so on, the question remains as to who the principal deity is, the source of all others, and what the ideal means of attaining him is.

One possibility for resolving this dilemma Śrī Jīva suggests is to study the *Vedānta-sūtra*, for it was written with the view to determine the underlying unified teaching of all the Vedic literature. Vyāsadeva was the first in human society to ever attempt to demonstrate the concordance of revealed literature.[48] The Vedas have been called a jungle of sounds. From there, the lionlike king of this jungle, Śrī Vyāsa, called out the *Uttara Mīmāṁsā* along with his disciple Jaimini, who authored the *Pūrva Mīmāṁsā Sūtras*. These two demonstrated just how the apparently unrelated sounds of the *karma khaṇḍa* and *jñāña khaṇḍa* sections of the Vedas were intended to rule the world, taming people from their bestial nature, turning them systematically from the wild to their dutiful, religious, and ultimately transcendent potential.

Pūrva (earlier) *Mīmāmsā* deals with codes of working direction for human society, leading humanity to religion. *Uttara* (later) *Mīmāmsā,* or *Vedānta-sūtra,* is concerned with the final portion of the Vedas and is thus a treatise on Brahman, the transcendent absolute. *Pūrva Mīmāmsā* is no doubt also dealing with Brahman, yet it does so indirectly. *Vedānta-sūtra* demonstrates this, showing the concordance of the revealed scripture. The Vedas are all directly or indirectly dealing only with Brahman. There is no other topic contained therein. *Vedānta-sūtra*'s "But Brahman (Kṛṣṇa) is the only subject of the Vedas, and this is to be known by demonstrating concordance"[49] is in effect what the entire treatise is about—an attempt to demonstrate through

---

48. George C. Adams, Jr., *The Structure and Meaning of Bādarāyana's Brahma-sūtras,* p. 3.

49. *tat tu samanvayāt* (Vs. 1.1.4)

cryptic and concise language just what the long-winded Vedas and Purāṇas are all about.

But here also Śrī Jīva Goswāmī brings our attention to yet another difficulty we face in refining the *śabda-pramāṇa*. Vyāsa's *Sūtras* as mentioned are cryptic, and thus difficult to understand. In the *Sūtras* much is assumed on the part of the author as to the acquaintance of the student with the subject matter. Thus, although no one will disagree that the *Sūtras* are intended to reveal the essence of the Vedas, there are many interpretations of the *Sūtras*. The *Sūtras* are based on passages *(viṣaya vākya)* from the Upaniṣads, but Vyāsadeva does not mention in the *Vedānta-sūtra* which passages any particular *sūtra* is commenting upon. Thus the readers have been left to determine this themselves. It is no wonder then that Vyāsa, as mentioned in the *Śrīmad-Bhāgavatam*, felt his work was not yet complete even after compiling *Vedānta-sūtra*.[50]

It is in this discontentment of Vyāsa that Śrī Jīva finds the final resting place in this long and systematic search for the final word amid all that is known as *śabda*. The issue, he says, could be settled once and for all if we could find one scripture amid the entirety of the *śāstra* that is (1) Purāṇic in nature, (2) divinely composed, (3) representative of all the revealed scripture, (4) based on the *Vedānta-sūtra*, and (5) available in its complete form. After suggesting first the Veda, then the Purāṇas, followed by the *sāttvika* Purāṇas, Jīva Goswāmī has eliminated them all in his search for the perfect *pramāṇa*. On account of its cryptic style, lending to various interpretations, he has also eliminated the *Vedānta-sūtra*, seeking something that explains the *Sūtras* clearly, a commentary on the *Sūtras* not written by a human being handicapped by the four defects mentioned at the outset of this chapter. In eliminating these other scriptures he does not

50. SB. 1.4.30

by any means dismiss them altogether. Yet they do not individually or collectively serve as the spotless *pramāṇa* Śrī Jīva is after.

Yet does any book meet Śrī Jīva's fivefold criteria? Indeed there is one that does! The *Śrīmad-Bhāgavatam* perfectly fulfills the criteria. It is this book, the final work of Veda-Vyāsa, that puts the Vedic author's pen to rest, his heart satisfied that at long last his task was completed. This is so much so that without *Śrīmad-Bhāgavatam* no other single Vedic text, nor all other Vedic literature combined, offer much to humanity.[51] Thus with more than good reason Śrī Jīva Goswāmī describes *Śrīmad-Bhāgavatam,* the *Bhāgavata Purāṇa,* as the sovereign ruler of all *pramāṇas.*

In closing this chapter it is worth noting that the opinion of Jīva Goswāmī regarding *Śrīmad-Bhāgavatam* is gaining popularity. Many have understood the significance of *Śrīmad-Bhāgavatam* in terms of its place in Vedic literature. Although scholars do not agree with the practitioners as to the origins of the *Bhāgavatam,* nor that it was written by Vyāsa, this may be changing. In the least, some members of the academic community are meeting practitioners halfway.[52] Regarding the dating of the *Bhāgavata,* scholars do not all agree.[53] Recent evidence

---

51. (SB. 1.5.8)

52. Thomas Hopkins writes in "Bhakti in the *Bhāgavata Purāṇa,*" *Journal of Vaiṣṇava Studies,* Vol. 2 No. 3, "We do not know what hand or hands to credit for the monumental task of producing the *Bhāgavata.* Devotees will rightly say that it came from Kṛṣṇa...Scholars, however, without denying that the *Bhāgavata* is revelation, want to know also the human agents who put the revelation into its present form."

53. Ludo Rocher, "The Purāṇas " (Volume II), *A History of Indian Literature,* ed. Jan Gonda, (Wiesbaden: Otto Harrassowitz, 1986), pp. 102–103. Rocher writes, "Faced with endless speculations on the individual Purāṇas a number of scholars realized that there are serious limitations to our ability to date Purāṇas in their entirety...I submit that it is not possible to set a specific date for any Purāṇa as a whole."

substantiates the view that, in the least, the body of teaching that the *Bhāgavata* represents and its essence, found in the tenth canto, existed as early as the third century B.C.E.[54]

For a long time the *Śrīmad-Bhāgavatam* has been misconstrued to represent Śaṅkara's *advaitā-vedānta*, as has the entirety of Vedic literature. This is changing,[55] and much of the credit goes to Jīva Goswāmī and his modern-day followers.[56] The *Śrīmad-Bhāgavatam*, the very essence of the Vedas, is not about Śaṅkara's monism at all. Its glory and message constitute the balance of *Tattva-sandarbha*.

---

54. In his insightful article, "*Bhāgavata Purāṇa* in Stone," *Journal of Vaiṣṇava Studies*, Vol. 3 No. 3, Dennis Hudson writes "Evidence suggests that the archaic language of the Purāṇa's esoteric division needs to be taken seriously as reflecting an archaic body of teaching that may go back to 400 B.C.E...at least the lore of Books 9–10 of the *Bhāgavata Purāṇa* together with the *vyūha* theology were present all over Bhārata from at least the 3rd century B.C.E."

55. See *Journal of Vaishnava Studies*, Vol. 2, No. 3 and Daniel P. Sheridan's *The Advaitic Theism of the Bhāgavata Purāṇa* for excellent examples of this trend.

56. The impact of A. C. Bhaktivedanta Swami Prabhupāda's "Hare Kṛṣṇa Movement" and its worldwide distribution of his *Bhāgavatam* translation has drawn considerable attention to the *Bhāgavatam* and its Vaiṣṇava interpretation. Bhaktivedanta Swami Prabhupāda is easily the most well-known modern-day follower of Jīva Goswāmī.

4

"The Vedas advise like a king, the Purāṇas like a friend, and Kāvya like one's beloved, but the Bhāgavatam like all three combined."

The Glory of Śrīmad-Bhāgavatam

The glories of *Śrīmad-Bhāgavatam* are many. It more than meets Jīva Goswāmī's fivefold criterion for the perfect *pramāṇa* mentioned in *anuccheda* eighteen. *Anuccheda* nineteen states that the *Bhāgavatam* manifested from the trance *(samādhi)* of Vyāsadeva. This insight of Jīva Goswāmī makes for a unique approach to understanding the significance of *Śrīmad-Bhāgavatam*. The trance of Vyāsa is discussed in *anucchedas* thirty through forty-nine in considerable detail. In this book, it forms an entire chapter, "The Trance of Vyāsa." In *anuccheda* nineteen, Śrī Jīva is content to mention it in passing, noting also that the *Bhāgavatam* was written by Vyāsa after he had compiled all of the Vedic literature including the *Mahābhārata* and the *Vedānta-sūtra.* Śrī Jīva concludes from this that the *Bhāgavatam* serves as a natural commentary on the *Vedānta-sūtra*. He develops this important point further in *anuccheda* twenty-one.

Jīva Goswāmī also mentions the Vedic nature of the *Bhāgavatam,* which can be understood from the fact that it begins by invoking the *gāyatrī-mantra. Gāyatrī* is the prototype of all Vedic *mantras*. From *gāyatrī* the Vedas are said to have emanated. *Gāyatrī* is a concise statement as to the significance of all the Vedas. That *gāyatrī* is invoked in the opening stanza of the *Bhāgavatam* signifies that the entire text is an explanation of *gāyatrī.* This is confirmed in several Purāṇas, all of which make similar statements as to the characteristics of the *Bhāgavatam*. Śrī Jīva begins in *anuccheda* nineteen to cite these Purāṇic references in order to identify the *Bhāgavatam*,[1] in doing so stressing its reference to *gāyatrī*.

In the *Matsya Purāṇa* we find: "That which is based on the *gāyatrī*, and thus describes the essence of *dharma*, and narrates the history of the killing of Vṛtrāsura is known as the *Bhāgavata*. This Purāṇa consists of eighteen thousand verses, and whoever makes a copy of it and gives it away on a golden throne during the full moon in the month of Bhadra will attain the supreme destination."[2]

Jīva Goswāmī explains that the reference to *gāyatrī* in the *Bhāgavatam* mentioned in the *Matsya Purāṇa* refers to the word *dhīmahi* (we meditate) found in the first stanza, *satyaṁ paraṁ dhīmahi*. This word, which is distinctly Vedic in nature, is found in the exact same form in the *gāyatrī* itself, *bhargo devasya dhīmahi*. Because the *gāyatrī* is Vedic in nature, it is not quoted in full in *Śrīmad-Bhāgavatam*. Doing so would have been inappropriate in the Purāṇic setting in which the *Bhāgavatam* appears, the Purāṇas being open to those unqualified to chant the Vedic mantras. It is the grace of the *Bhāgavata* that, although Vedic in nature, it nonetheless makes itself available to all.

Śrī Jīva is not alone in concluding that the *Bhāgavatam*'s first stanza invokes the *gāyatrī*. Most commentators on the *Bhāgavatam* concur. Śrīdhara Swāmī in particular seems to have paved the

---

1. There is another book also known popularly as the *Bhāgavata*: the *Devi-Bhāgavata*. Jīva Goswāmī labors considerably to demonstrate that the *Bhāgavata* referred to in the Purāṇas he cites is none other than the *Śrīmad-Bhāgavatam*.

2. *yatrādhikṛtya gāyatrīṁ varṇyate dharma-vistaraḥ/*
vṛtrāsura-vadhopetaṁ tad bhāgavatam iṣyate//
ikhitvā tac ca yo dadhyād hema-siṁha-samanvitam/
prauṣṭha-padyāṁ paurṇamāsyāṁ sa yāti paramāṁ gatim/
aṣṭādaśa-śahasrāṇi purāṇaṁ tat prakīrtitam // (Ma. P. 53.20–22)

way for Jīva Goswāmī in his commentary on the first verse on the *Bhāgavatam*. Therein Śrīdhara Swāmī states, "In opening the *Śrīmad-Bhāgavatam* with the word *dhīmahi,* which is found in the *gāyatrī,* it is to be understood that this Purāṇa deals with spiritual knowledge *(brahma-vidyā)* as does *gāyatrī.*"

As far as the *Bhāgavatam*'s being based on *gāyatrī,* and thus explaining this *mantra,* Jīva Goswāmī cites two statements from the *Bhāgavatam*'s first verse that correspond with the *gāyatrī* and serve to illuminate the *gāyatrī*'s meaning. The phrases *janmād-yasya yataḥ* (from whom the world is manifest) and *tene brahmā hṛdā* (who nourished the creator with spiritual inspiration from within his heart) explain respectively the spiritual substratum of the material world, Brahman, and its ability to awaken spiritual knowledge within the *jīva* souls. These explanations of the nature of Brahman, the absolute truth, correspond with the *gāyatrī*'s explanation of the same found in the words *tat savitur* (that light of consciousness underlying the world) and *dhiyo yo naḥ pracodayāt* (may he mercifully inspire our thoughts in meditation upon him). Śrīdhara Swāmī states similarly in his *Bhāvārtha-dīpikā* commentary on *Śrīmad-Bhāgavatam* 1.1.1: "The phrase *tene brahmā hṛdā* indicates the meaning of *gāyatrī* in terms of its inspiring the intellect."

When *gāyatrī* says *"tat savitur,"* the question arises as to who *savitur* refers to. Is it the sun, fire, or some other personality represented by another prominent feature of nature? Persons chant *gāyatrī* with different conceptions as to just who *savitur* refers to. The definitive answer is given in the *Bhāgavatam,* which as the Purāṇas state is based on *gāyatrī* and serves as a commentary on it. The *Bhāgavatam* says that *savitur* is *janmādy asya yataḥ,* he from whom the world takes its birth *(janma)* and he by whose energy it is maintained and ultimately destroyed *(ādi). Savitur* thus refers to none other than Brahman, who is represented partially by sun, fire, and so on, being the light of lights. As *savitur* can refer to the light of the sun, which lights the world, in a deeper sense it can also refer to our conscious nature as *jīva* souls, which lights the world, being one with Brahman.

What is the meaning of *dhiyo yo naḥ pracodayāt*? Who is *gāyatrī* referring to when it says "he who inspires our intellect"? To this the *Bhāgavatam* replies *"tene brahmā hṛdā ya ādi-kavaye."* It is the one who nourished the heart of the creator Brahmā with spiritual insight, Bhagavān himself, Śrī Kṛṣṇa.

Later in this chapter, Śrī Jīva will discuss the significance of *gāyatrī* in relation to the *Bhāgavatam* in greater detail. Here in *anuccheda* nineteen he discusses this topic in brief, following the lead of Śrīdhara Swāmī. Śrīdhara Swāmī's commentary cites three Purāṇic verses that describe the *Bhāgavatam*. These verses are cited by Śrī Jīva in the following *anuccheda*. Before moving to the next *anuccheda,* Śrī Jīva states that *Śrīmad-Bhāgavatam* will reveal that the ultimate *dharma,* or engagement for human society, is meditation on Bhagavān. In stating this, he is commenting upon the word *dharma-vistaraḥ* found in the verse from *Matsya Purāṇa* cited above. There it was mentioned that the *Bhāgavatam* is characterized as that book in which *dharma* is described to its fullest extent. This is the type of *dharma* found in *Śrīmad-Bhāgavatam,* "This *Bhāgavatam* propounds the highest *dharma,* which is free from any ulterior motive,"[3] i.e., meditation in service to the absolute truth.

The *Skanda Purāṇa* and the *Agni Purāṇa* both glorify the *Bhāgavatam* thus: "That which is based on the *gāyatrī,* and thus describes the essence of *dharma,* and narrates the history of the killing of Vṛtrāsura is known as the *Bhāgavata.* It describes incidents dealing with both humans and gods that took place dur-

---

3. *dharmaḥ projjhita-kaitavo 'tra…* (SB. 1.1.2)

ing the Sāraswata *kalpa*. This Purāṇa consists of eighteen thousand verses, and whoever makes a copy of it and gives it away on a golden throne during the full moon in the month of Bhadra will attain the supreme destination."[4]

These lines from the *Agni* and *Skanda Purāṇas* differ only from the *Matsya Purāṇa* verse quoted above in that they mention the Sāraswata *kalpa*. During the Sāraswata *kalpa* histories concerning spiritual knowledge are recorded. The word *kalpa* refers to the Vedic time period consisting of one day of the creator, Brahmā. It may sometimes refer as well to shorter periods of time within the duration of Brahmā's day such as the change of Manus, *manvantaras*. In either case, the period of time is quite long by human calculation. Brahmā's day consists of one thousand *yuga* cycles (4,336,000,000 years). The Lord incarnates again and again, and his pastimes, when performed in different *yugas* or *kalpas* as the case may be, may vary in details. Thus there is variation in their performance. These variations appear to those not trained in the *guru paraṁparā* as inconsistencies in the Vedic literature, while in fact they amount to descriptions of pastimes occurring at different times as far apart as from one *kalpa* to another. Saraswatī is the goddess of learning. Thus the Sāraswata *kalpa* is one in which the histories dealing with the highest knowledge occur, such as those recorded in the *Bhāgavatam*.

Common to all three of the above Purāṇic quotations is the reference to giving the *Bhāgavatam* away on a golden throne.

---

4. *yatrādhikṛtya gāyatrīṁ ityādi/*
sārasvatasya kalpasya madhya ye syur narāmarāḥ/
tadvṛttāntodbhavaṁ loke tac bhāgavataṁ smṛtam//
likhitvā tac ca itiādi ca/
aṣṭādaśa-sahasrāṇi purāṇaṁ tat prakīrtitam//
(Sk. P.2.39–42 & Ag. P. 272.6-7)

We hear of no other book that the *śāstra* says should be given away on a golden throne. This is a singling out of the *Bhāgavatam* by the other Purāṇas, indicating that it is the king of scriptures *(grantha rāja)*. As a king should be honored with a throne, similarly the *Bhāgavatam* should be so revered. The throne of the *Bhāgavatam* is a *siṁhāsana*, or lion's throne. As the lion is the king of beasts, so the *Śrīmad-Bhāgavatam* is meant to rule over the beasts of our senses that call us to the wild of sensual abandon. It will tame us and then set us free in the suprasensual plane of Bhagavān.

Another characteristic of the *Bhāgavatam* common to both of these verses is one found in still another similar Purāṇic text. Jīva Goswāmī refers to this Purāṇa as "one quoted by the commentator," presumably Śrīdhara Swāmī. This text may be, as are many today, one that was at the time of Jīva Goswāmī not found in any edition of the then current manuscripts. He did apparently see it, however, in Śrīdhara Swāmī's commentary on the first stanza of the *Bhāgavatam*. The common characteristic is the slaying of Vṛtrāsura, a history found in the *Bhāgavatam*, and thus mentioned on account of its being a distinguishing trait. The citation is as follows: "The *Bhāgavata* is that scripture in which descriptions of the spiritual knowledge *(brahma-vidyā)* of Hayagrīva and the slaying of Vṛtrāsura are mentioned. It begins with a reference to *gāyatrī* and consists of twelve cantos and eighteen thousand verses."[5]

The significance of mentioning the *brahma-vidyā* of Hayagrīva along with the slaying of Vṛtrāsura is that there is no reference to Hayagrīva and *brahma-vidyā* in the *Devī-Bhāgavatam*. In discussing the killing of Vṛtrāsura, the *Śrīmad-Bhāgavatam*

---

5. *grantho 'ṣṭādaśa-sāhasro dvādaśa-skandha-sammitaḥ/*
hayagrīva-brahma-vidyā yatra vṛtra-vadhas tathā/
gāyatryā ca samārambhas tad vai bhāgavataṁ viduḥ//

alone mentions the fact that *brahma-vidyā* was given by Hayagrīva to one through whom it was eventually passed to Indra (in the form of *nārāyaṇa-varman,* an impenetrable *mantric* shield nondifferent from Nārāyaṇa himself). Indra's success against Vṛtrāsura depended upon acquiring from that same Hayagrīva a particular weapon.

Here Jīva Goswāmī wants to further emphasize that the ultimate *pramāṇa* is *Śrīmad-Bhāgavatam* and not the *Devī-Bhāgavatam*. It appears that this and the previous *anuccheda* are primarily making this important distinction. Śrī Jīva says that the name "Hayagrīva" refers to the sage Dadhīci who manifested *brahma-vidyā* in the form of *nārāyaṇa-varman*.

"Hayagrīva" could refer to a number of persons. *Śrīmad-Bhāgavatam* mentions a demon named Hayagrīva in the sixth and eighth cantos.[6] In the second and seventh cantos, Hayagrīva is mentioned as an *avatāra* of Viṣṇu.[7] Again in the sixth canto *Bhāgavatam* narrates the story of Dadhīci, referring to him as "horse-headed" (Aśvaśira).[8] "Hayagrīva" also means "one who has the head of a horse." Thus the question arises as to which Hayagrīva is being referred to. Is it the demon, the *avatāra,* or Dadhīci? The answer to this lies in the connection between Hayagrīva and *brahmā-vidyā* mentioned in the verse under discussion.

According to *Śrīmad-Bhāgavatam,* Dadhīci was approached by the Aśvinī-kumāras, who asked for *brahma-vidyā*. Dadhīci agreed to give it to them. They, however, were Ayurvedic physicians, and although *brāhmaṇas,* in Indra's estimation based on the *smṛti* they were not fit to receive *brahma-vidyā.* This was due to their occupation, which put them in intimate contact with

---

6. SB. 6.6.31, 6.10.19, 8.10.21.
7. SB. 2.7.11, 7.9.37.
8. SB. 6.9.52.

both unclean persons and unclean practices on a regular basis. Dadhīci was warned not to give them spiritual knowledge if he wanted to keep his head. The Aśvinī-kumāras, being physicians, assured him that they could restore his head should it be cut off. To prove this they cut off his head, preserved it, and put in its place the head of a horse. Through the horse's mouth Dadhīci spoke *brahmā-vidyā* to them, and afterwards Indra cut off his horse-head. The Aśvinī-kumāras then replaced Dadhīci's original head.

Later when Indra was fighting the formidable Vṛtrāsura, Nārāyaṇa advised him to go to the magnanimous Dadhīci and ask for his bones from which Indra could make a thunderbolt weapon and defeat Vṛtrāsura. At that time Nārāyaṇa mentioned the *nārāyaṇa-varman* as if to instill faith in Indra as to the prowess and magnanimity of Dadhīci. Jīva Goswāmī says that because the term *"hayagrīva-brahma-vidyā"* occurs alongside the phrase "slaying of Vṛtrāsura," it indicates that *brahma-vidyā* is a reference to *nārāyaṇa-varman* and "Hayagrīva" is a reference to Dadhīci.

Another verse quoted by Śrīdhara Swāmī in his commentary on *Śrīmad-Bhāgavatam* (6.9.52) confirms that *nārāyaṇa-varman* and *brahma-vidyā* are synonymous. "Dadhīci, the son of Atharvan, having been properly received by the Aśvinī-kumāras, taught them the Pravargya ceremony along with *brahma-vidyā* for fear of not breaking his promise to them."[9] Again, the conclusion Jīva Goswāmī effectively draws is that all of the Purāṇic verses cited above glorify the *Śrīmad-Bhāgavatam* and refer to it alone.

Continuing his glorification of *Śrīmad-Bhāgavatam,* Jīva Goswāmī says that the *Bhāgavatam* is very dear to Bhagavān

9. *etac chrutvā tathovāca dadhyaṇṇ ātharvaṇas tayoḥ/*
pravargyaṁ brahmavidyāṁ ca satkṛto śatya śankitaḥ// (*Bhāvārtha-dīpikā*)

and thus it must be as transcendental as the Lord is. *Bhāgavatam* is pleasing both to the Lord and to his devotees, whose only interest is that which is transcendental. *Śrīmad-Bhāgavatam* is therefore the most *sāttvika (paraṁ sāttvika)* of the Purāṇas. Jīva Goswāmī indicates here that the *Bhāgavatam* is not merely a *sāttvika* Purāṇa, it is *paraṁ-sattva,* dealing only with that which is purely transcendental. The material mode of goodness *(sattva-guṇa)* promotes spiritual thinking, while it is at the same time material and thus something that must be transcended. The term *paraṁ-sattva* refers not to the material mode of goodness, but to the transcendental *(paraṁ),* or *nirguṇa,* condition beyond all material qualities yet full of transcendental qualities such as are possessed by Bhagavān and his devotees. *Śrīmad-Bhāgavatam* refers to itself similarly in the twelfth canto, *Śrīmad-Bhāgavatam amalaṁ purāṇam. Śrīmad-Bhāgavatam* is the *amalaṁ,* or spotless (free from the modes of material nature), Purāṇa.

Jīva Goswāmī cites verses from the *Padma Purāṇa* to further establish that the *Bhāgavatam* is purely transcendental due to its capacity to bring pleasure to Hari (Bhagavān). "O King, do you discuss the *Bhāgavatam* which contains descriptions of Hiraṇya-kaśipu and his son Prahlāda before the Lord in the temple?"[10] Here Gautama is speaking to Mahārāja Ambarīṣa. The sage continues, "One should listen throughout the entire night to recitations of the Lord's glories found in scriptures such as *Bhagavad-gītā, Viṣṇu-sahasra-nāma,* and the *Bhāgavata Purāṇa* spoken by Śukadeva Goswāmī. These scriptures please the Lord very much, and thus they should be recited attentively."[11] In the

---

10. *purāṇaṁ tvaṁ bhāgavataṁ paṭhase purato hareḥ/*
caritaṁ daitya rājasya prahlādasya ca bhūpate// (Pa. P. *uttara khaṇḍa)*

11. *rātrau tujāgaraḥ kāryaḥ śrotavyā vaiṣṇavī kathā/*
gītā nāma sahasraṁ ca purāṇaṁ śukabhāṣitam/
paṭhītavyaṁ prayatnena hareḥ santoṣa kāraṇam// (Pa. P. *uttara khaṇḍa)*

Padma Purāṇa this is further emphasized thus: "O Ambarīṣa, if you desire to transcend birth and death, always listen to and recite the Purāṇa taught by Śukadeva Goswāmī."[12]

Śrī Jīva ends *anuccheda* twenty with a quotation from the *Skanda Purāṇa:* "He who stays awake reciting the *Bhāgavatam* with devotion in the presence of the Lord (in the temple) attains the abode of Viṣṇu along with his entire family."[13]

Anucchedas twenty-one and twenty-two explain the significance of two important verses found in the *Garuḍa Purāṇa.* These verses cannot be found in any of the existing manuscripts of this Purāṇa. They are, however, quoted by the Goswāmīs in other works and appear in the *Caitanya-caritāmṛta* as well. As mentioned in the introduction, several of the verses cited in *Tattva-sandarbha* are not found in any existing manuscripts.

Śrī Jīva Goswāmī's discussion of the *Garuḍa Purāṇa* verses cited in this section makes it clear that the claims of the verses are easily supportable. Thus Śrī Jīva's explanation of these verses serves to strengthen the well-founded conviction that this and other such verses were actually in earlier manuscripts. He saw them in the writings of other Vaiṣṇavas, most probably those of Śrīdhara Swāmī, Madhvācārya, and Rāmānuja.

Existing manuscripts aside, *Garuḍa Purāṇa* states: "That which is known as *Śrīmad-Bhāgavatam* is the natural commentary on *Vedānta-sūtra,* and from it one can know the purpose of the *Mahābhārata*. The *Śrīmad-Bhāgavatam* reveals the purport of the *gāyatrī mantra,* and it supplements the Vedas. It is the

---

12. *ambarīṣa śuka-proktaṁ nityaṁ bhāgavataṁ śṛṇu/*
paṭhasva sva-mukhenāpi yad icchasi bhava-kṣayam"//
(Pa. P. *uttara khaṇḍa)*

13. *srīmad-bhāgavataṁ bhaktyā paṭhate hari-sannidhau/*
jāgare tat-padaṁ yāti kula-vṛnda-samanvitaḥ//
(Sk. P. *Dvārakāmāhātmya, Prahlāda Saṁhitā)*

Sāma Veda of the Purāṇas, and it is directly spoken by Bhagavān himself. It consists of twelve cantos, numerous chapters, and eighteen thousand verses."[14] Here we find perhaps the most important statement of this chapter—the *Bhāgavatam* is a commentary on *Vedānta-sūtra* as well as on the *gāyatrī*, and it explains the purpose of the *Mahābhārata*.

Although other verses cited also describe the relationship between *gāyatrī* and the *Bhāgavatam*, *Garuḍa Purāṇa* is more specific in this regard—the entire *Bhāgavatam* is the purport of *gāyatrī*. Thus although Jīva Goswāmī has already discussed how the first verse of *Bhāgavatam* explains *gāyatrī*, here he will go into greater detail. Before doing so he explains how the *Bhāgavatam* explains the purpose of *Mahābhārata*, and in what way it is a commentary on the *Vedānta-sūtra*.

That the *Bhāgavatam* is a natural commentary on the *Sūtras* is foundational to the Gauḍīya *sampradāya*. At the time Jīva Goswāmī wrote *Tattva-sandarbha*, the Gauḍīya *sampradāya* had no commentary on the *Sūtras*. The reason for this was that Śrī Caitanya considered the *Bhāgavatam* Vyāsa's own commentary on his *Sūtras*, and thus, although an *ācārya* himself, Śrī Caitanya saw no need to write a Vedāntic commentary.

It was considered at that time that to establish one's school of thought as "Vedic" one needed a commentary on the *Vedānta-sūtra*. Śrī Caitanya brought in this sense a refreshing insight to the religious and scriptural history of India, although it did not go unchallenged. Long before that challenge and the *sampradāya*'s reply in the form of Baladeva Vidyābhūṣaṇa's

---

14. *artho'yaṁ brahma sūtrāṇāṁ bhāratārtha-vinirṇayaḥ/*
gāyatrī-bhāṣya-rūpo 'sau vedārtha paribṛṁhitaḥ//
purāṇānāṁ sāma-rūpaḥ sākṣād bhagavatoditaḥ/
dvādaśa-skandha yukto 'yaṁ śata-viccheda-samyutaḥ/
grantho 'ṣṭādaśa sāhasraḥ śrīmad-bhāgavatābhidhaḥ// (G. P.)

masterful *Govinda Bhāṣya,*[15] *Ṣaṭ-sandarbha* firmly established through logic and scripture that the *Śrīmad-Bhāgavatam* is the perfect commentary on Vyāsa's *sūtras.* Books being a much rarer commodity at the time, one cannot help but conjecture that the challengers had not the opportunity to consider Śrī Jīva's treatise.

Jīva Goswāmī considers Vyāsa's *sūtras* to be notes on that which he realized within his heart after having written all of the Vedic literature. The *Bhāgavatam* is those notes written out in longhand. In *Tattva-sandarbha* Jīva Goswāmī rests with this explanation. Having referred to the authority of the *Garuḍa Purāṇa,* he gives his explanation in brief. It seems that for him this is sufficient to make his case. It must however be remembered that *Tattva-sandarbha* is an introduction to his complete treatise, *Ṣaṭ-sandarbha.* Later in the *Paramātmā-sandarbha* Śrī Jīva gives an extended explanation of this point in his commentary on the first verse of the *Bhāgavatam.* There he reveals that all four *adhyāyas* of the *Vedānta-sūtra* are represented in seed in the first verse of *Śrīmad-Bhāgavatam,* and that the first verse itself serves as a commentary on the first five *sūtras* of the first *adhyāya.*

---

15. *Govinda Bhāsya* was written in Jaipur by Baladeva, who at the time was commissioned by Viśvanātha Cakravartī Ṭhākura to represent the dignity of the Gauḍīya *sampradāya.* The practices of the Gauḍīyas in Jaipur, amounting to worshipping Kṛṣṇa before Nārāyaṇa and worshipping Kṛṣṇa along with Rādhā, were objectionable to the Śrī *sampradāya.* In challenging the authority of the Gauḍīyas in general and their practice in particular, they asked the then quite young Baladeva to produce a commentary on the *Vedānta-sūtra* if he was to debate with them at all. He did so in a mere seven days having heard the commentary from the deity of Rūpa Goswāmī, Govindajī. It thus became known as "Govinda Bhāṣya," the speech of Govinda, and Baladeva was crowned with the prestigious title "Vidyābhūṣaṇa," the ornament of knowledge. He opens his commentary by acknowledging that the *Śrīmad-Bhāgavatam* itself is the natural commentary on the *Sūtras.*

Śrī Jīva seems more concerned about explaining *Garuḍa Purāṇa*'s statement about the *Bhāgavatam*'s revelatory relationship with *gāyatrī* and how the *Bhāgavatam* sheds light on the significance of the *Mahābhārata* (spending considerably more time discussing these two glories of the *Bhāgavatam*). The followers of Jīva Goswāmī, however, have written extensively about the *Bhāgavatam* as a natural commentary on the *Vedānta-sūtra*. Viśvanātha Cakravartī discusses it in his commentary on the first verse of the *Bhāgavatam*.[16] In recent times, Haridas Śāstrī has written *Vedānta Darśana*, in which he has shown how Vyāsa's every *sūtra* is most perfectly explained by citations from *Śrīmad-Bhāgavatam*. *A Vaiṣṇava Interpretation of the Brahma-sūtras* by Rampada Chattopadhyaya contains an excellent chapter dedicated to explaining this point. There is no dearth of insight among Gauḍīya Vaiṣṇavas as to how *Śrīmad-Bhāgavatam* is the natural commentary on the *Sūtras* of Vyāsa. Their explanations all attest to the fact that Śrī Caitanya's insight in this regard is one of the most significant contributions to the school of Vedānta. Commentaries on the *Sūtras* are many, but Śrī Jīva accepts only those that are in consonance with Vyāsa's self-revealed natural commentary—*Śrīmad-Bhāgavatam*.

The *Bhāgavatam*, being the final composition of Vyāsa, was written after the *Mahābhārata*. There is some confusion about this chronology, and Śrī Jīva will clear it up in his discussion of Vyāsadeva's *samādhi*. Here, in *anuccheda* twenty-three, he explains how the *Bhāgavatam* reveals Vyāsa's intent while writing his classic epic, *Mahābhārata*.

The *Bhāgavatam* and *Mahābhārata* alike, says Śrī Jīva, deal only with Bhagavān. Considering the *Nārāyaṇīya* section of the *Mahābhārata* as the most significant, Jīva Goswāmī notes that

---

16. For an English explanation of this see Swāmī B.V. Tripurāri, "Chaitanya's Bhāgavata," *The Gaudiya*, Vol. 2 No. 3. (1994).

Mahābhārata offers the highest knowledge, namely knowledge of the glory of Nārāyaṇa (Bhagavān). "O *brāhmaṇa*, rich in austerity, just as butter is churned from milk and the scent of sandalwood from the wind in Malaya, the Upaniṣads from the Vedas, and nectar from medicinal herbs, similarly by churning the ocean of truth with the staff of knowledge, out of the one hundred thousand verses of the *Mahābhārata* we are left with your nectarine words based on topics related to Nārāyaṇa."[17]

It is within the *Mahābhārata* that we find the *Bhagavad-gītā*, considered by all to be the essence of the epic. While *Bhagavad-gītā* is spoken by Kṛṣṇa, Śukadeva's *Bhāgavatam* is spoken about Kṛṣṇa, his nature and innermost thoughts. The inner meaning of the *Gītā* can thus be drawn only from acquaintance with the *Bhāgavatam* and Kṛṣṇa's inner nature.

Kṛṣṇa concludes the *Gītā* by telling Arjuna to forgo *dharma*. Thus the *Gītā* is ultimately not about *dharma*. What is it about? It is about *prema*. Kṛṣṇa tells Arjuna to forsake *dharma* and surrender unto him.[18] In doing so, he uses the word *"vraja,"* which means to "go," or "come." Kṛṣṇa is saying, "Come to me," "Take refuge in me." According to Sanskrit *alaṅkāra* (rhetoric), *dhvani* is when the very sound of a word suggests an ornamen-

---

17. *idaṁ śata-sahasrād dhi bhāratākhyāna-vistarāt/*
āmathya matimanthena jñānodadhim anuttamam//
navanītaṁ yathā dadhno malayāc candanaṁ yathā/
āraṇyaṁ sarva-vedebhy oṣadibhyo 'mṛtaṁ yathā//
samuddhṛtam idaṁ brahman kathāmṛtam idaṁ tathā/
tapo-nidhe tvayoktaṁ hi nārāyaṇa-kathāśrayam//

(M. Bh. Mokṣadharma 170.11.14)

18. *sarva-dharmān parityaja mām ekaṁ śaraṇaṁ vraja/*
ahaṁ tvāṁ sarva-pāpebhyo mokṣayiṣyāmi mā śucaḥ//

"Abandoning all types of religious duties *(dharma)*, surrender unto me alone. Do not fear, for I will protect you from any consequences." (Bg. 18.66)

tal meaning. Here, *"vraja"* can thus be taken as a suggestion as to what it means to go with Kṛṣṇa. It means to go to Vraja, or Vṛndāvana, where Kṛṣṇa *līlā* fully expresses itself.[19] The essence of Vraja is described only in *Śrīmad-Bhāgavatam*. When Kṛṣṇa uttered *"vraja"* his preaching came to a close. He himself was transported to the *bhāva*, or transcendental emotion, of the land of Vraja, where preaching ends in a life of *prema*. Thus from the *Bhāgavatam* we can get the deepest understanding of the message of the *Gītā*, which is the message of the *Mahābhārata* and all the Vedas.

Jīva Goswāmī mentions a story from the Vedic literature presumably so well-known at the time that he sees no necessity to cite a reference for it. The story illustrates the weightiness of the *Mahābhārata*. Once Vyāsa gathered together Brahmā and all of the demigods and *ṛṣis* and asked them to place both the *Mahābhārata* and the Vedas on a scale to see which was heavier. The scales tipped in favor of the *Mahābhārata*. It thus became known as *Mahābhārata* because of its greatness *(mahattva)* and its heaviness *(bhārāva)*.[20]

The purport of the Vedas is found in the *Mahābhārata*, woven throughout stories that appear to be mundane. *Mahābhārata* is equal to the Vedas in terms of its message, yet greater in terms of its mode of expression. This is directly stated in the *Śrīmad-Bhāgavatam*: "Your friend, the great sage Kṛṣṇa-

---

19. Śrīla Bhakti Rakṣaka Śrīdhara Deva Goswāmī, *Śrīmad Bhagavad-gītā: Hidden Treasure of the Sweet Absolute.* (Nabadwip, India: Dayādhara Gaurāṅga Dāsa Brahmacārī, 1985).

20. *nirṇayaḥ sarva-śāstrāṇāṁ bhārataṁ parikīrtitam/*
bhārataṁ sarva-vedāś ca tulām āropītāḥ purā//
devair brahmādibhiḥ sarvairṣibhiś ca samanvitaiḥ/
vyāsasyaivājñayā tatra tv atiricyate bhāratam/
mahattvād bhāravattvāc ca mahābhāratam ucyate//

dvaipāyana Vyāsa, has already described the glories of the Lord in the *Mahābhārata* with the idea of drawing the attention of the masses to topics concerning the Lord (*Bhagavad-gītā*) by placing them within descriptions of worldly pleasures."[21] We also find the following, "The sage Vyāsa compiled the *Mahābhārata* out of compassion for the lowborn, to elevate those who are not qualified to read the Vedas, deluded as they are as to what is the proper behavior and the ultimate good."[22] In this way, *Śrīmad-Bhāgavatam* sheds light on the significance of the *Mahābhārata* by revealing the intentions of its author.

Having commented on the *Bhāgavatam*'s relationship with *Vedānta-sūtra* and *Mahābhārata* in accordance with the two *Garuḍa Purāṇa* verses under discussion, Jīva Goswāmī returns to a discussion of the relationship between the *Śrīmad-Bhāgavatam* and *gāyatrī*. *Garuḍa Purāṇa* states: "*Śrīmad-Bhāgavatam* is a commentary on the *gāyatrī mantra*." Because the *Bhāgavatam* is discussing Bhagavān exclusively, to a greater extent and in greater detail than any other Vedic literature, it serves as an explanation of *gāyatrī*, which is itself a meditation on Bhagavān. But *gāyatrī* is understood by others to be meditation upon a number of things other than Bhagavān. Thus Śrī Jīva labors to demonstrate that *gāyatrī*, like *Śrīmad-Bhāgavatam*, is an exclusive meditation on Bhagavān.

Without citing any reference, Śrī Jīva states that *Viṣṇu-dharmottara Purāṇa* describes that Bhagavān alone is the subject

---

21. *munir vivakṣur bhagavad-guṇānāṁ sakhāpi te bhāratam āha kṛṣṇaḥ/*
yasmin nṛṇāṁ grāmya-sukhānuvādair matir gṛhītā nu hareḥ kathāyam//
(SB. 3.5.12)

22. *strī śūdra dvija bandhūnaṁ trayī na śruti-gocarā/*
karma śreyasi mūḍhānaṁ śreya evaṁ bhaved iha/
ti bhāratam ākhyānaṁ kṛpayā muninā kṛtam// (SB. 1.4.25)

of *gāyatrī*. Apparently, *Viṣṇu-dharmottara* discusses how the *Bhāgavatam*'s first verse explains *gāyatrī*, for Jīva Goswāmī states that he will give a similar explanation of this *Bhāgavatam* stanza. Here he is referring to his own explanation, which is based on the *Agni Purāṇa* and appears in his *Paramātmā-sandarbha*. In *Tattva-sandarbha*, Śrī Jīva cites the *Agni Purāṇa* to further establish that *gāyatrī* is concerned solely with Bhagavān.

"The 'light' *(bhargo)* found in *gāyatrī* is the Supreme Brahman, for the 'light' means consciousness."[23] The word *bhargo* in *gāyatrī* comes from the root *bhṛij* indicating action that requires heat or light. *Gāyatrī* is speaking of the light of the world which could be construed as reference to the sun or fire upon which we are so dependent. But it is not by sunlight or the illumination of fire that we see. It is not by this kind of light that we live. We ourselves are in a deeper sense the illuminating influence of the world. It is consciousness that sees, and this without the help of anything material. It is not that because we have eyes we can see. We are the seer. Experience is the prerogative of consciousness alone. Yet our consciousness is dependent upon another, the supreme consciousness, *paraṁ* Brahman. This then is the "light" of *gāyatrī* indicated by the word *bhargo*. This light is *vareṇyaṁ* (that which is most desirable, excellent) to us. Although we are conscious, we are nonetheless dependent entirely upon he who is self-illumined by dint of his own *svarūpa śakti*.

Agni Purāṇa continues, "That light is Bhagavān Viṣṇu, who is the cause of the entire world. Some worshippers understand it to indicate Śiva, Sūrya, or others. Others take it to be indicative of Agni, the god of fire. Yet it is actually Viṣṇu alone, who

---

23. *taj jotiḥ paramaṁ brahma bhargas tejo yataḥ smṛtaḥ//* (Ag. P. 216.3)

assumes the forms of these different gods for various functions, who is glorified in the Vedas as Brahman."[24]

Śrī Jīva notes that the *Bhāgavatam* directly mentions *gāyatrī* twice, once in the opening stanza and again at the close of the *Bhāgavatam*. In the final canto of *Śrīmad-Bhāgavatam,* we find *gāyatrī* again indicated by the word *dhīmahi,* as it was at the outset, *satyaṁ paraṁ dhīmahi*. The last line of this verse gives an import of *gāyatrī* comparable with that found in the *Agni Purāṇa*. The *Bhāgavata*'s verse "Let us meditate upon the purest Supreme Brahman, who is beyond all misery,"[25] is thus comparable to the *Agni Purāṇa*'s verse, "Let us meditate upon the eternally pure Supreme Brahman, the perpetual light, who is the supreme controller, by contemplating 'I am of the same light as the Supreme Brahman,' and in this way attain *prema (vimuktaye)*."[26] Here *ahaṁ jyotiḥ paraṁ brahma* ("I am the light of the Supreme Brahman") indicates that one must understand oneself to be consciousness (Brahman) to worship *(dhyāyema)* Brahman, just as one must acquire the mentality of an Indian to truly experience India. That *dhīmahi* is in the plural, as it appears in both *Śrīmad-Bhāgavatam* and *gāyatrī,* indicates that it is advocating worship, or devotion to the supreme, not becoming the supreme. The many *jīvas* should meditate upon the one supreme Brahman. It is also significant that *Bhāgavatam* opens and closes with *gāyatrī,* for examining the concordance between

---

24. *taj jhotir bhagavān viṣṇur jagajjanmādikāraṇam/*
śivaṁ kecit paṭhanti sma śakti-rūpam vadanti ca/
kecit sūryaṁ kecid agniṁ daivatāny agni-hotriṇaḥ//
agny-ādirūpo viṣṇur hi vedādau brahma gīyate/ (Ag.P. 216.7–9)

25. *tac chuddhaṁ vimalaṁ viśokam amṛtam satyaṁ paraṁ dhīmahi//* (SB. 12.13.19)

26. *nitayaṁ śuddhaṁ paraṁ brahma nitya bhargam adhīśvaram/*
ahaṁ jyotiḥ paraṁ brahma dhyāyema hi vimuktaye// (Ag. P. 216.6)

the opening and closing statement of any text is part of the six-fold traditional means of determining its meaning.[27]

Śrī Jīva, however, raises a technical argument against his own postulate based on the rules of Sanskrit grammar. In the verse from *Agni Purāṇa* just cited, the word *bhargam* appears. If it is referring to *bhargo* in *gāyatrī*, explaining that it indicates the Supreme Brahman, one would expect that in *gāyatrī* the word would appear in the same form, i.e., "*bhargam.*" This is the regular accusative singular ending of a word ending in *a* (*adanta* stem). Jīva answers this objection with a reference to the *ādi* grammarian Pāṇini, who has given license for Vedic irregularity.[28]

Someone may object further to the idea that *gāyatrī* refers to Brahman, rather than the sun, based on statements of the *Bhāgavatam* itself. Therein Yājñavalkya worshipped the sun,[29] indicating this to be the object of worship during the three *sandhyās.*[30] Later in the same canto, in relation to the meditation of Yājñavalkya, we also find *sūryātmano hareḥ*[31] uttered by Śaunaka. These references, Jīva Goswāmī instructs, are to be understood not as an advocacy of sun worship, rather of wor-

---

27. *upakramopasaṁhārāv abhyāso 'pūrvatā phalam/*
arthavādopapattī ca liṅgaṁ tātparya-nirṇaye//

"The method by which the essence of any *śāstra* can be ascertained consists of examining (1) the opening and closing statements, (2) that which is repeated throughout, (3) that which is unique about the text, (4) the result or fruit of applying the text, (5) that which the author states is its meaning, and (6) reasoning.

28. *Pāṇini-sūtra* 7.1.39

29. SB 12.6.67–69

30. *Gāyātri* is chanted thrice daily: dawn, noon, and dusk. These are the three *sandhyas*.

31. SB.12.11.28

ship of the Paramātmā dwelling within the sun, Sūrya Nārāyaṇa. *Agni Purāṇa* states, "By meditation upon the sun one can realize the Lord dwelling therein, but the supreme abode *(paramaṁ padaṁ)* is that of Viṣṇu *(sadāśiva)*."[32] The idea here is that through meditation the *purūṣa* can be realized, not that which we can already see with our eyes (the sun). Yet the sun, visible as it is, can help us. It can serve as a starting point for our meditation, wherein we think that the Lord is present as the sun watching over us at all times. However, eventually the sun will burn out. But the abode of the Lord is itself Brahman and thus imperishable and the true object of meditation. This is the object of meditation found in *gāyatrī* and *Śrīmad-Bhāgavatam*.

Śrīmad-Bhāgavatam's characteristic of being "based upon *gāyatrī*" as mentioned in other Purāṇas quoted earlier is also mentioned in the *Agni Purāṇa*. In this section *Agni Purāṇa* also describes the characteristics of other Purāṇas. About the *Śrīmad-Bhāgavatam* it says: "It is the opinion of the *Agni Purāṇa* that *gāyatrī* is solely concerned with the Supreme Lord, who is the creator, preserver, and destroyer of the world. The *Śrīmad-Bhāgavatam,* which is known for being based upon the *gāyatrī* (which is thus also about the Supreme Lord, *janmādy asya yataḥ*), reigns victorious all over the earth."[33]

Concluding this discussion, Jīva Goswāmī refers back to the *Skanda Purāṇa*'s statement that the *Bhāgavatam*'s stories are associated with the Sāraswata *kalpa*. The presiding deity of this

---

32. *dhyānena puruṣo 'yaṁ ca draṣṭavyaḥ sūrya-maṇḍale/*
satyaṁ sadāśivaṁ brahma tad viṣṇoḥ paramaṁ padam//
(Ag. P. 216.16–17)

33. *agneḥ puraṇaṁ gāyatrīṁ sametya bhagavat-parām/*
bhagavantaṁ tatra matvā jagaj-janmādikāraṇam//
yatrādhikṛtya gāyatrīm iti lakṣaṇa-pūrvakam/
śrīmad-bhāgavtaṁ śaśvat pṛthvyāṁ jayati sarvataḥ// (Ag. P.)

kalpa is the goddess Sarasvatī, who has speech about Bhagavān as her distinguishing characteristic. Thus, that the *Bhāgavatam* and *gāyatrī* are identified with Saraswatī is most appropriate. *Gāyatrī*'s association with Sarasvatī is mentioned thus in the *Agni Purāṇa*: "*Gāyatrī* is named such because it is a song that reveals the *śruti, smṛti,* the divine light of consciousness, and the life force. It is known as Sāvitrī, or the daughter of the sun, because of its illuminating power. Because this *gāyatrī* is the daughter of the sun and the essence of speech, which is ruled by fire, it is also called Sarasvatī."[34]

Gāyatrī and *Śrīmad-Bhāgavatam* are thus synonymous, and thereby *Bhāgavatam* is the essence of revealed scripture. After such an explanation of but part of *Garuḍa Purāṇa*'s two verses, one is moved to accept that they are indeed authentic. Jīva Goswāmī is systematically demonstrating the truth of the *Purāṇa*'s statement, and he is not finished yet. *Garuḍa Purāṇa* states next, "It is the *Sāma Veda* of the Purāṇas." This is a glorification stating that just as the *Sāma Veda* is the best of the Vedas, so the *Bhāgavatam* is the best of Purāṇas. Previously, Śrī Jīva has shown how the *Bhāgavatam* is the best of the Purāṇas. Here he will discuss it again in brief, shedding even more light on the glory of *Śrīmad-Bhāgavatam*.

Why is the *Sāma Veda* the best of the Vedas? The *Sāma Veda* deals primarily with that which the Vedas are ultimately about—worship. It is filled with hymns; it is the Veda of song. Although it is primarily derived from the *Ṛg Veda* (only seventy-eight of its verses are not found also in the *Ṛg Veda),* it is nonetheless the best of the Vedas according to the *Garuḍa Purāṇa* because it brings out that theme that is central to all of

---

34. *gāyaty ukthāni śastrāṇi bhargaṁ prāṇaṁs tathaiva ca/*
tataḥ smṛteyaṁ gāyatrī sāvitrī yata eva ca/
prakāśinī sa savitur vāgrūpatvāt sarasvatī// (Ag. P. 216.1–2)

the Vedas. In the same way, the *Bhāgavatam* brings out directly that which all of the Purāṇas are ultimately speaking about. While some Purāṇas seem to indicate *tāmasika* or *rājasika* ends, they are ultimately aimed at gradually bringing one to the transcendental result of love of God. This is their underlying theme. Jīva Goswāmī here quotes an unidentified verse, "In the *Vedas, Rāmāyaṇa, Purāṇas,* and *Mahābhārata,* it is Hari who is praised in the beginning, middle, and end."[35] Thus as the *Sāma Veda* is the best of the Vedas, *Bhāgavatam* is the best of the Purāṇas. Its glory is further described in this connection in the *Skanda Purāṇa* thus: "If one keeps hundreds and thousands of scriptures in his house in Kali-yuga yet does not keep the *Bhāgavatam* what good will this do? If one in Kali-yuga does not keep the *Bhāgavatam* in his house, how can he be considered a Vaiṣṇava? Even if such a person is a *brāhmaṇa,* he should be considered lower than a dog-eater. O Nārada, wherever the *Bhāgavatam* is kept in Kali-yuga, Hari goes there with all the demigods. O sage, those pious souls who recite even a single verse of the *Bhāgavatam* daily reap the fruits of having studied all eighteen Purāṇas."[36]

Garuḍa Purāṇa also tells us the *Bhāgavatam* is glorious also on account of its having been spoken directly by Kṛṣṇa. It is

---

35. *vede rāmāyaṇe caiva purāṇe bhārate tathā/*
ādāv ante ca madhye ca hariḥ sarvatra gīyate//

36. *śataśo 'tha sahasraiś ca kim anyaiḥ śāstra-saṁgrahaiḥ/*
na yasya tiṣṭhate gehe śāstraṁ bhāgavataṁ kalau//
kathaṁ sa vaiṣṇavo jñeyaḥ śāstraṁ bhāgavataṁ kalau/
gṛhe na tiṣṭhate yasya sa vipraḥ śvapacādhamaḥ//
yatra yatra bhaved vipra śāstraṁ bhāgavataṁ kalau/
tatra tatra harir yāti tridaśaiḥ saha nārada//
yaḥ paṭhet prāyato nityaṁ ślokaṁ bhāgavataṁ mune/
aṣṭādaśa-purāṇānaṁ phalaṁ prāpnoti mānavaḥ//
(Sk. P. *viṣnu khaṇḍa* 16.40, 42, 44, 331)

thus *śruti-sāram ekam,* the essence of the *śruti. Śrīmad-Bhāgavatam* concludes itself by stating, "Let us meditate upon the Supreme Lord *(satyaṁ paraṁ)*... who revealed the *Bhāgavatam* to Brahmā."[37]

That it was Śrī Kṛṣṇa himself, rather than Viṣṇu, who spoke the four original verses of the *Bhāgavatam* to Brahmā is proved by Jīva Goswāmī in his *Bhagavat-sandarbha.* There he cites the *Bhāgavatam* and *Gopāla-tāpanī śruti.* There is a distinction between *Bhāgavata,* or Bhagavān, and the *puruṣa,* from whom Brahmā took birth. *Śrīmad-Bhāgavatam* is the *Bhāgavata Purāṇa,* not the "*Puruṣa Purāṇa.*" It is that which was spoken by Bhagavān about himself. The first *puruṣa-avatāra* did not speak the *Bhāgavatam* in four verses to Brahmā, it was Bhagavān himself *(svayam bhagavān)* in the dress of a cowherder *(gopa-veṣa).* Śrī Kṛṣṇa mentioned to Uddhava that he spoke the *Bhāgavatam* to Brahmā as well.[38] And Sūta Goswāmī describes the incident similarly.[39] This is certainly an extraordinary opulence of the *Bhāgavatam,* to have been directly spoken by *svayam bhagavān.*

Later the *Bhāgavatam* was expanded by Śukadeva into eighteen thousand verses spread over twelve cantos and numerous chapters *(śataviccheda).* The actual number of chapters is 335. There is, however, some controversy regarding this number. Jīva Goswāmī deals with this controversy in his *Laghu-vaiṣṇava-toṣanī.*[40] Here in *Tattva-sandarbha* he elects not to lengthen his treatise unnecessarily by discussing it. Instead he concludes

---

37. *kasmai yena vibhāsito 'yam atulo jñāna-pradīpaḥ purā/* (SB. 12.13.19)

38. SB. 3.4.13

39. SB. 12.13.10

40. Śrīdhara Swāmī appears to describe the *Bhāgavatam* as consisting of 332 chapters. In his explanation of Sanātana Goswāmī's *Vaiṣṇava Toṣanī* commentary on SB. 10.12.1, Jīva Goswāmī explains Śrīdhara Swāmī's term *dvātriṁśat triśataṁ,* which appears to indicate 332 chapters, as indicating 335. His explanation is based on the rules of Sanskrit grammar.

anuccheda twenty-two by reminding us how fitting the Purāṇa's words "mounted on a throne of gold" are in relation to this king of scriptures. It is the sovereign ruler of all scriptures that should be studied repeatedly by all, as stated in the *Skanda Purāṇa,* "Of what use are hundreds and thousands of other scriptures (in comparison with the *Bhāgavatam*)?"[41]

Jīva Goswāmī begins *anuccheda* twenty-three with a citation from *Śrīmad-Bhāgavatam* in which the *Bhāgavatam* describes itself through the mouth of Sūta Goswāmī. Here Sūta Goswāmī answers the query of Śaunaka in the first chapter as to who will protect the principles of religion once Kṛṣṇa has left the world. "This Purāṇa has arisen just like the sun for those bereft of sight in the Kali-yuga."[42] This verse explains that the *Bhāgavatam* embodies the religion and knowledge that Kṛṣṇa himself embodies. Other than this self-illumined *Bhāgavatam,* no scripture is capable of shedding light on the ultimate nature of reality.

The *Bhāgavatam* is accepted as such by many great souls, who have themselves written commentaries on it or extracted sections of it to demonstrate its significance. Jīva Goswāmī lists several commentaries and digests. *Tantra-bhāgavata* is for all intents and purposes a commentary, while the *Hanumad-bhāṣya, Vāsānabhāṣya, Sambandhokti, Vidvat-kāmadhenu, Tattva-dīpikā, Bhāvārtha-dīpikā, Paraṁahaṁsa-priyā, Śuka-hṛdaya,* and others are actual commentaries. This is Śrī Jīva's list of ancient commentaries among which only Śrīdhara Swāmī's *Bhāvārtha-dīpikā* is available today. *Muktā-phala, Hari-līlā,* and *Bhakti-ratnāvalī* are listed as *nibandhas,* or digests. The *Caturvarga-cintāmaṇi* praises the *Bhāgavatam* in the same way the *Matsya Purāṇa* has in the verse cited earlier, and in the same book the *Bhāgavatam*'s ad-

41. *śataśo 'tha sahasraiś ca kim anyaiḥ śāstra-saṁgrahaiḥ/* (Sk. P. 16.40)

42. *kalau naṣṭa-dṛśām eṣa purāṇārko 'dhunoditaḥ//* (SB. 1.3.43)

vocacy of congregational chanting of the holy names of God *(saṅkīrtana)* as the *yuga dharma* is accepted.[43]

Śrī Jīva notes that Śaṅkara did not comment on the *Bhāgavatam*. Yet if the *Bhāgavatam* was as readily accepted as Jīva Goswāmī makes it appear, surely Śaṅkara would have commented upon it. The fact that he did not has contributed to the academic theories that date the writing of the *Bhāgavatam* after the time of Śaṅkara (eighth century C.E.), theories that, although once widely accepted, are now in question. Śrī Jīva offers another scenario regarding Śaṅkara's relationship with the king of scriptures, one that turns Śaṅkara's apparent disinterest in the *Bhāgavatam* into just the opposite—glorification of *Śrīmad-Bhāgavatam*.

Śaṅkara is accepted by the Vaiṣṇavas as an incarnation of Śiva. Out of deference to the *Bhāgavatam*, which so directly opposed his doctrine of illusion *(māyāvāda)*, Śaṅkara did not venture to cloud with the gray skies of his bleak doctrine the pristine pages of this scripture, in which the *līlās* of Śrī Kṛṣṇa shine forth like the brilliance of the sun. It was at the behest of Viṣṇu that Śiva ventured to propagate his *māyāvāda* doctrine,[44] and the *Bhāgavatam*, in pursuit of Viṣṇu's order, was not to be tampered with. Yet as Śrī Jīva points out, Śaṅkara deeply appreciated the *Bhāgavatam*, and the *Bhāgavatam* also contains considerable praise of Śaṅkara (Śiva). Śaṅkara's appreciation is found in his poems such as *Govindāṣṭaka*, in which *līlās* found only in *Śrīmad-Bhāgavatam* are glorified. Thus it was most certainly available at the time of Śaṅkara, and his direct avoidance of it, as well as his covert glorification of *Śrīmad-Bhāgavatam*, serve as evidence as to this most famous *ācārya*'s appreciation for the essence of all revealed scripture.

43. *kaliṁ sabhājayanty āryāḥ* (SB. 11.5.36)

44. Pa. P. *uttara khanda* 25.7

Madhvācārya, whom Jīva Goswāmī considers to have been formally in the *sampradāya* of Śaṅkara, on coming in contact with the *Bhāgavatam*, rejected the *māyāvāda* doctrine. Subsequently, Madhva wrote his own commentary on the *Bhāgavatam* known as *Bhāgavata-tātparya*, in which he comments only upon those verses which seem to lend support to Śaṅkara's interpretation of Vedānta. In doing so, Madhva demonstrated clearly that the *Bhāgavatam* does not support Śaṅkara's *māyāvāda* doctrine. Although Śaṅkara himself did not comment upon the *Bhāgavatam*, several of his followers did, and such editions were prominent during the time of Madhva. In this connection, Śrī Jīva mentions the commentary of Puṇyāraṇya, which is not available today.

Śrī Jīva mentions Madhvācārya with a noteworthy tone of respect, for the Gauḍīya Vaiṣṇavas derive their validity as a *sampradāya* to some extent from Madhva. A verse from *Padma Purāṇa* states that there are four *sampradāyas.* They stem from Brahmā, Rudra, Sanat Kumāra, and Lakṣmī respectively. The implication of this verse (which is not found in any current editions of the Purāṇa) is that without initiation into one of these *sampradāyas*, one's doctrine is not considered authoritative.[45] Even a new creed must have its connection with one of these *sampradāyas* to have validity. Śaṅkara himself has stated this strongly in his *Gītā* commentary. "A man who does not belong to a *sampradāya* must be ignored, as one would ignore a fool."[46]

Madhva appeared in the Brahmā *sampradāya*, and the Gauḍīyas trace their connection with his lineage. This connec-

---

45. Cited in *The Vedānta Sūtras of Bādarāyaṇa with Commentary of Baladeva*, (New Delhi: Munshiram Manoharlal Publishers Pvt. Ltd., 1979), Appendix 2, p. 3.

46. Gita Press edition, p. 310. Cited by A. K. Majumdar in *Caitanya: His Life and Doctrine*, p. 266.

tion is, however, not based on concurrent doctrine. The Gauḍīyas differ on at least ten points of philosophy from the Madhva *sampradāya*. Yet they have adopted the appellation "Brahmā Madhva Gauḍīya *sampradāya*." They have done so based on Mādhavendra Purī's connection with the Madhva *sampradāya*.[47] Mādhavendra Purī was the guru of Śrī Caitanya's guru. On doctrinal terms, however, the Gauḍīyas do agree with the refutation of *māyāvāda* so strongly presented in Madhva's *Bhāgavata-tātparya* and, of course, Madhva's high regard for the authority of the *Bhāgavata*.

Thus the *Bhāgavatam*'s statements about itself are appropriate, as evidenced by their acceptance by the greatest religious thinkers of India's spiritual heritage. Śrī Jīva cites several passages from *Śrīmad-Bhāgavatam* itself with regard to its glory. "Vyāsadeva explained the *Bhāgavatam* to his son Śukadeva who was perfectly self-controlled. It represents the essence of the Vedas and Itihāsas."[48] "The beautiful *Bhāgavatam* is considered to be the essence of Vedānta. One who relishes it will have no taste for anything else."[49] It is a book of philosophy, yet at the same time not dry and heady. It is sweet and charming, as it addresses the heart of the reader. "O connoisseurs of that which

---

47. Kavikarṇapūra in his *Gaura-gaṇoddeśa-dīpikā* affirms this as does the later Baladeva Vidyābhūṣana who was initiated in the Madhva *sampradāya* before embracing the Gauḍīya doctrine. In both his gloss on his own *Govinda Bhāṣya* and his *Prameya-ratnāvalī*, he lists the *guru-paramparā* of Śrī Caitanya linking him formally to the Madhva-*sampradāya*. For a refutation of the arguments questioning the validity of these writings, see O. B. L. Kapoor, *The Philosophy and Religion of Śrī Caitanya*, (New Delhi: Munshiram Manoharlal Publishers Pvt. Ltd., 1977), Chap. 3.

48. *tad idaṁ grāhayām āsa sutam ātmavatāṁ varam/*
sarva-vedetihāsānāṁ sāraṁ sāraṁ samuddhṛtam// (SB. 1.3.41)

49. *sarva-vedānta-sāraṁ hi śrī-bhāgavatam iṣyate/*
tad-rasāmṛta-tṛptasya nānyatra syād ratiḥ kvacit// (SB. 12.13.15)

is sweet, relish the juice of *Śrīmad-Bhāgavatam* repeatedly. It is the ripened fruit of the wish-fulfilling tree of Vedic knowledge. Having emanated from the lips of Śukadeva, it is sweeter still [as parrots *(śuka)* pick only the ripest fruit]."[50] Śrī Sūta Goswāmī mentions its glory in his opening statements: "Let me offer my obeisances unto Śukadeva, the son of Vyāsa and the guru of the most learned. He spoke this confidential Purāṇa, the essence of the *śruti*, out of compassion for those struggling in the darkness of material existence and desiring release, having realized it himself."[51]

The position of Śukadeva is significant, for he, the speaker of the *Bhāgavatam*, was respected by all. "Sages of pure heart and high minds who had the capacity to purify even holy places assembled along with their disciples—Atri, Vasiṣṭha, Cyavana, Śaradvān, Ariṣṭanemi, Bhṛgu, Aṅgira, Parāśara, Viśvāmitra, Paraśurāma, Utathya, Indrapramada, Idhmavāhu, Medhātithi, Devala, Ārṣṭiṣeṇa, Bharadvāja, Gautama, Pippalāda, Maitreya, Aurva, Kavaṣa, Kumbhayoni, Dvaipāyana, the worshippable Nārada along with other *devarṣis, brahmarṣis,* and *rājarṣis,* including Aruṇā and more. Mahārāja Parīkṣit greeted these leaders of various clans who were filled with joy, bowing his head before them and offering praise again and again, informing them of his intentions."[52] Mahārāja Parīkṣit told them, "O

---

50. *nigama-kalpa-taror galitaṁ phalaṁ śuka-mukhād amṛta-drava-saṁyutam/ pibata bhāgavataṁ rasam ālayaṁ muhur aho rasikā bhuvi bhāvukāḥ//* (SB. 1.1.3)

51. *yaḥ svānubhāvam akhila-śruti-sāram ekam*
adhyātma-dīpam atititīrṣatāṁ tamo 'ndham/
saṁsāriṇāṁ karuṇayāha purāṇa-guhyaṁ
taṁ vyāsa-sūnum upayāmi guruṁ munīnām// (SB. 1.2.3)

52. *tatropajagmur bhuvanaṁ punānā mahānubhāvā munayaḥ sa-śiṣyāḥ/ prāyeṇa tīrthābhigamāpadeśaiḥ svayam hi tīrthāni punanti santaḥ//*

learned persons, taking refuge in your counsel I ask of you a most important question about duty: What is the duty of one who is about to die? What should he pursue as the goal of his life? Please consider this amongst yourselves."[53] At that time, as if in response to the king's inquiry, "Śukadeva, the son of Vyāsa, appeared as an *avadhūta*, who wandered at will over the earth. He bore no sectarian markings, was self-satisfied, and was surrounded by children (who had no idea of his exalted position)."[54] Much to his entourage's surprise, "The assembled sages all stood up out of respect, and Śukadeva appeared like the full moon surrounded by the stars of all the assembled sages."[55] Even the learned Vyāsa and Nārada, Śukadeva's guru and *parama* guru respectively, sat to hear his explanation of *Śrīmad-Bhāgavatam*. That he was chosen to be its principal speaker is thus another of the innumerable glories of *Śrīmad-Bhāgavatam*.

---

atrir vasiṣṭhaś cyavanaḥ śaradvān ariṣṭanemir bhṛgur aṅgirāś ca/
parāśaro gādhi-suto 'tha rāma utathya indrapramadedhmavāhau//
medhātithir devala ārṣṭiṣeṇo bhāradvājo gautamaḥ pippalādaḥ/
maitreya aurvaḥ kavaṣaḥ kumbhayonir dvaipāyano bhagavān nāradaś ca//
anye ca devarṣi-brahmarṣi-varyā rājarṣi-varyā aruṇādayaś ca/
nānārṣeya-pravarā sametān abhyarcya rājā śirasā vavande//
sukhopaviṣṭeṣv atha teṣu bhūyaḥ kṛtapraṇāmaḥ svacikīrṣitaṁ yat/
vijñāpayām āsa viviktacetā upasthito 'gre 'bhigṛhīta pāṇiḥ// (SB. 1.19.8–12)

53. *tataś ca vaḥ pṛcchyam imaṁ vipṛcche viśrabhya viprā iti kṛtyatāyām/*
sarvātmanā mriyamāṇaiś ca kṛtyaṁ śuddhaṁ ca tatrāmṛśa tābhi yuktāḥ//
(SB. 11.19.24)

54. *tatrābhavad bhagavān vyāsa-putro yadṛcchayā gām aṭamāno 'napekṣaḥ/*
alakṣya-lingo nija-lābha-tuṣṭo vṛtaś ca bālair avadhūta-veṣaḥ// (SB. 11.19.25)

55. *sa saṁvṛtas tatra mahān mahīyasāṁ brahmarṣi-rājarṣi-devarṣi-saṅghaiḥ/*
vyarocatālaṁ bhagavān yathendur graharkṣa-tārā-nikaraiḥ parītaḥ//
(SB. 1.19.30)

Because the glory of *Śrīmad-Bhāgavatam* is so great, Śrī Jīva states that those verses that assert the superiority of other Purāṇas are to be balanced against the glory of the *Bhāgavatam*. Those verses are only relatively true; that is, they are pertinent only to those whose worship is governed by the particular mode of material nature that such Purāṇas govern. Here Jīva Goswāmī says, "Enough! What is the need for any further argument? *Śrīmad-Bhāgavatam* is Kṛṣṇa's own representative." He then quotes the *Bhāgavatam* itself. "This *Bhāgavata Purāṇa* is as brilliant as the sun. It has arisen just after the departure of Śrī Kṛṣṇa from the world to his abode, accompanied as he was with religion and knowledge. Those who have lost their way in the dense darkness of Kali-yuga can get light from this Purāṇa."[56] The *Bhāgavatam* is full of all good qualities. "Devoid of all cheating religion this *Bhāgavatam* propounds the highest truth."[57] Vopadeva's *Muktāphala* states, "The Vedas advise like a king, the Purāṇas like a friend, and Kāvya like one's beloved, but the *Bhāgavatam* like all three combined."[58] Thus while someone may consider other Purāṇas to be dependent upon the Vedas, the *Bhāgavatam* declares that this is not so for itself, for it is the essence of all the *śruti*. "How did it happen that Mahārāja Parīkṣit met this great sage (Śukadeva), making it possible for this, the *sātvatī śruti* (*Śrīmad-Bhāgavatam*), to be sung by him?"[59] Moreover, the fact that it was written by Vyāsa after he had completed all of the other Purāṇas also underscores the

---

56. *kṛṣṇe sva-dhāmopagate dharma-jñānādibhiḥ saha/*
kalau naṣṭa-dṛśām eṣa purāṇārko 'dhunoditaḥ// (SB 1.3.43)

57. *dharmaḥ projjhita-kaitavo 'tra paramaḥ* (SB. 1.1.2)

58. *vedāḥ purāṇaṁ kāvyaṁ ca prabhur mitraṁ priyeva ca/*
bodhayantīti hi prāhus trivṛd bhāgavataṁ punaḥ// (Muktāphala)

59. *kathaṁ vā pāṇḍave yasya rājarṣer muninā saha/*
saṁvādaḥ samabhūt tāta yatraiṣā sātvatī śrutiḥ// (SB. 1.4.7)

Bhāgavatam's importance, as per logic—that which is spoken last is to be accepted as conclusive.

Having established that *Śrīmad-Bhāgavatam* meets his five-fold criterion mentioned in the previous chapter and more, Śrī Jīva concludes that when cited in context the *Bhāgavatam* alone is sufficient to serve as conclusive support for that which he will claim in *Ṣaṭ-sandarbha.* He then outlines the format of his presentation to come. He says that his own prose will serve as *sūtras,* and the *Bhāgavatam* as the subject under discussion. This is the aforementioned style in which the *Vedānta-sūtra* is written *(adhikaraṇa).* Śrī Jīva's explanation of the *Bhāgavatam* verses cited constitute a type of commentary *(bhāṣya).* He explains the *Bhāgavatam* such that one will understand not only the significance of the *Bhāgavatam,* but the nature of its composition as well. From the study of *Ṣaṭ-sandarbha,* one will understand how the diverse sections of the *Bhāgavatam* fit together as an organic whole, and how it was written with a single purpose in mind. Such a treatise is invaluable, for it can save us from certain conjectures as to the unsystematic nature of the *Bhāgavatam*'s composition.[60]

The *"bhāṣya"* of Jīva Goswāmī follows the views of the predecessor *ācāryas*, such as Śrīdhara Swāmī, Rāmānuja, and Madhvācārya. However, Śrī Jīva states that he will cite only those portions of the revered Śrīdhara Swāmī's commentary that follow the natural spirit of the *Bhāgavatam* and its Vaiṣṇava conclusions. Because Śrīdhara Swāmī's commentary is interspersed with monistic Advaitin interpretations, those sections will not be drawn upon for support. They were written not as conclusions that represent the true spirit of the *Bhāgavatam,* but as a tact employed to attract the followers of Śaṅkara to the

60. See Dasgupta, *A History of Indian Philosophy IV* (Cambridge, England: Cambridge University Press, 1949), p. 26.

Bhāgavatam. They are the bait by which Śrīdhara Swāmī attempted to hook the monists on Kṛṣṇa *līlā*, and thus free them from drowning in the whirlpool of endless impersonal meandering.

This is an important point, for as mentioned earlier Śrī Caitanya greatly appreciated Śrīdhara Swāmī's commentary. Here Jīva Goswāmī is not deviating from his master's opinion, he is qualifying it. Śrīdhara Swāmī's greatness is not brought into question, rather it is brought out further in terms of the specific nature of his contribution. It is one that was appreciated deeply by the "hidden *avatāra*" that Śrī Caitanya was. The *sannyāsa* of Śrī Caitanya is also explained by Kṛṣṇadāsa Kavirāja Goswāmī in this light—as a trick he employed to induce the world to accept his doctrine.[61]

It would be difficult to construe Śrīdhara Swāmī's doctrine as one in support of *advaita-vedānta*, for tradition informs us that the Śaṅkarites themselves questioned his commentary, one in which the eternality of the Lord, his form, pastimes, and entourage are all stressed from the outset. It is said that in Benares Śrīdhara Swāmī's *Bhāvārtha-dīpikā* was placed before Kāśīnātha, Lord Śiva, and only when the deity spoke a verse in support of the commentary[62] was it accepted. It was after this that the Advaitins then embraced Śrīdhara Swāmī, attempting to adjust his devotional explanations around their nondevotional conclu-

---

61. *ataeva avaśya āmi sannyāsa kariba/*
sannyāsi-buddhye more praṇata ha-iba//

"I should accept *sannyāsa*, for then people will offer me respect, thinking I am of the renounced order." (Cc. Ādi 17.256)

62. *śuko vetti vyāso vetti rāja vetti na vetti vā/*
śrīdharo hi sarvaṁ vetti śrī nṛsiṁha prasādātaḥ//

"Sukadeva knows the meaning of the *Bhāgavatam*, as does Vyāsa. Parikṣit Mahārāja may or may not know, but Śrīdhara Swāmī knows everything by the mercy of Lord Nṛsiṁha."

sions. Furthermore, the heart of Śrīdhara Swāmī is revealed in his purely devotional commentaries on the *Viṣṇu Purāṇa* and the *Bhagavad-gītā*. Thus Śrī Jīva states that he will also draw from those writings which represent the Swāmī's actual understanding of the *Bhāgavatam*.

Rāmānujācārya wrote no commentary on the *Bhāgavatam*. His doctrine of *viśiṣṭādvaita* is, however, a devotional one. His *Śrī-Bhāṣya* commentary on Vyāsa's *Vedānta-sūtra* and many of his other works directly oppose the nondevotional explanation of Śaṅkara. Jīva Goswāmī acknowledges Rāmānuja's devotional doctrine as having its origin in the goddess Śrī (Lakṣmī). He and his Vaiṣṇava followers are mentioned in the *Bhāgavatam* as those hailing from the southern Draviḍa provinces: "Devotees of the Lord can be found everywhere, but they are numerous in the Draviḍa provinces."[63] Thus Jīva Goswāmī will also quote Rāmānujācārya, yet at the same time he states that he will quote only that of Rāmānuja which follows the spirit of the *Bhāgavatam*. Śrī Jīva does not cite those writings that emphasize the *ācārya*'s own deity (Nārāyaṇa) over Kṛṣṇa, such as those writings found in his commentary on the *Viṣṇu Purāṇa*, which for the Rāmānuja sect is most important.

Regarding Madhva, Śrī Jīva again underscores his contribution in the course of articulating the methodology he has adopted in *Ṣaṭ-sandarbha*. Stating that he will cite other Purāṇas and the Vedas that he has seen, as well as those he has not seen, Śrī Jīva refers to the writings of the venerable Madhva. Madhva cites various ancient texts in *Bhāgavata-tatparya, Bhārata-tātparya,* and *Brahma-sūtra bhāṣya* which he saw in earlier editions of the Purāṇas. Śrī Jīva qualifies that the reason for his

---

63. *nārāyaṇa-parāyaṇāḥ kvacit kvacin mahā-rāja draviḍeṣu ca bhūriśaḥ* (SB. 11.5.38)

citing many texts other than the self-supporting *Bhāgavatam* is to give further support to his own words regarding his understanding of the *Bhāgavatam*. He then proceeds in profuse praise of Madhva. He is "the founder of the philosophy of Tattvavada, the topmost amongst the knowers of the Vedas," and "His disciples and granddisciples were also of considerable renown, not only in the southern regions, but elsewhere as well." Śrī Jīva then quotes Madhva's own words found in his *Mahābhārata* commentary, *Bhārata-tātparya:* "After becoming accomplished in the knowledge of revealed scripture by the illuminating light of Vedānta and having seen various versions of the *Mahābhārata* in different parts of the country, I will analyze these and speak just as Vyāsa, the Lord himself, spoke."[64]

The *śruti* texts from Madhva's writings that Śrī Jīva quotes that were not available in their original form at the time of Jīva Goswāmī are from the *Caturveda-śikha*. The Purāṇa texts are from the *Garuḍa* and other Purāṇas no longer available, the *Saṁhitā* texts are from the *Mahā-saṁhitā* and others, and the Tantric texts are from *Tantra-bhāgavata* and *Brahma-tarka*.

Anucchedas twenty-seven and twenty-eight discussed above bring the *Tattva-sandarbha*'s *pramāṇa khaṇḍa* to a close. In them Jīva Goswāmī shows his respect for the previous *ācāryas* and discusses the method of his approach. But he makes it clear that he will present his own understanding, that which was taught by Śrī Caitanya, who accepted the *Bhāgavatam* with a fuller embrace than any other *ācārya*.

While other Vaiṣṇavas accept the *Bhāgavatam* and its devotional conclusions in general, it is the *Bhāgavatam*'s deliberation

64. *śāstrāntarāṇi saṁjānan vedāntasya prasādataḥ/*
deśe deśe tathā granthān dṛṣṭvā caiva pṛthag-vidhān//
yathā sa bhagavān vyāsaḥ sākṣān nārāyaṇaḥ prabhuḥ/
jagāda bhāratādyeṣu tathā vakṣye tadīkṣayā// (*Bhārata-tātparya* 2.7–8)

on aesthetic experience in transcendence, or *rasa,* that Śrī Caitanya was concerned with. It is a *rasa-śāstra* intended for those who are expert in relishing *rasa, rasikā bhuvi bhāvukāḥ.*[65] This is what Jīva Goswāmī will bring out in his *Bhakti* and *Prīti-sandharbhas,* and this is what he differs on more than anything else from the commentaries of the previous *ācāryas.* His is not so much a difference as it is a development of thought, a penetration into the deepest esoteric meaning of the *Śrīmad-Bhāgavatam.* This is the unique contribution of the Gauḍīya Vaiṣṇava *sampradāya* to the world of religious thought.

65. SB 1.1.3

PRAMEYA KHAṆḌA

5

"The absolute is one inasmuch as it is a unity unto itself. There is no other. Yet its completeness necessitates the expression of the joy of its unity. This is not a necessity owing to incompleteness, rather celebration of its completeness."

The Trance of Vyāsa

Śrī Jīva Goswāmī begins *anuccheda* twenty-nine with the word *atha,* now, indicating that he will begin the *prameya khaṇḍa.* Having completed the *pramāṇa khaṇḍa,* he will now begin to discuss that which he will prove by citing the *Bhāgavatam.* "*Prameya*" means that which is to be discussed and demonstrated. The subject matter of *Tattva-sandarbha*'s *prameya khaṇḍa* is the nature of absolute truth as it is described in *Śrīmad-Bhāgavatam.*

In *anucchedas* twenty-nine through forty-nine Jīva Goswāmī demonstrates from *Śrīmad-Bhāgavatam* the Gauḍīya *sampradāya*'s metaphysic, which he terms *acintya-bhedābheda,* inconceivable simultaneous oneness and difference. There are a number of metaphysics based on Vedānta. The most well-known is perhaps *advaita-vedānta* of Śaṅkara. Other forms of Vedānta postulated by the Vaiṣṇava *sampradāyas* include *viśiṣṭādvaita-vāda* of Rāmānuja, *dvaita* of Madhva, *dvaitādvaita* of Nimbārka, and *śuddhādvaita* of Viṣṇu Swāmī, later represented by Vallabhācārya. While these metaphysics are based to some extent on the *Bhāgavatam,* Jīva Goswāmī and the Gauḍīya *sampradāya*'s *acintya-bhedābheda* is based squarely upon *Śrīmad-Bhāgavatam,* which as we have heard, is the natural commentary on the *Vedānta-sūtras.*

Jīva Goswāmī arrives at the conception of *acintya-bhedābheda* by first analyzing the way in which one should understand *Śrīmad-Bhāgavatam.* In this he has taken a novel approach. No other scholar or *ācārya* has thought to examine the contents of *Śrīmad-Bhāgavatam* from this particular angle, yet it is such an obvious one at the same time. What could be more direct and simple yet perfect a means of understanding the *Bhāgavatam*'s message than examining the minds of its principal speaker and author, Śukadeva Goswāmī and Vedavyāsa respectively, revealed as they are within the text? This is what Jīva Goswāmī has done in *Tattva-sandarbha.*

In the *anucchedas* under discussion, Śrī Jīva analyses the *samādhi* of Vyāsa that gave rise to his writing of the *Bhāgavatam,* demonstrating how his resultant realization corresponds with the realization of both Śukadeva and Sūta Goswāmī. Śukadeva heard the *Bhāgavatam* from his father, Vyāsa, and Sūta Goswāmī heard it from Śukadeva when Śukadeva spoke it to Mahārāja Parīkṣit. Later Sūta reiterated it to the sages at Naimiṣāraṇya headed by Śaunaka Ṛṣi.

The chronology of the *Bhāgavatam*'s recitation can be confusing. Did it arise from the trance of Vyāsa, or as already mentioned, was it originally spoken by Kṛṣṇa to Brahmā? If it was written by Vyāsa before he spoke it to Śukadeva, then who wrote the current edition consisting of eighteen thousand verses, in which the setting is Sūta Goswāmī speaking to the sages at Naimiṣāraṇya? Jīva Goswāmī clears up this confusion in *Ṣaṭ-sandarbha*. Kṛṣṇa spoke it to Brahmā in four seed verses,[1] and Brahmā passed it on to Nārada. Nārada in turn passed the seed conception to Vyāsa who realized its significance in trance, taught it to Śukadeva, and later compiled it in its present form after Śukadeva had spoken it and Sūta Goswāmī had reiterated it. All of these events are explained throughout *Ṣaṭ-sandarbha*. In discussing them, Jīva Goswāmī demonstrates that the realization of Vyāsa's trance corresponds with the gist of the essen-

1. Jīva Goswāmī demonstrates this in his *Bhagavat-sandarbha.*

tial four verses spoken by Kṛṣṇa, as well as with the realization of all of the principal speakers and listeners mentioned within the text. Thus he makes a very convincing case as to the actual meaning of *Śrīmad-Bhāgavatam*—that it is a dissertation on the absolute truth as represented in the Vedas, in which the ultimate reality is inconceivably one with and different from itself at the same time, *acintya-bhedābheda*.

Śrī Jīva first discusses the blissful realization of Śukadeva, which is revealed in the praise offered to him by Sūta Goswāmī found in the twelfth canto. "Let me offer my obeisances unto my guru, Śukadeva Goswāmī, the son of Vyāsa, who can destroy all inauspiciousness within the world. At first he was absorbed in the bliss of Brahman realization, leaving aside all worldly concerns. Later, however, he was attracted to the enchanting pastimes of Ajita (Kṛṣṇa who is unconquerable). Having been attracted thus, he spoke out of compassion the *Bhāgavata Purāṇa*, which is centered on Śrī Kṛṣṇa and thus illuminates the nature of reality like a glowing lamp."[2]

In explaining the significance of this verse in which the import of the *Bhāgavatam* is described in brief, Śrī Jīva cites the *Bhāvārtha-dīpikā* of Śrīdhara Swāmī. Following the revered Swāmī's lead, he explains that "inauspiciousness" indicates both renunciation resulting from indifference to worldliness and aversion to Kṛṣṇa that turns one to a life of acquisition and false proprietorship. Both *jñāna*, the culture of knowledge that leads to detachment from the world, and *karma*, which implicates one in exploiting the world, were thus transcended in the realization of Śukadeva. Sūta Goswāmī says that Śukadeva is

---

2. *sva sukha-nibhṛta-cetās tad vyudastānya-bhāvo*
'pyajita-rucira-līlākṛṣṭa-sāras tadīyam/
vyatanuta kṛpayā yas tattva-dīpaṁ purāṇaṁ
tam akhila-vṛjina-ghnaṁ vyāsa-sūnuṁ nato 'smi// (SB. 12.12.69)

capable of enabling us to do the same through his compassionate discourse, *Śrīmad-Bhāgavatam.* It is notable that Śukadeva's realization of Kṛṣṇa *līlā* is described herein as being superior to the realization of Brahman, having attracted Śukadeva deeper into transcendence from his worldly indifference resulting from Brahman realization.

Śrī Jīva concludes from Śukadeva's attraction to Kṛṣṇa *līlā* that the *prayojana,* or goal of life, is not mere liberation from worldliness, but positive attachment within transcendence to the personification of transcendence, Śrī Kṛṣṇa. Kṛṣṇa *prema,* or love of Kṛṣṇa, is the fruit of all transcendental culture. Devotion to Kṛṣṇa is the *abhidheya,* or means, by which such transcendental love, which leaves in its wake both worldliness and liberation, is realized. This devotion consists primarily of hearing and chanting about him.

Just how Śukadeva came to hear about the pastimes of Kṛṣṇa, which are the essence of the *Bhāgavatam,* is described in the *Brahmavaivarta Purāṇa.*[3] Although here Śrī Jīva mentions this incident only in relation to the word *vyāsasūnuṁ* (the son of Vyāsa) found in Sūta's words of praise for Śukadeva, later in *anuccheda* forty-nine he will relate the incident in greater detail. In this section he mentions only that the appellation *vyāsasūnuṁ* indicates (based on the account of *Brahmavaivarta)* that Śukadeva was free from illusion from the very moment of his birth (as well as within the womb) due to a benediction from Kṛṣṇa. The implication is that although liberated and completely detached from worldly life and family attachments, he nonetheless became attracted to the transcendental pastimes *(līlās)* of Śrī Kṛṣṇa. Hearing of those *līlās* transported him into a life of love within transcendence beyond mere realization of impersonal Brahman.

---

3. This story is not found in any of the current editions, but it was apparently within the manuscript in Jīva Goswāmī's possession.

Śukadeva's realization is also described by Śukadeva himself in the second canto of *Śrīmad-Bhāgavatam*. Jīva Goswāmī refers to three verses uttered by Śukadeva in the first chapter as a means of cross-referencing that which is described by Sūta Goswāmī in the *praṇāma mantra* under discussion. Śukadeva Goswāmī says, "O king, for the most part the topmost transcendentalists who have transcended Vedic rules and regulations take pleasure in describing the glories of Śrī Kṛṣṇa. At the end of the Dvāpara-yuga, I studied this *Bhāgavata Purāṇa* which is the essence of all the Vedas from my father, the author of the Vedas, Kṛṣṇa-dvaipāyana Vyāsa. O saintly King, I was fully Brahman realized, yet I was attracted to the delineation of the supermost *līlās* of Kṛṣṇa that constitute the *Śrīmad-Bhāgavatam*."[4]

As Śukadeva realized the ultimate reality described in *Śrīmad-Bhāgavatam*, so did Vyāsa before him under the inspiration of Nārada. Sūta Goswāmī describes this in the first canto of the *Bhāgavatam* in eight verses (the sixth of these is a question posed by Śaunaka). Jīva Goswāmī's detailed explanation of these verses constitutes the heart of this chapter. The context in which these verses appear in *Śrīmad-Bhāgavatam* is Sūta Goswāmī's reply to Śaunaka as to the response of Vyāsa to Nārada's instructions and life story given in the previous chapters. "After hearing from Nārada, what did Vyāsadeva do?" asked Śaunaka. On the western banks of the Saraswatī...he sat down in his *āśrama* and began to meditate.[5]

---

4. *prāyeṇa munayo rājan nivṛttā vidhi-ṣedhataḥ/*
nairguṇya-sthā ramante sma guṇānukathane hareḥ//
idaṁ bhāgavataṁ nāma purāṇaṁ brahma-sammitam/
adhītavān dvāparādau pitur dvaipāyanād aham//
pariniṣṭhito 'pi nairguṇya uttama-śloka-līlayā/
gṛhīta-cetā rājarṣe ākhyānaṁ yad adhītavān// (SB. 2.1.7–9)

5. SB. 1.7.1–3

Sūta Goswāmī then explained the nature of the *samādhi* of Vyāsa. As we shall see, it was not *nirvikalpa samādhi,* in which the absolute is realized without realizing its attributes, rather it was *savikalpa samādhi,* in which the ultimate reality replete with qualities, form, and pastimes is realized. It is difficult to imagine identifying an object separately from its attributes. The time that elapses between perceiving an object and its attributes is too short to measure. In relation to God realization, however, it is possible to realize the absolute (Brahman) without simultaneously realizing its attributes. As mentioned earlier, such was the realization of Śukadeva before hearing the *Bhāgavatam.* Vyāsa's realization was then passed on to Śukadeva, elevating him from *nirvikalpa samādhi* to *savikalpa samādhi.*

Before discussing Śrī Jīva's explanation of the eight verses concerning Vyāsa's trance, the verses themselves are cited below in English. Readers can thus refer back to them in the course of studying Śrī Jīva's explanation. The original Sanskrit for these verses is footnoted after each of the verses as they appear in the *bhavānuvāda* format.

> (1) Thus he [Vyāsa] absorbed his mind in *bhakti-yoga* free from material contamination and realized the *pūrṇa-puruṣa* along with his subordinate, material energy.
>
> (2) [He further realized that] the living entity *(jīva),* although transcendental to the three modes of material nature, thinks himself to be a product of them by virtue of identifying with them and thus suffers under their influence.
>
> (3) Thus Vyāsa composed the *Śrīmad-Bhāgavatam (sātvata-saṁhitā)* for the people in general, who are unaware that *bhakti-yoga* directed to the transcendental Godhead is the means of their deliverance from grief.
>
> (4) If a person merely hears the message of *Śrīmad-Bhāgavatam,* devotion to Kṛṣṇa, the *parama puruṣa,* will manifest within him and free him from lamentation, fear, and illusion.

(5) After initially compiling *Śrīmad-Bhāgavatam*, Vyāsa revised it and then taught it to his son (Śukadeva), who was situated in renunciation.

(6) [Having heard this from Sūta Goswāmī] Śrī Śaunaka asked Sūta: "Why did Śrī Śukadeva Goswāmī, who was already living in renunciation and self-realized, rejoicing within, and unconcerned with his surroundings, study such a vast literature?"

(7) Sūta Goswāmī replied: "Sages such as Śukadeva who take pleasure in the self and are free from bondage, nonetheless relish unmotivated devotion to Urukrama (Kṛṣṇa). Such are the virtues of Hari."

(8) Śukadeva Goswāmī, the son of Vyāsa, was captivated by the virtues of Hari, and thus studied *Śrīmad-Bhāgavatam*, becoming dear to Viṣṇu's (Kṛṣṇa's) devotees.

Jīva Goswāmī understands the first of the eight consecutive *Bhāgavatam* verses discussing the *samādhi* of Vyāsa in this way: "Thus Vyāsa fixed his mind in a trance of *prema-bhakti* as he had been instructed to do by Nārada. Free from material conceptions, he recalled in *līlā-smaraṇam* the pastimes of Śrī Kṛṣṇa, the *pūrṇa-puruṣa,* along with his *svarūpa-śakti.* He realized, that is, the Lord's eternal abode, Goloka, and at the same time he saw Śrī Kṛṣṇa's secondary *śakti, māyā,* keeping her distance from the Lord."[6]

"Bhakti-yogena" mentioned in this verse refers to *prema-bhakti,* or devotion in its mature stage of development. *Bhakti* as discussed in Śrīla Rūpa Goswāmī's scientific book of devotion, *Bhakti-rasāmṛta-sindhu,* describes three developmental stages of the culture of pure devotion, *sādhana-bhakti, bhāva-bhakti,* and *prema-bhakti. Sādhana-bhakti* is devotional apprenticeship. When, in the course of culturing *sādhana-bhakti,* the first

---

6. *bhakti-yogena manasi samyak praṇihite 'male/*
apaśyat puruṣaṁ pūrṇaṁ māyāṁ ca tad-apāśrayam// (SB. 1.7.4)

ray of the sun of pure transcendental energy enters the *sādhaka*'s heart, the dawn of *prema* arises. This is the stage of *bhāva-bhakti.*[7] At that time one has realized *bhakti* proper, and its continued culture develops into the full experience of *prema-bhakti,* mature love of Godhead. It was in a trance of *prema-bhakti (bhakti-yogena)* that Vyāsa realized that which belittles mere liberation, or *nirvikalpa samādhi.* What he realized could not have been merely *sādhana-bhakti* which retires upon realization of the absolute. He realized a mature stage of *bhakti,* which has its expression within transcendence.

Jīva Goswāmī cites his principal *pramāṇa* to demonstrate that *bhakti* does indeed continue beyond liberation from material qualities. In the fifth canto of *Śrīmad-Bhāgavatam* we find in a conversation between Śukadeva and Mahārāja Parīkṣit the following statement of Śukadeva: "Mukunda (Kṛṣṇa) easily grants liberation, but he rarely bestows devotion."[8] Here Mahārāja Parīkṣit is doubting his standing in relation to Śrī Kṛṣṇa. Śukadeva Goswāmī herein assures him that the favor his family received from Kṛṣṇa was extraordinary. Kṛṣṇa, the Supreme Godhead, became the chariot driver of Parīkṣit's grandfather Arjuna, subordinating himself to his devotee. This is one of the characteristics of *prema-bhakti, śrīkṛṣṇākarṣiṇī,*[9] it attracts and conquers even Kṛṣṇa. Thus Kṛṣṇa does not bestow it often or to those who worship him with a view to achieve liberation. It is bestowed upon those who care not for getting, even when that getting is liberation from the material world. It is also noteworthy that this verse points out that *nirvikalpa samādhi* depends upon some form of *bhakti,* or worship of God. Without some

---

7. *śuddha-sattva-viśeṣātmā prema-sūryāṁśu-sāmya-bhāk* (Brs. 1.3.1)
8. *muktiṁ dadāti karhicit sma na bhakti-yogam* (SB. 5.6.18)
9. Brs. 1.1.7

bhakti, liberation is mere imagination,[10] and liberation itself is a far cry from *prema*. When one can approach the absolute without any concern for getting, the absolute gives itself to such devotees. This rare state of transcendental exchange between the Lord and his devotee was realized by Vyāsa in his trance of *prema-bhakti*.

The word *praṇihite*, perfectly poised, in this verse indicates that Vyāsa attained the highest *samādhi* by taking to heart the instructions of Nārada. Nārada informed Vyāsa that he was qualified to contemplate the *līlās* of Śrī Kṛṣṇa.[11] This is only possible for the most highly qualified devotees. Nārada told Vyāsa of his qualifications in this regard, thus giving him permission to engage in *līlā smaraṇam*.[12] *Smaraṇam*, or continual meditation upon the *līlās* of Śrī Kṛṣṇa, is the perfection of devotion, indicated by the word *praṇihite*.

The word "*pūrṇa*" indicates completeness or perfection, and as an adjective of *puruṣa (pūrṇa-puruṣa)* it refers to Bhagavān and not the *puruṣa avatāra*, the aspect of Bhagavān (Paramātmā) who rules over *māyā*. It refers to Śrī Kṛṣṇa, of whom the *puruṣa avatāra* is but a plenary portion. Śrī Jīva quotes the *uttara khaṇḍa* of *Padma Purāṇa* wherein the word *puruṣa* is described as synonymous with Bhagavān, "The words Bhagavān and *puruṣa* both refer to Vāsudeva, the soul of all, who is free from all limiting adjuncts."[13] Śrīdhara Swāmī's *Bhārvātha-dīpikā*, which comments on two verses from the

---

10. *ye 'nye 'ravindākṣa vimukta-māninas*
tvayy asta-bhāvād aviśuddha-buddhayaḥ// (SB. 10.2.32)

11. *samādhinānusmara tad-viceṣṭitam* (SB. 1.5.13)

12. *śuci-śravāḥ satya-rato dhṛta-vrataḥ* (SB. 1.5.13)

13. *bhagavān iti śabdo 'yam tathā puruṣa ity api/*
vartate nirupādhiś ca vāsudeve 'khilātmani"// (Pa. P. *uttara khaṇḍa)*

Bhāgavatam's second canto, is also cited to further substantiate this understanding. The verses are as follows: "One who desires domination over a kingdom or an empire should worship the Manus. One who desires victory over an enemy should worship the demons, and one who desires sense gratification should worship the moon. But one who desires nothing of material enjoyment should worship the Supreme Personality of Godhead. A person of broad intelligence, whether filled with material desire, without any material desire, or desirous of liberation, should with great determination approach the Supreme Lord through *bhakti-yoga*."[14] Śrīdhara Swāmī comments that the *parama puruṣa* mentioned in the first of these verses indicates the Paramātmā, "whose sole limiting adjunct is the *prakṛti*, or material nature," while the same word appearing in the consecutive verse indicates "he who is free from all limiting adjuncts." The first verse speaks of the *pūrṇa puruṣa* and his administrators *(devas)* in relation to the material world (Paramātmā), whereas the second verse describes the *pūrṇa-puruṣa* who is worshipped by *bhakti-yoga* (Bhagavān). The second *pūrṇa-puruṣa* thus refers to Kṛṣṇa who has nothing to do with the material world. Thus the *pūrṇa-puruṣa* that Vyāsa realized was Bhagavān, Śrī Kṛṣṇa, and not the Paramātmā feature of Bhagavān as one might misconstrue.

Śrī Jīva begins *anuccheda* thirty-one by stating further that if the word *pūrvaṁ* found in some editions of the *Bhāgavatam* is accepted in place of *pūrṇa*, his understanding still holds. He bases this argument upon the etymological interpretation of the

---

14. *rājya-kāmo manūn devān nirṛtiṁ tv abhicaran yajet/*
kāma-kāmo yajet somam akāmaḥ puruṣaṁ param//
akāmaḥ sarva-kāmo vā mokṣa-kāma udāra-dhīḥ/
tīvreṇa bhakti-yogena yajeta puruṣaṁ param// (SB. 2.3.9–10)

word *puruṣa* found in the *śruti,* which explains it as "the one who existed prior *(pūrvaṁ)* to everything."[15] Thus if one accepts the reading as *puruṣaṁ pūrvaṁ* rather than *puruṣaṁ pūrṇaṁ* the meaning is the same. In either reading it is Bhagavān Śrī Kṛṣṇa who Vyāsa realized in *samādhi.* That the *pūrṇa-puruṣa* is Śrī Kṛṣṇa is brought out more clearly as Śrī Jīva develops his analysis of Vyāsa's meditation.

Seeing the *pūrṇa-puruṣa,* Śrī Kṛṣṇa, in trance means that Vyāsa saw the Lord along with his own *svarūpa-śakti.* Śrī Jīva gives the example of seeing the full moon. When one sees the full moon, one sees it along with its luster. The *svarūpa-śakti,* although not mentioned directly in the first verse describing Vyāsa's *samādhi,* is thus implied, for there is no meaning to seeing the primeval Godhead separately from his own internal *śakti.* It is this *śakti* that constitutes his essential nature. Kṛṣṇa in his fullest sense as *pūrṇa-puruṣa* is Kṛṣṇa alongside of Rādhā, the highest expression of his primal *śakti.* Thus Vyāsa saw the abode of Rādhā-Kṛṣṇa, Goloka, in all of its splendor, an abode which itself is nondifferent from the Lord.[16]

Śrī Jīva substantiates the above by citing another text from the same chapter of *Śrīmad-Bhāgavatam.* Arjuna tells Kṛṣṇa, "You are the original personality of Godhead. You are the controller of the creation, and at the same time you are transcendental to the material energy by dint of your *svarūpa-śakti,* or internal spiritual energy. Thus you are situated in your own self, full of transcendental bliss and knowledge."[17] The prime-

---

15. *pūrvam evāham ihāsam, tatpuruṣasya puruṣatvam*

16. *ārādhyo bhagavān vrajeśa-tanayas tad dhāma vṛndāvanaṁ (Caitanya-matta-mañjuṣā)*

17. *tvam ādyaḥ puruṣaḥ sākṣād īśvaraḥ prakṛteḥ paraḥ/ māyāṁ vyudasya cic-chaktyā kaivalye sthita ātmani//* (SB. 1.7.23)

val Godhead has his primary *śakti* by which he expands his pastimes, and these affairs are never touched by his secondary material energy, *māyā-śakti.*

Along with the Lord and his abode, Vyāsa also saw Kṛṣṇa's *māyā-śakti, māyāṁ ca tad-apāśrayam.* Jīva Goswāmī says that this *śakti* as described in Vyāsa's trance is Kṛṣṇa's inferior energy. It is important to note that *māyā,* although capable of creating an illusion, is herself real. She is not an illusion, but an objective reality manifest as the material world. She is like a servant of a king who remains outside the door while he consorts with his principal queen. *Māyā* never comes before Bhagavān. As stated in the second canto of *Śrīmad-Bhāgavatam,* "Māyā, being embarrassed to come before him, keeps away."[18] *Māyā-śakti,* who governs the affairs of the material world, is furthermore capable of being overpowered by the *svarūpa-śakti* by means of *bhakti-yoga,*[19] which is governed by the *svarūpa-śakti,* as are the affairs of the Lord in his abode.[20] *Māyā-śakti* is not very useful for the *jīva* souls. The *svarūpa-śakti,* however, facilitates both the *jīva*'s liberation from *māyā* and its spiritual life in the abode of the Lord.

Jīva Goswāmī comments that while the *māyā-śakti* is mentioned in the trance of Vyāsa, there is no mention of his seeing the *puruṣa* who rules over *māyā* (Paramātmā), nor is there any mention of his experiencing the undifferentiated aspect of the absolute (Brahman). The reason for this is that it is understood that realization of the Paramātmā aspect of Godhead is included in Bhagavān realization, as is realization of un-

---

18. *māyā paraity abhimukhe ca vilajjamānā* (SB. 2.7.47)

19. *anarthopaśamaṁ sākṣād bhakti-yogam adhokṣaje/*
lokasyājānato vidvāṁś cakre sātvata-saṁhitām// (SB 1.7.6)

20. *ātmārāmaś ca munayo nirgranthā apy urukrame/*
kurvanty ahaitukīṁ bhaktim ittham-bhūta-guṇo hariḥ// (SB. 1.7.10)

differentiated Brahman, these two being partial manifestations of Bhagavān.

The vision of Vyāsa is further described in the *Bhāgavatam*'s second consecutive verse concerning Vyāsa's *samādhi*. Śrī Jīva understands it thus: "Vyāsa saw that the *jīva* souls, although consciousness like the Lord, were nonetheless distinct from the Lord since they were deluded by the *māyā-śakti*, which although capable of deluding them, keeps her distance from the Lord. Due to the *jīva*'s delusion, it identifies with the three modes of nature considering itself to be a product of material nature and suffers the repeated miseries of birth and death. Seeing this, Vyāsa realized that if the *jīva* can misidentify with *māyā* and be deluded by her, the *jīva* not only is constituted of consciousness, but inherently possesses consciousness, or the power of identification and illumination. The *jīva* is thus itself an entity, rather than its individual identity being based on the influence of *māyā*."[21]

Vyāsa saw the Lord and his *svarūpa-śakti*, he saw the Lord's *māyā-śakti*, and here we find that he also saw the *jīva* souls, or *jīva-śakti*, struggling under the influence of *māyā*. Vyāsa saw the distinction between the Lord and the *jīva*. Without this distinction there is no question of there being any *prayojana*, or ultimate goal of love of God, nor is there any meaning to *abhidheya*, or the means of realizing the absolute through devotion. This is so because without two there is no meaning to love. Although two do become one in love, this dynamic oneness is not at the cost of individual existence. The individuality of the *jīva* and the Lord is necessary to experience love, which is a oneness only of two individuals' common experience, a oneness in which each is unconcerned about his own separate potential for experience. As stated earlier, the *prayojana* of the *Bhāgavatam* is

21. *yayā sammohito jīva ātmānaṁ tri-guṇātmakam/*
paro 'pi manute 'narthaṁ tat-kṛtaṁ cābhipadyate// (SB. 1.7.5)

love of Kṛṣṇa. Unless, therefore, the *jīva* exists eternally there is no possibility of such love. Moreover, if the *jīva* soul is itself an illusion as some philosophers claim, who will attain what? If there is no goal to achieve, there is no necessity of a means of achieving. Thus the existence of the *jīva* is essential to the philosophy of devotion espoused in *Śrīmad-Bhāgavatam*.

The *jīva* is described in this verse as "bewildered" *(sammohitaḥ)* and thus forced to "consider" *(manute)* itself to be a product of material nature. For something to have the potential of being bewildered and considering anything it must possess consciousness. Merely "being" consciousness is not sufficient. Śaṅkara's *advaita-vedānta* does not acknowledge the existence of the *jīva* in the ultimate issue. For Śaṅkara, the conception of the *jīva* is dissolved in enlightenment. Yet the *Bhāgavatam* describes the *jīva* as eternal, existing as such even after liberation. This verse explains that the *jīva* is both constituted of consciousness and has consciousness as its attribute at the same time. Jīva Goswāmī gives the example of a lamp, which has as its essential nature the power of illumination and it is thus illuminated and can at the same time illuminate other objects. He cites the *Bhagavad-gītā* in this connection: "The *jīva*'s original knowledge is covered by illusion, and thus he is bewildered."[22] The *jīva,* that is, has consciousness and the power of knowing, yet it is merely covered by *māyā.* Thus Śrī Jīva concludes that Vyāsadeva did not accept the notion that the Lord and the living entities are one and the same in every respect, their difference amounting only to a false perception based on the influence of *māyā*. It is worth adding that neither did he accept another important element of Śaṅkara's monism, the idea that the material world, or *māyā-śakti,* also has no real existence.

---

22. *ajñānenāvṛtaṁ jñānaṁ tena muhyanti jantavaḥ* (Bg. 5.15)

The bewilderment of the *jīva* soul is brought about by the *māyā-śakti*. Real as she is, she takes full responsibility for the suffering of the *jīvas* under her jurisdiction. Her Lord is not to blame. Bhagavān forever remains aloof from her affairs. The connection between the suffering of the living beings in this world and God is one that any theology must resolve. If God is all good, why does he either cause or allow suffering? In Gauḍīya Vaiṣṇava doctrine, God is not to blame. He does not directly cause the living entities to suffer, nor does he take any pleasure in their struggle, other than to the extent that it ever so indirectly brings the *jīvas* to happiness in the long run.

Punishment is the work of *māyā* alone, who is ashamed of her own task, knowing that it brings no direct pleasure to her Lord. As *Śrīmad-Bhāgavatam* states: "Foolish people, being bewildered by *māyā*, speak in terms of 'I' and 'mine.'" On account of her service of deluding the living beings, *māya* is ashamed to come before the Lord."[23] The significance of this verse is that *māyā* cannot take precedence over the Lord, while she can do so over the *jīvas* who are his parts and parcels. Why does she delude the *jīvas?* She cannot tolerate the fact that from a time without beginning *(anādi)* the *jīvas* have "turned away from him, devoting themselves to a separate existence." Thus to push them in his direction she inflicts suffering, "covering their real nature and causing them to identify with a false reality."[24] Her

23. Jīva Goswāmī remarks that should anyone question how insentient *māyā* could be "ashamed," the answer is that it is the presiding deity of *māyā* who feels so. To support the notion of a presiding deity of *māyā-śakti,* he cites a story from the *Kena Upaniṣad* in which the presiding deity of *māyā* is mentioned.

24. *bhayaṁ dvitīyābhiniveśataḥ syād īśād apetasya viparyayo 'smṛtiḥ//*

(SB. 11.2.37). This line also represents the two powers of *māyā, āvaraṇātmika* (deluding) and subsequently *vikṣepātmika* (covering).

pushing and his teaching in the form of *śāstra* make for the possibility of the *jīva* soul's gradual development of love of God.

In all of this it must be considered that *māyā* is a devotee of the Lord. Thus Kṛṣṇa cannot withhold his favor from her, whose task is to take charge of the creation, filled as it is with the misuse of will on the part of the *jīva*. Jīva Goswāmī says that the Lord so desires that the deluded *jīvas* turn to him, even if it be out of fear of him, that he instructs them in *Bhagavad-gītā* thus: "This divine *māyā* of mine consisting of the three modes of nature is insurmountable. Yet for those who take refuge in me, I enable them to cross over her jurisdiction."[25] Here the Lord is speaking to warn the materially conditioned *jīvas* that they must surrender unto him to escape *māyā*'s grip. While speaking, Kṛṣṇa is pointing to his own chest and saying, "Surrender to me (or you will suffer)." Here Śrī Jīva quotes another verse from the third canto of *Śrīmad-Bhāgavatam* to stress that just as from one side, through the punishment of *māyā*, he pushes the *jīva* souls in his direction, so also from the other side he makes information about himself available. Those who take advantage of this achieve liberation and a life of devotion. "In the association of pure devotees, discussions about my glories, which are pleasing to the ear and heart, take place. By taking part in these discussions people become free from illusion and are liberated. Such people gradually develop faith in me, and as they develop attraction for me (*rati* or *bhāva-bhakti*) they actually attain devotional service."[26] Thus the activities of the Lord and *māyā* are harmonious.

---

25. *daivī hy eṣā guṇa mayī mama māyā duratyayā/*
mām eva ye prapadyante māyām etāṁ taranti te (Bg. 7.14)

26. *satāṁ prasaṅgān mama vīrya-saṁvido*
bhavanti hṛt-karṇa-rasāyanāḥ kathāḥ/
taj-joṣaṇād āśv apavarga-vartmani
śraddhā ratir bhaktir anukramiṣyati// (SB. 3.25.25)

Having discussed the first and second verse describing Vyāsadeva's trance, Śrī Jīva draws from both of them to make a most significant point, building the foundation for *acintya-bhedābheda.* He has already analyzed that Vyāsa saw the *pūrṇa-puruṣa* Śrī Kṛṣṇa along with his essential nature (*svarūpa-śakti*). He also saw the reality of *māyā,* a nonessential *śakti* of the *pūrṇa puruṣa,* who keeps her distance from him. She is like his shadow. Then he saw the *jīva* and its delusion under the influence of *māyā.* Thus Śrī Jīva concludes that on the one hand Vyāsa saw that the Lord, who is pure consciousness, is the controller of *māyā.* She never takes precedence over him. On the other hand he saw the *jīva,* who shares the same conscious nature as the Lord but is nonetheless deluded by *māyā.* Thus the *jīva,* although in essence one with God, being consciousness, is at the same time different, as evidenced by the fact that *māyā* has taken precedence over it.

With this conclusion, Jīva Goswāmī proceeds in *anucchedas* thirty-five through forty-one to expose the principal shortcoming of the philosophical notion that the *jīva* and Brahman are one in every respect. Following the description of Vyāsadeva's trance, Śrī Jīva explains that it is incorrect to assume that the Brahman, who is pure consciousness, full of knowledge, and the support of the *māyā-śakti,* can at the same time be deluded by ignorance under the influence of *māyā.* The distinction between the *jīva* and God is that the former, although consciousness like the Lord, does come under the sway of *māyā.*

The Lord is like the sun, and the *jīvas,* who are his parts and parcels, are like the sun's rays. As the sun remains above the clouds, which the sun itself produces, so the Lord, the creator of the world and the support of the *māyā-śakti,* never becomes clouded. Yet the *jīvas,* like the sun's rays which are constituted of nothing other than sun, do come under the clouds of *māyā*'s influence. Thus the conclusion that the *jīva* and Brahman are one in every respect, a conclusion that displaces the notion of Bhagavān as the *pūrṇa-puruṣa* unaffected by *māyā,* is full of logical inconsistencies and cannot be supported from *Śrīmad-Bhāgavatam.*

The philosophy that Jīva Goswāmī is concerned with defeating here is of course that of Śaṅkarācārya's *advaita-vedānta,* also known as monism and labeled *māyāvāda* by the Vaiṣṇavas. As mentioned earlier, this philosophy was prominent at the time Śrī Jīva compiled *Ṣaṭ-sandarbha,* as it is today, although its influence is waning.

The arguments that Śrī Jīva puts forward will have greater meaning to one who has some background in *advaita-vedānta.* Jīva Goswāmī does not present any background information, assuming as he must have that his readers at the time were familiar with the doctrine of *māyāvāda.*

The *māyāvāda* doctrine posits that the *jīva* soul is itself the Godhead in every respect. To call oneself God may at first seem preposterous, yet it is to some extent understandable how one could reach the conclusion that the soul is itself the absolute truth, for life, or consciousness, is so wonderful, animating the world of insentient matter as it does. A mere touch of consciousness is infinitely greater than the sum total of matter. Our practical experience is that material manifestations derive meaning from contact with consciousness. The wonder of the world of matter is indeed the soul within it, without which it has no life and no one to appreciate what beauty it might hold on its own strength. Beauty, as it is said, lies in the eye of the beholder.

Yet acknowledging this, we are left to contend with the fact that matter has taken precedence over our souls, much like television: once we turn it on, it may take over our lives. So comprehensive is material nature's hold upon our souls that some of us reason, as ludicrous as it might seem, and in a sophisticated fashion, that we are not consciousness.[27] Ironically, while in one sense the *māyāvadā* doctrine equates the *jīva* with Godhead, in doing so it does away with both God and soul and has thus often been described as cryptic Buddhism.[28]

Māyāvādins posit three levels of reality: *pāramārthika* (absolute reality), *vyāvahārika* (practical reality), and *prātibhāsika* (apparent reality). Absolute reality is that which always exists *(sat)*. That which never exists is termed *asat*. Practical reality is the world of our experience. Apparent reality is likened to misconstruing a rope for a snake. The perceived snake does not exist, yet it does inasmuch as it is perceived and causes one to become fearful. Thus it is neither real or unreal; it is *mithyā*. This apparent reality is what we might call a hallucination.

According to the Māyāvādins, a portion of Brahman comes under the influence of *māyā*, and that portion is then known as *jīva*. Its individuality is based not on its essential nature, but its material embodiment, the influence of *māyā*. Brahman also manifests within *māyā* as *īśvara*, or the personal God who is the controller of *māyā*. Although this personhood of God is merely a product of material designation, it is nonetheless conscious of itself within *māyā* and unaffected by *māyā*'s influence. Māyāvādins divide *māyā* into *vidyā* (knowledge portion) and *avidyā* (ignorance portion). As such *īśvara*, the *śāstra*, and the worship of *īśvara*, being manifestations of the *vidyā* portion of *māyā*, all serve to free the *jīva* from *avidyā*. Freed from ignorance, the *jīva* leaves the practical reality behind, merging with the absolute and realizing itself to be Brahman.

---

27. Jīva's argument against the Śūnyavādis, or Buddhists, which is based on the *Bhāgavatam* and our everyday experience, will be discussed in the next chapter.

28. Gregory J. Darling, *An Evaluation of the Vedāntic Critique of Buddhism*. (New Delhi: Motital Banarsidass Pvt. Ltd., 1987), pp.118–122.

Māyāvāda is a very sophisticated philosophy, and it can appear to be based on the *śāstra,* or *śabda-pramāṇa.* Yet the *amala-pramāṇa, Śrīmad-Bhāgavatam,* puts forth a very different philosophy, one that is free of the logical inconsistencies of *advaita-vedānta.*

That the *māyāvāda* doctrine is not based on the *śāstra pramāṇa* is revealed by Jīva Goswāmī's unique approach to *Śrīmad-Bhāgavatam.* It is very difficult to draw a monistic conclusion from the *Bhāgavatam.* As mentioned earlier, Śaṅkara himself out of reverence for the *Bhāgavatam* did not touch it with his interpretive pen, nor would it have been easy for him to do so, although some of his so-called followers have attempted. Here in the *prameya khaṇḍa* Śrī Jīva demonstrates how to understand *Śrīmad-Bhāgavatam,* such that all of the quoting of the *māyāvāda* philosophers of both the *śruti* and *smṛti* is revealed to be just short of the devil's quoting scripture to support his case. That is, their quotes are out of context inasmuch as they do not conform with the experience of Vyāsa in his *samādhi.*

Māyāvādins often attempt to support their theory on the basis of the theories of *pariccheda* (limitation) and *pratibimba* (reflection). By the theory of limitation the Māyāvādins understand the *jīva* to be merely a result of Brahman being limited by the adjunct of the material body. They maintain that just as sky when placed in an earthen pot is sky within a pot, yet when the pot is broken it merges with the totality of sky, so similarly Brahman when limited by the adjunct of *māyā* considers itself to be an individual, but when it is liberated from the bodily conception it merges with Brahman. As Śaṅkara sees it, Bhagavān is relegated to the realm of *māyā,* for an absolute in which there is no "other" does not allow for a Godhead with pastimes and devotees. Śaṅkara's is a static absolute, devoid of movement and variety. It rests in eternal slumber.

The theory of reflection reaches the same conclusion, but is a different attempt to explain the greatest problem with the *māyāvāda* philosophy, that of the experience of the world and the *jīva,* which in this theory do not ultimately exist. Because Brahman is undifferentiated and without any other, *māyā* cannot ultimately exist, nor can the *jīva,* yet our experience is that they do. In the theory of reflection the *jīva* is ultimately Brahman, formless, and all-pervading, yet appearing as a *jīva* due to the reflection of Brahman.

The analogies of *pratibimba* and *pariccheda* are mentioned in the *śruti,* yet according to Śrī Jīva, they are misapplied by the Māyāvādins. Thus he proceeds to expose the misunderstanding of the Māyāvādins, and in so doing demonstrates how to understand those passages from scripture that on the surface seem to support Śaṅkara's *advaita-vedānta* interpretation of the analogies of limitation and reflection.

Regarding the theory of reflection, Śrī Jīva argues that if Brahman is all pervading as it is, how then can it at any time be reflected? And if it somehow could, upon what would it reflect, being itself all pervading? That which is attributeless, all pervading, and without parts (Brahman) cannot be reflected. If one argues that the sky, which is analogous to Brahman, can be reflected in water, Jīva Goswāmī replies that sky itself is not reflected in water, rather it is the stars, moon, sun, clouds, refracted light, etc. alone that are reflected and never the sky itself.

Regarding the theory of limitation, Śrī Jīva points out that if something is attributeless it cannot have any relationship with limitation, for what will one limit? Brahman, which is all pervasive, cannot be divided, and that which is said to be without parts cannot be perceived in the first place. Śrī Jīva argues that if the proposed limitations of *māyā (upādhis)* that cause Brahman to appear as *jīva* occur at the *vyavahārika* level, or the level of practical reality, then such limitations cannot affect Brahman, which is said to be the absolute reality, lying beyond the level of practical reality. On the level of Brahman there is no practical reality. Thus the practical reality cannot touch the absolute reality in which the practical realm has no representation. Thus how can the proposed limitation upon Brahman take place, and what is its cause?

For there to be any kind of knowledge, even the so-called false knowledge of material designation, there must be a knower and that which is known. Knowledge requires a subject and object. What then is the subject and object of the false knowledge that produces the concept of the *jīva,* a limitation upon Brahman, or its reflection? This false knowledge has no subject because neither the ultimate reality or the practical reality can be its subject. This is so because ultimate reality is said to be that which is misunderstood. It is not the subject of false knowledge because it is considered the object of misunderstanding. Furthermore, because it is absolute truth, nothing false or erroneous can exist within it.

At the same time, this so-called false knowledge can have no object. Ultimate reality cannot be its object because anything that could be the object of false knowledge also ultimately does not exist. Nothing in practical reality can be the object of this false knowledge either, for practical reality itself is said to be the result of false knowledge. Thus the false knowledge of the Māyāvādins conceived of as a limitation upon or reflection of Brahman is a kind of knowledge that has no subject and no object, no knower and no known. This is meaningless, for the so-called false knowledge is itself false! It is more deluding than *māyā* itself.

If the designation of *jīva* brought about by either the so-called limitation or reflection of Brahman is considered to take place at the level of ultimate reality, then it cannot be done away with. Contemplating *śruti* texts such as *tat tvam asi* (thou art that) and understanding them to indicate that the *jīva* is in every respect one with Brahman will never do away with that which is actually real. If to avoid this problem one states that it is by the power, or *śakti,* of Brahman that the limitations or material designations covering Brahman are removed, then Śrī Jīva says we have no problem with this. Of course, removal of the material designation covering the portion of Brahman known as *jīva* does not do away with the *jīva* in uniting it with Brahman. Such is the philosophy of the *Bhāgavatam,* in which Brahman in its fullest expression is Bhagavān, the transcendent Lord, replete with *śaktis* that do not compromise his nonduality, yet make for the possibility of a dynamic absolute full of movement that amounts to the celebration of its own joy. Brahman, that is, moves not out of incompleteness, but in celebration of its fullness. Thus if one makes this argument, one has inadvertently admitted to the *śakti* of the absolute, a tenet not acceptable to Śaṅkara, who considered that a Brahman with power, or *śakti,* would not be nondual in the strictest of terms. As alluded to here in brief, we shall see that in the metaphysic of *acintya-bhedābheda* the nonduality of the absolute is maintained even while acknowledging its innumerable *śaktis,* one of which the eternal *jīva* is constituted of.

If the limitations upon Brahman proposed by the Māyāvādins are said to be *mithyā,* or appearing at the *prātibhāsika* level of apparent reality, then the division *māyā* is said to create must also be *mithyā* and could have never been brought about by an effect in practical or ultimate reality. How can that which is said to occur at the level of apparent reality bring about the effect of the world of our practical experience? An effect must be present in its cause. We might perceive a rope to be a snake, but that so-called snake will never bite us. If the cause is *mithyā,* then the effect must also be so, thus the apparent reality of the Māyāvādins can never give rise to the practical reality of our experience.

In posing this argument Śrī Jīva characterizes the Māyāvādins as those who base their theory on the analogy of a dream.

Some Māyāvādins liken this material world to an unreal dream state, upon awaking from which the world no longer exists and one realizes oneself to be Brahman. Yet if this is so, one cannot substantiate the dream by using examples of empirically real things from practical reality such as jars and space, as in the case of *pariccheda* wherein the jar is compared to the *upādhi* brought about by material nature and the space to Brahman contained within, or in the case of *pratibimba* wherein the jar containing water is said to reflect the sky.

Why is this so? Because in the analogy of the dream we do not find the kind of one-to-one correspondence between the dream state and the experience of the material world that is necessary for a valid analogy. For an analogy to be valid there must be correspondence between the example and that which it seeks to exemplify. For example, even the Māyāvādins accept that in the material world one can obtain tangible results from action *(karma)*. Yet in a dream one cannot achieve any tangible result, such as appeasing one's appetite by dreaming of eating sumptuously.

If one argues that objects such as jars and space of our practical experience are also ultimately unreal when considered from the level of absolute reality, and therefore there is correspondence between the dream state and the material world, the Gauḍīya Vaiṣṇavas reply that, although the practical reality may be ultimately unreal in this theory, it does have empirical value and is of a different nature than the apparent reality, in which everything has only illusory value. Thus the analogy remains invalid.

It may be argued further that one can only dream of those things which one has experience of. Because one cannot dream about that which one has no experience of, the experiences of our dream, however distorted, must have some connection with reality. We would never experience the apprehension that a rope is a snake unless we have had some experience of a snake. Thus if this world is a dream, the experiences we have here must exist in some form in absolute reality. This being so, Māyāvādins cannot invoke this analogy, for their conception of absolute reality has nothing within it that remotely resembles anything in the world of our material experience.

If in order to avoid the problems discussed above, one argues that the false knowledge that somehow limits Brahman is an independent existence, one compromises the theory of nonduality. If one argues that this false knowledge ultimately does not exist, in an attempt to salvage the monistic doctrine of nonduality, the question arises as to who the knower of ultimate knowledge is. It cannot be the *jīva* if the *jīva* is merely a product of false knowledge and thus does not ultimately exist. If the knower is the ultimate reality itself, then it must possess inherently the power, or *śakti,* of knowing. This again is the philosophy of *Śrīmad-Bhāgavatam.* A philosophy that is free from the logical inconsistencies of Śaṅkara's *advaita-vedānta* and is also scripturally supportable.

Jīva Goswāmī offers one more argument to demonstrate that the *māyāvāda* theory in general suffers from the fallacy of mutual dependence. He says that in this theory Brahman is said to be pure consciousness and untouched by *māyā*'s influence. Yet that same Brahman is considered to be the *jīva,* who is covered by ignorance due to *māyā*'s influence. Brahman is also considered to be *īśvara* out of whom *māyā* arises. Yet this *īśvara* is considered the projection of the *jīva* as a result of being under the influence of ignorance, or *māyā.* The same *īśvara* is also considered to be the *jīva* when falling under the sway of *māyā.* Thus *avidyā,* or ignorance, is said to exist within Brahman, while knowledge is found in *īśvara,* who is designated as such by the influence of ignorance. The bottom line of all of this is that the very embodiment of knowledge is also considered to contain ignorance.

If it had been *advaita-vedānta* that Vyāsa realized, Vyāsa would have seen something much different than he did. He would have seen that Brahman only *appeared* to be divided due to ignorance. The consequence of this apparent division of Brahman in the form of the world of misery would have been seen to be surmountable by the culture of knowledge. Furthermore, if the pastimes of Bhagavān were ultimately unreal, a mere appearance of *īśvara* at the level of practical reality, this would contradict the realization of Śukadeva Goswāmī, who although Brahman-realized became attracted to the pastimes of Kṛṣṇa, considering them transcendental and trancendentally superior to the realization of nondifferentiated Brahman. It is significant that the word Brahman is not even mentioned in the vision of Vyāsa. As mentioned earlier, Jīva Goswāmī points out that Brahman is not mentioned because it is understood to be an aspect of Bhagavān, rather than the personhood of Godhead being a reflection of impersonal Brahman appearing only in the Māyāvādin's concept of practical reality.

Having rejected the *māyāvāda* theory, employing logic and ultimately evidence from the *Bhāgavatam*, Śrī Jīva acknowledges in *anuccheda* forty-two that the doctrines of *pariccheda* and *pratibimba* are nonetheless analogies found in the *śruti*. How then should they be understood? They should be understood not in their primary sense, but in their secondary sense. They should be understood to indicate only partial similarity between the example and that which they seek to exemplify. This is confirmed in the *Vedānta-sūtra* as follows: "The *jīva* is not a reflection of Brahman in the same way that the sun is reflected in water, because Brahman is all pervasive and not limited as the sun is. Nor can Brahman be divided by *upādhis* as earth can be divided by water, for Brahman has no perceivable characteristics. These comparisons are thus not appropriate in their primary sense. They are to be understood in their secondary sense. For example, as the sun is great, so is the Lord. Its reflection, however, is small, as is the *jīva*. Why is this so? Because the purport of the scriptures is fulfilled by understanding them in this way."[29]

As mentioned, there are several *śruti* texts that employ analogies of reflection and limitation in explaining the nature of Brahman. They are misunderstood by the Advaitins, taken as they are in their primary sense. We can understand the scripture both in terms of its direct *(mukhya-vṛtti)* or indirect *(gauṇa-vṛtti)* meaning. To construe an interpretation from the scriptures that supports the Māyāvādin theory, one is faced with the formidable task of interpreting the innumerable passages that speak about the transcendental Lord, his qualities, form, pastimes, and the virtues of devotion (the vast majority of scriptural texts) in terms of a secondary meaning. To avoid this, Śaṅkara has introduced his concept of *saguṇa* Brahman, or Brahman with material qualities appearing in practical reality as *īśvara* and *jīva*. This is his speculation, one that is not supported anywhere in *Vedānta-sūtra*.[30] Employing this speculation, Māyāvādins are able to interpret all of the direct statements about the Lord and those emphasizing difference between *jīva* and Brahman as discussions regarding practical reality and their so-called *saguṇa* Brahman.

The above aphorisms of *Vedānta-sūtra* tell us to take the theories of *pariccheda* and *pratibimba* as analogies that are meant to demonstrate that the *jīva*, although similar to the Lord, is at the same time very different. Taken otherwise, to indicate that

---

29. *ambuvad agrahanāt tu na tathātvam*
vṛddhi hrāsa bhāktvam antarbhāvād ubhaya sāmañjasyād evam
(Vs. 3.2.19–20)

30. George C. Adams, Jr., *The Structure and Meaning of Bādarāyaṇa's Brahma-sūtras,* (New Delhi: Motilal Banarsidass Publishers Pvt. Ltd., 1993), p. 56.

the *jīva* and Brahman are one in every respect, they are inappropriate analogies lacking necessary correspondence, and the conclusion drawn from them as to the identity of Brahman and *jīva* are incongruous with the spirit of the entirety of the *śāstra*. The analogy of reflection, for example, lacks correspondence between Brahman and the sun. While sun can be reflected due to its being at a distance from water, Brahman, being all pervasive, cannot. As the *śruti* itself says, "Brahman is colorless, reflectionless."[31]

However, taken in a secondary sense, as we often take worldly metaphors such as in comparing a man to a lion, such scriptural statements make sense. When we say, "The man is a lion," we do not mean it in its primary sense, rather that he has certain qualities of a lion, such as courage and strength. Similarly, the sun is great. It is vast and moving freely throughout the sky. Its reflection on the other hand is small and dependent upon the sun, as well as influenced by the size of that which it is reflected in. If we change the size of the reflected area, the size of the reflection will also change, yet the sun itself remains unchanged and independent. Similarly, the Lord is great and unaffected by any limiting *upādhi,* while the *jīva* is affected by its material designation under the influence of *māyā*. Thus although both the sun and its reflection are light, and Brahman and *jīva* are consciousness, they are at the same time different. In this way the analogy of reflection should be understood.[32]

Jīva Goswāmī ends this discussion in *anuccheda* forty-three with the conclusion that those scriptural texts that advocate oneness between Brahman and *jīva* (such as the famous *tat tvam asi,* considered by Śaṅkara to be the *mahā-vākya,* or supreme ut-

---

31. *tad acchāyam aśarīram alohitaṁ* (Praśna Up. 4.10)

32. All of these arguments are more fully developed in *Paramātma-sandarbha.*

terance, of the *śruti)* must be understood in terms of Vyāsa's trance, thereby avoiding the contradictory views of oneness and difference. This means that he accepts all of the scriptural statements and sees no contradiction between those that advocate oneness and those that advocate difference between *jīva* and Brahman. Rather than either of these extremes, which are difficult to support from the entirety of scripture, he accepts just what the scripture says. The *jīva* is one with Brahman, and the *jīva* is different from Brahman. How is this so? It is occurring by the inconceivable *śakti,* or power, of Brahman, which is inherent in its ultimate feature as Bhagavān. Brahman, that is, has inconceivable *śakti* of which the *jīva* souls are constituted, and by which it is one with them and different from them simultaneously, just as sun and its rays are one yet different at the same time.

Just as a person might refer to his hand as his body and be correct, similarly *śāstra* sometimes says that the *jīva* is Brahman in statements like *tat tvam asi* (you are that). Yet at the same time, there is more to be said about one's hand. If we say that it is the body, we are correct, but moreover it is also a hand, and as such, a part of one's body. Similarly, the *jīva* is Brahman, but unless we understand the nature of Brahman as revealed in Vyāsa's trance we will not understand statements like *tat tvam asi* correctly. We will do a disservice to our body if we do not understand that our hand, although our body, has a service to render to the body at the same time. Similarly, we will do a disservice to the absolute in concluding we are *Brahman* in every respect.

What is the nature of Brahman? It has inconceivable *śakti* by which it can move and yet be all pervasive at the same time. It is nondual, yet possessed of *śakti,* or power, and its inconceivable *śakti* does not compromise its nonduality. As mentioned earlier, the absolute moves not out of incompleteness but out of celebration of its fullness. Brahman is not still, motionless, eternally slumbering. It is full in itself and celebrating eternally. This is the *līlā* of Bhagavān that Śukadeva realized and Vyāsa saw in his trance.

For Śrī Jīva, the absolute is one and different at the same time. It is both static (one) and dynamic (different) simultaneously. Its static nature necessitates its dynamism. These two are not incompatible if we properly understand either of them. The absolute is one for Śrī Jīva inasmuch as it is a unity unto itself. There is no other. Yet its completeness necessitates the expression of the joy of its unity. This is not a necessity owing to incompleteness, rather celebration of completeness. The expression of the ultimate unity is brought about by the primary *śakti*, or power, of the absolute. This expression is the absolute's essential nature.

It is the opinion of Śrī Jīva that because one cannot conceive of the *śakti* of the absolute as one with the absolute, reality is *bheda*, or different. Yet because it is equally impossible to conceive of this *śakti* as different from the absolute, we call reality *abheda*, or nondifferent. This simultaneous one and different nature of reality, being beyond the power of human comprehension, is thus also *acintya*, or inconceivable.

It is important to note that the inconceivable simultaneous one and different nature of the absolute is inconceivable to those whose consciousness is covered. Covered consciousness only peers out of its confinement through the crack in the wall that amounts to reasoning power. Reasoning dictates that no one thing can be one and different simultaneously. Yet the plane of consciousness proper is not restricted as the world of our present experience is. In the plane of consciousness, the polar opposites of one and different do not cancel one another out resulting in a void or motionless, undifferentiated consciousness. They are synthesized into a higher reality that harmonizes both concepts. As vast possibilities exist in the mental realm, so even greater possibilities abound in the plane of consciousness. In dreams we can walk through the walls of the physical world of sense experience, yet in the plane of enlightened consciousness, we can go beyond the confines of our imagination. If one has ever thought himself a fool, never more so than when he insists "impossible."

Foolish we may be, yet many among us are reasonable nonetheless. I venture here to say that a good number of such reasonable persons have indicated in their own language similar notions of reality to that which Śrī Jīva and the *Bhāgavata* speak of. For Freud, the opposites of good and bad coexist in perfect harmony in the subconscious. It is due to the limitations of the physical plane that only one can be expressed at a time, that the two appear mutually exclusive. In science, we know that the quantum physics reality exists, yet it can only be expressed in classical physics terminology. The quantum reality remains thus just beyond our world even while it is our world.

Edward Dimock has given us much to help digest Śrī Jīva's *acintya* in our quantum quandary, invoking Heisenberg, Bell, Schrodinger, Hawking, and others. His efforts do much to narrow the gap between that which we have learned is reasonable and is thus "real" and that which Śrī Jīva posits as ultimate reality.[33] Śrī Jīva's world is no more unbelievable than that of quantum theory, which is widely accepted but far beyond our ability to conceptualize. We may know that waves and particles are one and different, but this truth still does not compute.

---

33. Edward C. Dimock, Jr., "Lilā," *Journal of the History of Religions* (Chicago: University of Chicago Press, 1989), p. 159. For more along these lines, see Swāmī B. V. Tripurāri, *Rasa: Love Relationships in Transcendence* (Eugene, Oregon: Clarion Call Publishing, 1994), chapter four.

When it comes to understanding and conceptualizing the spiritual reality, the whole picture of reality, the problem is with ourselves. This is so much so that whatever we touch turns to matter. Śrī Jīva insists appropriately that we must forego attempting to understand reality with our imperfect equipment. We must be and become consciousness to understand consciousness. Simultaneously, we must remain distinct from the absolute to love it. It is through this love that the absolute is understood to the fullest extent.

Śrīmad-Bhāgavatam, and therefore ultimately all the *śāstra,* is telling us this. The absolute is not like Śaṅkara's *advaita,* nor Madhva's *dvaita.* Nor is it qualified nondifference, as in the theory of Rāmānuja *(viśiṣṭādvaita)*; nor one sometimes and different sometimes as considered by Nimbārka *(bhedābheda)*; nor pure nonduality as taught by Viṣṇu Swāmī *(śuddhādvaita).* It is one and different simultaneously by the strength of its own inconceivable power—*acintya-bhedābheda-tattva.*

Jīva Goswāmī proceeds from here to further analyze Vyāsadeva's trance. However, before doing so, in *anucchedas* forty-four and forty-five, he describes through logic that which he will demonstrate from the *Bhāgavatam* in his continued analysis. Here he points logically to that which follows from his discussion of the *sambandha* he has explained thus far.

Sambandha-jñāna is the knowledge of relationship, a conceptual orientation—what the relationship is between God and the world, the world and the *jīvas,* the *jīvas* and God, and so on. This has been described, giving rise to the metaphysic of *acintya-bhedābheda.* That which follows logically from one's conceptual orientation is subsequent action, or the means *(abhidheya),* by which one actualizes the goal *(prayojana),* in this case the *jīva* soul's highest prospect in life.

Although *Tattva-sandarbha* is primarily concerned with *sambandha,* as are *Bhāgavata, Paramātmā,* and *Kṛṣṇa-sandarbhas,* in

Tattva-sandarbha everything is given in seed. Thus here Śrī Jīva sows the seeds of that which he will also discuss in great detail in *Bhakti* and *Prīti-sandarbhas*. He does so first with logical reasoning, following this with further evidence from the *samādhi* of Vyāsa.

Śrī Jīva says that because of the difference between the *jīva* and the Lord, the latter being the support of *māyā* and the former deluded by her, devotion is the only means *(abhidheya)* for the *jīva*'s deliverance from delusion. The means is not knowledge, as the Advaitin would have it, but devotion, consisting primarily of hearing and singing about he who is the shelter of all. Furthermore, it is Bhagavān alone who instructs the *jīvas*, and in so doing relieves them of suffering. He is of the highest nature, as opposed to the *jīvas* who are only similar with him in terms of being conscious like him, and therefore he alone is the worshippable object. He deserves the highest love. Awakening this Kṛṣṇa *prema* is the goal, *prayojana*, set forth in *Śrīmad-Bhāgavatam*.

Jīva Goswāmī is saying that Kṛṣṇa is the ultimate object of love. How is this so? In this world, we love in reality only ourselves, our souls. The tiny *jīva*, a unit of consciousness likened to a ray of the sun of Bhagavān, projects itself throughout the material body and beyond it into those things which it, as a result of this projection, comes to think of as its own. My body, my wife, my husband and children, my house, and so on are all thought of as such only because it is our very self that we have projected into them. Ultimately we love our bodies because we are within them. The spark of life within each of us is where the beauty we are in search of lies, not in the material body. Yet deluded by material identification, we look for ourselves within matter. Thus we try to make the body that which we ourselves are —units of beauty, eternality, and so on. Yet we do this with another objective in mind, to find perfect love.

It is love for which we live. Finding love is finding firm ground in life. Even when this love is misdirected towards the body, it affords the greatest security in the material world. When we find our love, nothing else matters. Although we are a unit of God, and similar to him in essence, we are emanations from him, dependent upon him. He is our support, and loving him provides the ultimate support for the life of the liberated *jīva*. We love our bodies only because we (consciousness) are animating them, and this consciousness is lovable because it is emanating from Kṛṣṇa. Kṛṣṇa is the reservoir of beauty and thus the ultimate object of love.

It is significant that Śrī Jīva has described the goal of life to be love of Kṛṣṇa and not Kṛṣṇa himself. Kṛṣṇa is the ultimate object of love, while love of Kṛṣṇa is itself the goal. As the *jīva* is drawn toward love of Kṛṣṇa, so Kṛṣṇa himself is drawn to that love expressed by the pure *jīva* endowed with *svarūpa-śakti,* the very energy of devotion. Thus devotion is both the means *(sādhana-bhakti)* and the goal *(prema-bhakti)*. It draws the *jīva* to Kṛṣṇa and Kṛṣṇa to the *jīva*. This notion, that it is love of God and not God himself that is the highest goal, is the unique contribution of the Gauḍīya *sampradāya* to the world of religious thought. In the tradition's depiction of this love, it is Rādhā, Śrī Kṛṣṇa's feminine counterwhole, who embodies the highest love. She is the devoted aspect of divinity and thus acts as both deity and ideal of devotion. It is the spirit of Rādhā's love for Kṛṣṇa that devotees aspire for. Cultivating this transcendental loving emotion is the means, attaining it the goal.

In *anuccheda* forty-six, Śrī Jīva, turns our attention to the third verse of Sūta Goswāmī, which describes Vyāsa's *samādhi*. In this verse, devotion is described as the only remedial measure for the *jīva*, resulting as it does ultimately in love. "Vyāsa saw that the material miseries were in reality superfluous to the *jīvas*. The *jīvas*, however, cannot understand this themselves, and thus Vyāsa compiled the *Śrīmad-Bhāgavatam* for their benefit. *Śrīmad-Bhāgavatam* advocates *sādhana-bhakti* as the remedial means *(abhidheya)* to material suffering and promotes *prema-bhakti* as the goal."[34]

Śrī Jīva explains that Vyāsa realized that *bhakti* was the means to free the *jīvas* from misery, and thus he wrote *Śrīmad-Bhāgavatam* to teach *sādhana-bhakti*. It is *sādhana-bhakti* that is referred to in this verse as opposed to the *prema-bhakti (bhakti-yogena)* of Vyāsa's trance. *Sādhana-bhakti* consists primarily of hearing and chanting about Bhagavān. Because it can be taught, it is not the mature stage of *bhakti*. *Prema-bhakti*, the highest love, cannot be taught. It depends solely upon the grace of Kṛṣṇa. Only when one achieves it can it be said that one is free from all miseries *(anarthas)*. Yet because *sādhana-bhakti* is the means to acquire grace, it can be said to directly mitigate all misery, as this verse states. It may also be construed that *sādhana-bhakti* removes worldly misery without the help of anything else, while the material condition itself is removed by its effect of *prema*.

Śrī Jīva cites two verses from the eleventh canto of *Śrīmad-Bhāgavatam* to confirm that *bhakti* is sufficient in and of herself to both remove misery and grant boons. "Whatever benefits are derived from the performance of rituals, austerity, the culture of knowledge, renunciation, yoga, charity, virtue, or any other pious means, can be attained by my devotee without effort through *bhakti* aimed at realizing me. This is so whether he desires heaven, liberation, my abode, or anything else."[35] Con-

---

34. *anarthopaśamaṁ sākṣād bhakti-yogam adhokṣaje/*
lokasyājānato vidvāṁś cakre sātvata-saṁhitām// (SB. 1.7.6)

35. *yat karmabhir yat tapasā jñāna-vairāgyataś ca yat/*
yogena dāna-dharmeṇa śreyobhir itarair api//
sarvaṁ mad-bhakti-yogena mad-bhakto labhate 'ñjasā/
svargāpavargaṁ mad-dhāma kathañcid yadi vāñchati// (SB. 11.20.32–33)

versely, knowledge and other such means are themselves dependent upon *bhakti*: "O Lord, those who take trouble to acquire only wisdom, disregarding the higher path of devotion, only waste their time, like those who engage in husking the chaff."[36] Whatever can be achieved by any other means can be achieved by *bhakti* alone, and any other means requires the element of *bhakti* for it to bear the desired fruit. That which cannot be attained by any other means, *prema*, is the ripened fruit of *bhakti*. Thus in this third verse the *abhidheya* has been directly established, as it was indirectly established in the previous two verses.

As mentioned earlier, the *prayojana* was indirectly indicated in the second of Sūta Goswāmī's verses. In the fourth verse this *prayojana* is further stressed, as is the fact that the *pūrṇa-puruṣa* mentioned in the first verse is none other than Śrī Kṛṣṇa. In this fourth verse, Sūta Goswāmī mentions the effects of hearing *Śrīmad-Bhāgavatam*, another experience of Vyāsadeva. "Simply by hearing *Śrīmad-Bhāgavatam*, *prema-bhakti*, unalloyed love for Śrī Kṛṣṇa the original *pūrṇa-puruṣa*, becomes manifest, and secondarily the fire of lamentation, illusion, and fear are extinguished."[37]

In this verse the word *bhakti* refers to *prema* as it did in the first of Sūta's verses. *Prema* is the goal of the *sādhana-bhakti* mentioned in the previous verse. While *sādhana* consists of hearing and chanting about the Lord as he is described in *Śrīmad-Bhāgavatam*, *prema* is the fruit of this exercise. As stated herein, *prema-bhakti* "sprouts up" *(utpadyate)* by the watering process

---

36. *śreyaḥ-sṛtiṁ bhaktim udasya te vibho*
kliśyanti ye kevala-bodha-labdhaye/
teṣām asau kleśala eva śiṣyate
nānyad yathā sthūla-tuṣāvaghātinām// (SB. 10.14.4)

37. *yasyāṁ vai śrūyamānāyaṁ kṛṣṇe parama pūruṣe/*
bhaktir utpadyate puṁsaḥ śoka-moha-bhayāpahā // (SB. 1.7.7)

of hearing *Śrīmad-Bhāgavatam*. The idea is that *prema* is beyond cause and effect. Nothing can cause it and nothing can stop it. It is its own cause, being the function of the Lord's *svarūpa-śakti*, his own inner nature, and as such it is independent as is he. *Prema*'s primary characteristics are that it causes one to love Kṛṣṇa and guides one in that love. Its secondary concomitant effect is that it removes all misery, *śoka-moha-bhayāpahā*, freeing the *jīva* from all grief brought about by misidentifying with material nature, *ātmānam tri-guṇātmakam*.

The grief of the *jīva* is deeply rooted in its initial bewilderment *(sammohitaḥ)*. *Padma Purāṇa* describes the various stages of *karma*, from that which is unmanifest *(aprārabdham)* to that which is bearing fruit at present *(prārabdham)*.[38] All stages of our karmic bondage are cleared by the execution of that *sādhana-bhakti* which culminates in *prema-bhakti*. Although *sādhana-bhakti* is sometimes considered to remove all such *karmic* traces in and of itself,[39] this is ultimately so only inasmuch as it leads to *prema*. Śrī Jīva cites the *Bhāgavatam* in making this point about *prema-bhakti*, "As long as one has not developed love for me, Vāsudeva, one will not be free from association with the body."[40]

Jīva Goswāmī says that the *parama puruṣa* mentioned in the fourth of Sūta's verses explaining Vyāsa's trance is the same as the *pūrṇa-puruṣa* mentioned in his first. The implied question of, "What form does the *pūrṇa-puruṣa* appear in?" is an-

---

38. *aprārabdha-phalaṁ pāpaṁ kūṭaṁ bījaṁ phalonmukham/*
krameṇaiva pralīyeta viṣṇu-bhakti-ratātmanām// (Pa. P.)

39. See Rūpa Goswāmī, *Bhakti-rasāmṛta-sindhuḥ*, translation by Tridandi Swāmī Bhakti Hridaya Bon Maharaja, (Vrindavana, India: Bon Maharaja, 1965), p.31.

40. *prītir na yāvan mayi vāsudeve*
na mucyate deha-yogena tāvat// (SB. 5.5.6)

swered here: *kṛṣṇe parama pūruṣe,* it is Kṛṣṇa. Who is Kṛṣṇa? Jīva Goswāmī says Kṛṣṇa is he upon hearing whose name those familiar with scripture will automatically think of the supreme person. It is he about whom the scripture repeatedly sings in verses such as the *Bhāgavatam*'s famous statement, "Kṛṣṇa, however, is the primeval Godhead, the source of Bhagavān."[41] This *parama puruṣa* is he who appears upon the recitation of his name. "It is he who has a dark complexion like that of a tamal tree, the child of Yaśodā, the supreme Brahman."[42] This is the popular meaning of the word Kṛṣṇa, the one that most readily comes to mind upon hearing his name. In today's world, many have heard his name, yet few are acquainted with the philosophy that underlies the *Bhāgavatam*'s Vedānta of aesthetics. The beautiful, dark-complexioned Kṛṣṇa, the cultivation of whose love ends all worldly misery, is the *parama puruṣa.*

In his fifth verse, Sūta Goswāmī explains that Vyāsa taught *Śrīmad-Bhāgavatam* to Śukadeva after having realized that the goal of life was love of God *(prema),* that the fullest expression of Godhead was Kṛṣṇa, and that hearing this message, which constitutes the essence of the Vedas, awakens that *prema.* Therefore, Vyāsa taught Śukadeva that the realization of Bhagavān Śrī Kṛṣṇa was trancendentally superior to the realization of undifferentiated Brahman. "Vyāsadeva, after compiling the *Śrīmad-Bhāgavatam* in short form, revised it and taught it to his son, Śrī Śukadeva, who was already Brahman realized."[43]

---

41. *kṛṣṇas tu bhagavān svayam* (SB. 1.3.28)

42. *tamāla-śyāmala-tviṣi śrī-yaśodā-stanandhaye/*
kṛṣṇa-nāmno rūḍhir iti sarva-śāstra-vinirṇayaḥ//

(Attributed to Lakṣmīdhara's *Namākumuḍī* and recorded in Cc. Antya 7.86).

43. *sa saṁhitāṁ bhāgavatīṁ kṛtvānukramya cātma-jam/*
śukam adhyāpayām āsa nivṛtti-nirataṁ muniḥ// (SB. 1.7.8)

Here the phrase *kṛtvānu kramya cātma-jam*, explains that Vyāsa had already written *Śrīmad-Bhāgavatam* as one of his eighteen Purāṇas in an abbreviated form. After having done so, he was inspired by Nārada to revise the work. Thus the statement found in both the *Skanda* and *Matsya Purāṇas* as to the *Mahābhārata* being compiled after the eighteen Purāṇas,[44] and the *Bhāgavatam*'s own statement as to its being compiled after the *Mahābhārata*,[45] are harmonized in this verse.

It is also significant, Śrī Jīva points out, that Śukadeva is described here as being absorbed in a life of renunciation *nivṛtti-niratam̐*. He was Brahman realized, and thus there was no chance of his being distracted by mundane affairs. This again underscores the transcendental significance of Kṛṣṇa *līlā*.

Following this fifth verse in the discussion of Vyāsa's trance, Śaunaka asked Sūta Goswāmī why Śukadeva, although already self-realized, underwent the trouble of studying *Śrīmad-Bhāgavatam*.[46] After Sūta Goswāmī's five verses discussing Vyāsa's trance, Śaunaka asks this question. Śaunaka's question is the sixth verse concerning Vyāsa's trance. Sūta replied in two verses, which conclude the discussion. The first of these verses explains the nature of Vyāsa's experience arising from his *samādhi*, an experience that is shared by all who take pleasure in the self. In this verse Sūta gives the logic as to why Śukadeva underwent the study of *Śrīmad-Bhāgavatam*. "All who partake of the bliss of the self, rather than the so-called happiness of attachment to that which does not endure and is thus foreign to the self, even though free from material attach-

44. *aṣṭādaśapurāṇāni kṛtvā satyavatī-sutaḥ/*
cakre bhāratam ākhyānam̐ vedārthair upabṛm̐hitam//
(Sk. P. *prabhāsa khaṇḍa* 2.94)

45. SB. 1.5.3

46. SB. 1.7.9

ments such as family and friends, nonetheless take pleasure in devotional service to Kṛṣṇa. Thus *ātmārāmas* like Śukadeva, having transcended the study of all subjects, nevertheless enjoy studying *Śrīmad-Bhāgavatam*. This is so because the very nature of Śrī Kṛṣṇa, who is described therein, is that he is beyond cause and effect and thus transcendental. Thus Śukadeva, not for the sake of gaining anything, being full in himself, took pleasure in hearing more about Brahman in the form of the narration of *Śrīmad-Bhāgavatam* in which the Lord's *līlās* are described."[47]

In this verse the word *"nirgrantha"* means "beyond all rules and regulations," "free from bondage resulting from false ego." *"Granthā"* also means book or scripture. Śukadeva was beyond all scripture. He had realized Brahman. His devotion was *"ahaitukī,"* motiveless. He was not in need of anything, yet he took the time to study *Śrīmad-Bhāgavatam*. Sūta in using these words affirms that Śaunaka's question was indeed a good one. Why would someone who was already beyond scripture, beyond false ego, transcendental to all scriptural do's and don'ts, without motive, and having nothing to gain, take up the study of scripture? Sūta answers, "Because that is the nature of the qualities of Hari (Kṛṣṇa)." The qualities of Kṛṣṇa are transcendental to such an extent that even self-realized souls will be attracted to them. There is no reason or cause as to why he became attracted to them, for they themselves are beyond cause and effect, being transcendental. It is the very nature of Kṛṣṇa *līlā* that it is attractive to even the self-realized.

While the first verse in reply to Śaunaka's question describes the nature of Vyāsa's trance, the next of Sūta's verses confirms that the experience of Śukadeva was the same as that of his father. "Śukadeva, the son of Vyāsadeva, although

---

47. *ātmārāmāś ca munayo nirgranthā apy urukrame/*
kurvanty ahaitukīṁ bhaktim ittham-bhūta guṇo hariḥ// (SB.1.7.10)

trancendentally situated nonetheless had his mind attracted to the qualities of Kṛṣṇa, and thus he·studied *Śrīmad-Bhāgavatam* and held the devotees of the Lord dear to his heart."[48]

Jīva Goswāmī explains, as per the *Brahmavaivarta Purāṇa*, that Śukadeva was unwilling to leave his mother's womb for fear of *māyā*. He somehow petitioned his father, Vyāsa, to call Kṛṣṇa. Although Kṛṣṇa's transcendental significance was not entirely understood by Śukadeva, he knew that Kṛṣṇa was able to grant liberation. Kṛṣṇa came and revealed himself to Śukadeva while he was still within the womb. Thus achieving liberation, he came out and went to the forest. It is significant that Śukadeva's Brahman realization was dependent on Kṛṣṇa's mercy.

Vyāsa then devised a means to capture his son. He sent a woodcutter to the forest, asking him to sing verses from the *Bhāgavatam*, in the hope that Śukadeva would hear them. It so happened that Śukadeva did, and he asked from where the verses came. The woodcutter took him to the hermitage of Vyāsa, where he then heard the entire *Bhāgavatam*.

The specific verses that Śukadeva heard are not mentioned by Jīva Goswāmī, and the section of *Brahmavaivarta Purāṇa* describing this incident is no longer available. Śrī Jīva only says that they were selected sections in which the glory of Śrī Kṛṣṇa is particularly mentioned. However, from the Gauḍīya oral tradition we can get some idea of what these verses were.[49] The

48. *harer guṇākṣipta-matir bhagavān bādarāyaṇiḥ/*
adhyagān mahad ākhyānaṁ nityaṁ viṣṇu-jana-priyaḥ// (SB.1.7.11)

49. Bhakti Rakṣaka Śrīdhara Mahārāja suggests in his recorded lectures entitled *Sermons of the Guardian of Devotion Vol. I* that one of the verses was SB. 10.1.2, in which the nature of Kṛṣṇa *līlā* in terms of its power to cure the disease of *māyā* is described along with the qualifications of the speaker of the *Bhāgavatam* (free from material desire). Others have suggested 10.21.7, which describes the beauty of Kṛṣṇa entering the Vṛndāvana forest.

particular verses aside, the significant point here is that Śukadeva heard only these verses. At that time he had no formal education, thus he had not studied Sanskrit grammar. Yet simply by hearing the poetry of the *Bhāgavatam* he became attracted to this transcendental literature. The mere sound of the *Bhāgavatam* caused him to forget about nondifferentiated Brahman. Such is the power of the *Bhāgavatam*. Later he actually underwent a formal study of the literature. He was prepared to do this to further relish that sound he had heard in the forest. If Śukadeva Goswāmī, the best of the *ātmārāmas*, or those interested in the pleasure of the self, was prepared to undergo the rigorous study of *Śrīmad-Bhāgavatam*, how important must this scripture be? Can we, who are all *ātmārāmas* in the common sense of the term, pursuers of self-pleasure, afford not to do the same in the serious pursuit of our highest potential?

Self-pleasure is the interest of all *jīvas*, but most *jīvas* pursue this aim without knowing who or what they are. Śukadeva knew what he was and what we all are, consciousness in search of ourselves. We are all but trying to find within matter the qualities inherent in ourselves. Śukadeva was a step ahead of the common *jīva*. He knew he was Brahman. Yet upon hearing *Śrīmad-Bhāgavatam*, he came to know that there was more to his being Brahman than he had realized—*para brahma*, Śrī Kṛṣṇa, in whom the best of the seekers of self-pleasure take shelter.

Thus Śrī Jīva Goswāmī concludes his discussion of Vyāsadeva's *samādhi*, resting in concordance with where he began. Both the principal author and the principal speaker's minds have been revealed, and the realization of Śukadeva and that of Vyāsa have proven to be one and the same. If we are to understand the significance of *Bhāgavatam*, we must do so in consideration of their shared insight. Any other attempt to understand its significance is a deviation from the true path.

6

"Who has not seen Śrī Jīva's ideal portrayed in art as the charming, flute-bearing cowherd, Kṛṣṇa, surrounded by his gopī lovers? Yet few have pondered the philosophy that serves as the canvas for this art of love."

The Ultimate Shelter

In the previous chapter Jīva Goswāmī revealed the manner in which one should approach the *Bhāgavatam*—through due consideration of that which was experienced by Vyāsa in his *samādhi*. Examining the vision of Vyāsa through the words of Sūta Goswāmī casts light upon the three categories of *sambandha, abhidheya,* and *prayojana.*

We learned in the previous chapter that the *jīvas* are eternally subordinate to Bhagavān; Bhagavān is the substratum of *māyā*; *māyā* has bewildered the *jīvas*; the Paramātmā and Brahman features of the absolute are included within Bhagavān, being aspects of himself; and so on. All of this constitutes *sambandha,* or the knowledge of how things are related. We also learned that the means, or *abhidheya,* for achieving the goal of life is *bhakti,* or devotion on the part of the *jīvas* directed towards Bhagavān. The goal, or *prayojana,* we learned, is attainment of love of God, Kṛṣṇa *prema*. Thus, as we heard in the closing *anuccheda* of the *maṅgalācaraṇa* about the *sambandha, abhidheya,* and *prayojana* in brief, in chapter five we heard of them in greater detail.

Now in this chapter beginning with *anuccheda* fifty, Śrī Jīva says that, having ascertained the manner in which the *Bhāgavatam* should be understood, he will discuss in much greater detail the *sambandha, abhidheya,* and *prayojana* in the following *sandarbhas.*

Tattva-sandarbha serves as an introduction to the other five treatises, and while in an introductory fashion it reveals the *sambandha, abhidheya,* and *prayojana* of the *Bhāgavatam,* it deals primarily with a *sambandha* of its own. That is, it reveals both the subject matter and the medium of its expression around which the other *sandarbhas* revolve. The subject is the absolute truth, which, as we shall see in this chapter more clearly than we have seen thus far, is Śrī Kṛṣṇa. The medium of expression is *Śrīmad-Bhāgavatam.*

What is the relationship between the *Bhāgavatam* and the absolute truth? *Śrīmad-Bhāgavatam* reveals the nature of the absolute truth in its fullest expression. Jīva Goswāmī cites the *Bhāgavatam*'s second stanza, referring to Śrīdhara Swāmī's commentary: "The ultimate reality *(vastu)* is revealed in *Śrīmad-Bhāgavatam.*"[1] Śrīdhara Swāmī stresses that the term *vastu* in this verse is used in its highest sense, thus referring to the highest reality. It is not to be understood as it is by the Vaiśeṣikas as any existing real substance, essence, or object. In *Śrīmad-Bhāgavatam vastu* refers to the essence of all existence.

Śrī Jīva poses a question in *anuccheda* fifty-one, "What is the nature of the essence of reality, the *tattva* of *Śrīmad-Bhāgavatam*?" To answer this question he turns to his *pramāṇa,* citing the words of Sūta Goswāmī, "Those who actually know the truth describe it as *advaya-jñāna,* nondual reality."[2] This is the first line of a most important verse from the *Bhāgavatam*. Jīva Goswāmī practically bases his entire *Bhāgavata* and *Paramātmā-sandarbhas* on this verse, the second line of which, although not mentioned here, reveals further that that *tattva* is known variously as Brahman, Paramātmā, and ultimately Bhagavān. It is a reply to one of the six questions posed by Śaunaka in the first chapter of the *Bhāgavatam,* and it is found earlier in this book in essence in the concluding *anuccheda* of Śrī Jīva's *maṅgalācaraṇa.*

---

1. *vedyaṁ vāstavam atra vastu* (SB. 1.1.2)
2. *vadanti tattva-vidas tattvaṁ yaj jñānam advayam* (SB. 1.2.11)

Here the word *jñāna* means that the ultimate reality's essential nature is consciousness. Ultimate reality is called *advaya,* or nondual, because it exists for itself and by itself in that there is no other reality independent of it, either similar, as in the case of the *jīva-śakti* (being consciousness), or different, as in the case of *māyā-śakti* (being inert). Furthermore, ultimate reality is the only support for all of its *śaktis,* or potencies, which could not exist without it. Because it is the ultimate goal of life, it is by nature full of joy, and as such it is also eternal.

That consciousness is the essence of reality is a tenet of all Vedāntins. Reality, that is, is in the least that which cannot be denied. Such is the nature of consciousness, for denial itself is an act of consciousness. We have no experience of not existing. Our experience is that we exist, we are. No one ever naturally thinks "I am not." When we do think "I am" and think of the ramifications of this reality (as we unfortunately do not often enough), we have thought deeply. Whatever is in question, be it even the concept of "nothing," the very act of questioning is the prerogative of consciousness alone. Even the notion of an ultimate void has consciousness at its foundation. Thus the *Bhāgavatam*'s description of the ultimate reality begins with the declaration that its essential nature is that of consciousness; it experiences, and it is to be experienced.

When the *Bhāgavatam* says that the ultimate reality is consciousness that is nondual *(advaya),* as we have seen, it should not be misunderstood that it is referring to the concept of nonduality popularized by Śaṅkara. It is nondual in the sense that whatever exists is dependent upon it. The nature of this nondual reality has been described as being possessed of *śaktis,* as realized by Vyāsa. Thus the *tattva* is nondual with regard to these *śaktis* in that its *śaktis* are dependent upon itself. The *tattva* is both energetic *(śaktimān)* and energy *(śakti)* inseparably. Its three primary energies are external energy *(svarūpa-śakti*), marginal energy (*jīva-śakti*), and inferior energy (*māyā-śakti*). Because it is possessed of *śakti*, it is full of dynamic activity. The *Bhāgavatam* does not speak of the motionless, nondifferentiated nondual reality of Śaṅkara.

The *tattva* of the *Bhāgavatam* is also nondual in the sense of three Vedāntic philosophical categories: *svagata-bheda, svajātīya-bheda*, and *vijātīyabheda. Svagata-bheda* is nondifference within a particular object. If an object is made of parts that are different from the object itself, it is not nondual because it suffers from *svagata-bheda*, difference within itself. *Svajātīyabheda* means difference between objects of the same class. Two objects of the same class, such as a large glass and a small glass are, although both glasses and of the same class, different from one another and are thus not nondual. *Vijātīyabheda* means difference between objects of different classes, such as the difference between a glass and plate. The *tattva* of *Śrīmad-Bhāgavatam* is nondual in the sense that it is free from all of these types of difference.

For the Māyāvadins, the absolute is nondual because it is one substance without parts or qualities, what to speak of personality and all that goes along with the concept of God as a person. Thus for the Advaitins, Brahman is the absolute nondual reality being devoid of internal difference. It is also free from *svajātīyabheda* and *vijātīyabheda* because things of the same or different class do not ultimately exist in their conception.

But the *Bhāgavatam* speaks of a different conception of nonduality than the Advaitin's conception of Brahman, as we have seen from the trance of Vyāsa. Thus when it speaks of the person Kṛṣṇa, it is not speaking of what our experience of persons in the material world brings to mind. Kṛṣṇa's body is nondifferent from himself. Its parts are nondifferent from the whole. His body is nondual consciousness.

Although it may be difficult to conceive of form constituted of consciousness, we must remember that the possibilities that lie within consciousness are infinitely greater than those found in matter. Moreover, if matter can accept forms constituted of itself as we experience in this world, why then cannot consciousness itself, which causes matter to manifest forms and again revert to an unmanifest state, express itself in form, place, and pleasure pastimes? A world of material forms and places is possible only because of matter's connection with consciousness. As consciousness manifests material forms when in touch with matter, so similarly consciousness expresses itself in form when concentrated within itself. Kṛṣṇa's form is such: nondual consciousness in which all of the parts are nondifferent from the whole. It is thus free from *svagata-bheda*, or internal difference, as are his abode and associates, which are also manifestations of nondual consciousness.

His *avatāras*, which are all of the same class as him, are also nondifferent from him. They are aspects of his transcendent emotional being manifest for the sake of his devotees. Each of these manifest *avatāras* correspond with the spiritual emotions he has awakened in the hearts of his devotees. These *avatāras* do not exist independently of him. The *jīva* souls may also be loosely construed as being of the same class as Kṛṣṇa, for they too are consciousness. In this sense, they are nondifferent from him and dependent upon him as well. As for the material world, although of a different class being inert or unconscious, it is nondifferent from him because it is dependent upon him in every respect. It is his energy, which in the ultimate issue is nondifferent from its energetic source, for one cannot separate energy from the energetic as one cannot separate heat from fire or the sun's rays *(jīva-śakti)* or reflection (*māyā-śakti*) from itself.

This nondual reality is also joyful by nature. Consciousness alone gives pleasure. Although we think that material objects give pleasure, in reality it is only when we invest our consciousness in them that they afford any pleasure. The potential for happiness is thus inherent in consciousness. This consciousness must also be eternal, because happiness that ends is not happiness in the ultimate issue. Our happiness ends only because we are identifying it with the material objects that we project our consciousness into, and material objects come and go. If instead we look within consciousness itself, in which the potential for the experience of joy lies, we can find true joy. This joy culminates in identifying ourselves as particles of serving energy of the supreme consciousness, who is by nature full of joy and eternal. He is joy personified, loving whom all souls can find ultimate happiness that exists forever.

Although the *Bhāgavatam* maintains the nature of consciousness to be eternal, there are those who object. In *anuccheda* fifty-two, Śrī Jīva voices the objection of the Vijñānavādins, sometimes called Yogācāra Buddhists, who contend that consciousness is momentary.

The Vijñānavādins are idealists much like the philosopher Berkeley, who considered the world to be in the mind. According to the Vijñānavādins, as understood by Śrī Jīva, the objective world does not exist.[3] External objects exist only within our conscious mind, which itself changes as we shift from one thought to another by the force of *vāsanās,* or desires. As we project our consciousness by the force of desire, the external world seems to appear, when in fact it is merely a projection of our consciousness. If we stop desire, we stop the world and the false perception that we as an individual perceiver exist at all. Śrī Jīva states the Buddhists' objection thus, contrasting it with the *Bhāgavatam*'s description of an ultimate nondual conscious reality: "Why should we think that consciousness is eternal and

---

3. Gregory J. Darling in his *An Evaluation of the Vedāntic Critique of Buddhism* maintains that the Vijānavādins do accept the reality of the external world.

nondual in the way in which the *Bhāgavatam* describes, when we see that it is absolutely momentary, appearing in the shape of a blue object at one moment and that of a yellow object the next?"

This Buddhist notion of consciousness that is subject to change and transformation is different from the nondual, eternal consciousness described in the *Bhāgavatam*. In their objection, the Buddhists are speaking about the subtle mind, or *citta-vṛtti*, when they speak of consciousness. This mind is something that one can close down. When one does so through various practices, however, it is not that the conscious entity, the *jīva*, ceases to exist as the Buddhists maintain. The *jīva* exists independent of the mind as does its ultimate shelter, Bhagavān, ultimate nondual consciousness.

The Buddhists do not accept the existence of the *jīva*, nor that of its shelter Bhagavān. Thus in answering their objection, Śrī Jīva first stresses the nature of individual consciousness and that of Bhagavān as they are described in his *pramāṇa*, *Śrīmad-Bhāgavatam*. Then he proceeds to demonstrate both from the *Bhāgavatam* and our common experience that consciousness does exist beyond the mind as both the *jīva* and Bhagavān.

Jīva Goswāmī cites the twelfth canto of *Śrīmad-Bhāgavatam* to further establish that the *Bhāgavatam* does indeed say that the ultimate reality is eternal, nondual consciousness. "*Śrīmad-Bhāgavatam* is the essence of Vedānta. Its subject is that upon which all the Upaniṣads are based, characterized by the qualitative identity of the *jīva* with Brahman, and it is aimed at bringing about a unity in love between the *jīva* and Brahman."[4]

As Jīva Goswāmī has stressed in the last chapter the difference between the *jīva* and Brahman, here he stresses their one-

---

4. *sarva-vedānta-sāraṁ yad brahmātmaikatva-lakṣaṇam/*
vastv advitīyaṁ tan-niṣṭhaṁ kaivalyaika-prayojanam// (SB. 12.13.12)

ness. He says that the principal teaching of the Upaniṣads, upon which the *Vedānta-sūtra* is based, is that the *jīva* souls and the ultimate consciousness are one. By this he means that the Upaniṣads teach of the ultimate reality through a particular approach that stresses that the *jīva* soul is not matter but consciousness and in that sense one with Brahman, who when understood in terms of possessing *śakti* is known as Bhagavān. Statements such as *tat tvam asi*, "you are that," indicate this unity is one of quality, not quantity. We are of the same quality as Brahman. We share the same conscious nature with Brahman. As we are a unit of Brahman, we conscious beings are eternal as is he. By his *śakti* he pervades all, and we are a part of one of his eternal *śaktis* (*jīva-śakti*).

The Upaniṣads state that the Brahman with which we are one is "truth, knowledge, and infinity."[5] "Learning about Brahman, the unheard is heard,"[6] thus knowing Brahman nothing remains to be known. Brahman is the only cause of the universe, as stated in the *Chāndogya Upaniṣad*, "In the beginning Brahman alone existed."[7] Brahman is such that by its mere wish it can create, "Brahman glanced and willed to become many (and thus we exist)."[8]

After stressing our oneness with Brahman and its conscious nature, Śrī Jīva then reminds us, as per the trance of Vyāsa, that the *jīva* is not entirely one with Brahman. He cites the *Chāndogya Upaniṣad* once more, "By this living self (let me enter the *devatās* and create name and form)."[9] Here the pronoun *idam* (the in-

---

5. *satyaṁ jñānam anantaṁ brahma* (Tai. U. 2.1.1)
6. *yenāśrutaṁ śrutaṁ bhavati* (Ch. U. 6.1.3)
7. *sad eva saumyedam agra āsīt* (Ch. U. 6.2.1)
8. *tad aikṣata bahu syām* (Ch. U. 6.2.3)
9. *anena jīvenātmanā* (Ch. U. 6.3.2)

strumental case of which is *anena*), meaning "this," indicates our difference from the absolute, who is speaking. Yet *ātman*, meaning "self," implies our unity with the absolute.

Śrī Jīva gives an example to illustrate the way in which the Upaniṣads teach about Brahman. He says that just as one confined to a dark room for his entire life can be taught about the greatness of the sun first by being shown a ray of the sun and stressing that it is itself the sun, so similarly the Upaniṣads teach about Brahman by first stressing our oneness in quality with Brahman. Just as the rays of the sun are sun yet are not sun at the same time, the *jīva* is one and different from Brahman. One often says "Let's go sit in the sun." In this statement the speaker is really suggesting that we sit in the sun's rays and not the sun itself. Similarly, the *jīva* is sometimes referred to as Brahman, the supreme sun, which is all-pervasive, but in referring to the *jīva* as such the Upaniṣads are not intending to equate the tiny *jīva* in every respect with the all-pervading Brahman. Śrī Jīva discusses this in greater detail in his *Paramātmā-sandarbha*.

When in places the Upaniṣads tell us that Brahman has parts, it is speaking about Brahman in its ultimate feature as Bhagavān who is possessed of *śaktis*, one of which is the *jīva śakti*. In other places they teach that Brahman is without parts, referring in such passages to the undifferentiated Brahman, described metaphorically as the effulgence of Bhagavān.

As for the words *kaivalyaika prayojanam* mentioned in the previously quoted *Bhāgavatam* verse of the twelfth canto, Jīva Goswāmī says here it means *bhakti*, or love. It is commonly used by others to indicate absolute identity between the *jīva* and Brahman, but this cannot be the meaning, as Śrī Jīva will elaborate in *Prīti-sandarbha*.

Thus having further emphasized that the absolute truth of the *Bhāgavatam* is nondual, eternal consciousness possessed of the joy of love, Śrī Jīva returns to deal directly with the objection of the Vijñānavādins as to the so-called momentary nature of consciousness. In all of this Śrī Jīva is demonstrating the subject of the *Bhāgavatam* from an analysis of the position of the individual, or *jīva,* soul. He wants to show that consciousness exists beyond the mind, and that it underlies all of the mental and physical worlds of experience. This consciousness of which the *jīva* is constituted is of the same nature as its own substratum, which is the ultimate shelter or support of everything, the *advaya-jñāna tattva* of *Śrīmad-Bhāgavatam,* Śrī Kṛṣṇa.

Jīva Goswāmī quotes two verses from *Śrīmad-Bhāgavatam* which contain four arguments. Śrī Jīva says that they are in essence a commentary on an aphorism of *Vedānta-sūtra,* "The reference to the *jīva* has a different meaning."[10] The section in which this aphorism appears determines, as Śrī Jīva has maintained all along, that the *jīva,* although consciousness, is not the worshippable object which lies within the heart, the Paramātmā manifestation of Kṛṣṇa. The two *Bhāgavatam* verses he cites in which the *ātman* is mentioned should be understood in terms of the *Vedānta-sūtra* reference cited above, and thus *ātman* means *jīva,* or *jīvātmā,* who is similiar in nature to the Paramātmā and different from matter.

In the two *Bhāgavatam* verses Śrī Jīva cites, Pippalāyana responds to Mahārāja Nimi's inquiry about Brahman, the absolute, by first describing the *jīva,* who is equal to Brahman in quality. In other words, the *jīva* also has its support, which is the object of love and thus is quantitatively different. The *jīva* is in one sense the subject; matter, both subtle (psychic) and gross (physical), is the object of its perception. Yet the shelter of the *jīva* is the supersubject, in relation to which the *jīva* takes a position more akin to matter's position in relation to itself. As material objects are instruments to the *jīva,* the *jīva* is but an

---

10. *anyārthaś ca parāmarśaḥ* (Vs. 1.3.20)

instrument of the absolute, Bhagavān, albeit a conscious one. In his explanation of Pippalāyana's responce to Mahārāja Nimi, Śrī Jīva presents arguments to refute the idea that consciousness is momentary and further establishes the conscious nature of the *jīva* and Bhagavān. Thus Śrī Jīva invokes *Śrīmad-Bhāgavatam,* which through the logic of our everyday experience, refutes the Yogācāra's objection. Here the *Śrīmad-Bhāgavatam* invokes inference to refute those whose ultimate *pramāṇa* is the same *(anumāna).*

"The *ātman,* or pure *jīva,* was not born. Since it has no birth, it is also free from all other transformations that material manifestations alone undergo. Thus it does not die; it neither increases nor decreases. The evidence for this is that the *jīva* itself observes the increase and decrease of the material manifestation of the body (sixfold transformations). Although observing objects subject to transformation, the *jīva* is not subjected to the same changes. Just as the life air, *prāṇa,* does not change its position even though it appears to in the midst of the body's transformations, so the *ātman* exists at all times and in every body, remaining unchanged by the transformations of the body. The *jīva* is pure consciousness *(upalabdhi-mātraṁ)* and yet appears to undergo change due to the senses *(indriya-balena)* only.

"Life air *(prāṇa)* follows the *jīva* wherever it may go, whether appearing to take birth from an egg, fetus, seed, or perspiration. Similarly, the *jīva* remains unchanging, eternally the same despite its being in the midst of the transformations of material energy. Experience, which the Buddhists put considerable stock in, also leads us to the conclusion that consciousness is eternal and foundational to the material experience. For example, when we are in deep sleep without dreaming, both the physical world, represented by the senses, and the mental world, represented by dreams, for all intents and purposes close down. Although the psychic and physical worlds and their impression of material ego dissolve for one in deep sleep, he who is sleeping, upon awakening, remembers that he slept well. It is not that only void remains when the mind and physical world are merged into one another and even the sense of ego based on the bodily and mental configuration becomes dormant. It is consciousness that remains and witnesses that state of deep sleep. One cannot witness that which one has not experienced. The experience is vague only because of our embodiment, yet it serves to illustrate that consciousness exists aloof from the transformations of the body and is the basis of our material experience."[11]

The four arguments that Śrī Jīva finds in these verses are: (1) There is a distinction between that which undergoes transformation and that which is free from such transformations as origination and annihilation, (2) There is a distinction between that which is seen and the seer, (3) There is a distinction between the witness and that which is witnessed, (4) There is a distinction between that which suffers and the repository of love (this argument is implied).

Jīva Goswāmī explains that the *ātman,* or pure *jīva,* mentioned in the first of these verses described by the words "was not born," indicates that the *jīva* is distinct from the body which undergoes change in the form of birth, growth, maturation, giving off by-products (transforming), dwindling, and dying (vanishing). All material manifestations undergo these six

---

11. *nātmā jajāna na mariṣyati naidhate 'sau*
na kṣīyate savana-vid vyabhicāriṇāṁ hi/
sarvatra śaśvad anapāyy upalabdhi-mātraṁ
prāṇo yathendriya-balena vikalpitaṁ sat//
aṇḍeṣu peśiṣu taruṣv aviniściteṣu
prāṇo hi jīvam upadhāvati tatra tatra/
sanne yad indriya-gaṇe 'hami ca prasupte
kūṭa-stha āśayam ṛte tad-anusmṛtir naḥ// (SB. 11.3.38–39)

changes, but the *jīva,* or *ātman,* is described here as not being subject to them. The body alone undergoes these changes, not the *jīva*. The logic of this is that the *ātman* is the observer of these changes *(savana-vit)*. One who observes that which is changing cannot himself be undergoing the change. The *jīva* is the observer of all phases of time and thus of all things having a beginning and an end. It observes from childhood to youth and so on, in the bodies of either demigods or mortals.

The *jīvas* are spread throughout creation, appearing in a wide variety of bodies. Some of these bodies are large, some small. Some live for long periods, some for a relatively short time. In all instances of this variegated creation, however, the eternal *jīva* souls are animating the world of matter. Their essential and eternal conscious nature is not disturbed by the changes they induce in contact with material nature. Be one a man, god, animal, or plant in appearance, one is a *jīva* soul in every instance. Because we do not undergo transformation as the material body does, we are understood to be eternal, the constant observing factor of the ever-changing material phenomena. Because we not only are free from transformation, but observe the transformation of material nature as well, we are also inherently consciousness, which alone possesses the ability to perceive.

The unconditioned *jīvātmā* is *"upalabdhi-mātram,"* one whose nature is pure consciousness. Because we see that consciousness of a blue object appears and disappears, this does not have any bearing on the eternal nature of the conscious *jīva*. This example of transformation of consciousness from awareness of a blue object into awareness of a yellow one applies only to the mind and not the *jīva*. It occurs on account of the senses, *indriya-balena*. When we perceive an object, the mind takes the shape of that object, changing to another shape as we perceive another object. It is the soul, however, that perceives these changes of mind. Just as one might screw a blue light bulb into an electrical socket and get blue light, then a yellow one and get yellow light, so blue or yellow consciousness appear and disappear in the mind due to the senses, yet consciousness itself remains as constant as the electrical current. Consciousness, which is existence itself, is one. It appears as many due to the senses and subsequent mental modifications alone.

In the verses under discussion, "*prāṇa,*" or life air, is mentioned to illustrate that the *jīva,* like the *prāṇa,* is undivided. The *jīva,* or consciousness, appears to be divided and changing when in fact the apparent change is due only to the changing mind and senses. Similarly, the *prāṇa* is one yet when functioning it appears to be divided into five bodily airs.

The analogy of *prāṇa* is further developed in the second verse. This verse illustrates how the self is realized as the senses merge back into one another (the sense of smell and its corresponding sense object, earth, merging back into taste and taste's sense object, water, etc.). When one sleeps at night, the senses and the external world shut down. When we are in deep sleep devoid of dreams, the mind also closes down. At that time the *jīva* is no longer in the body because it is no longer conscious of it, consciousness being its only connection with the body. We are "in" the body only because we are consciously identifying with it. We cease to identify with it in dreamless sleep. At that time it is maintained by the Paramātmā. We return to it because of our *karma,* the force of material desire, which again prompts us to awaken from sleep. The *jīva* only appears to be changing in the waking and dream states. In the dream state consciousness appears to undergo changes due to impressions from the waking state that are stored in the mind. But when one is in deep sleep, the unchanging nature of the *jīva* is revealed.

The Buddhist, however, is not yet satisfied, for who is to say that anything other than the void remains when the body and mind close down? Where is the so-called changeless *jīva* at that time? This verse answers that our experience is upon waking that "we slept well." He who witnesses this restful state is the *jīva*. There can be no remembrance of a thing that one has no experience of. In this example, the experience that we slept well, we were peaceful, however vague, is nonetheless an experience, a hazy experience of the unchanging self that exists independent of the body and mind.

It is not that when we go to sleep we become self-realized. This example is given only to illustrate that the experience of deep, dreamless sleep shows us that consciousness exists when the body and mind are closed down. The means of permanently closing them down is stopping our *karma*, the force of material desire. When we do so through means of self-realization, it is not a void that we experience, it is the true eternal conscious nature of the self. When we do so through the culture of pure *bhakti*, we realize further the source and support of our own self, the reservoir of love, Bhagavān Śrī Kṛṣṇa, the supreme Brahman. One conscious identification, that of identifying with the body, brings about suffering, another, identifying with the self, ultimately reveals the repository of love.

It is to be understood that because the *jīva* suffers in its identification with matter, it cannot be the ultimate support. Thus the *jīva*'s suffering indirectly reveals that it also has a support. He who is our support is free from all suffering and is the perfect object of love. That we have a support is evidenced not only by the fact that we experience suffering, but by the fact that our bodies are maintained even when we leave them during deep sleep. Matter requires consciousness for its animation. The ultimate shelter thus maintains our lives materially, and when we develop a loving relationship with him, he does so spiritually as well.

Śrī Jīva concludes *anuccheda* fifty-five by restating the four arguments. In doing so he labels this type of reasoning *anvaya-*

vyatireka, or positive and negative concomitance. Having described the *tattva* (nondual consciousness) of the *Bhāgavatam* from the *vyaṣṭi*, or individual point of view, by analyzing the position of the *jīva*, in *anuccheda* fifty-six Śrī Jīva explains the same *tattva* from the *samaṣṭi*, or aggregate angle of vision. He says that the *Bhāgavatam* describes this *samaṣṭi* angle of vision by way of discussing the characteristics of a Mahāpurāṇa. In doing so, the *Bhāgavatam* calls its *tattva*, which is the ground of being, the ultimate shelter, *āśraya-tattva*.

In the second canto of the *Bhāgavatam*, Śukadeva Goswāmī lists the ten subjects that the *Bhāgavatam* discusses. These ten subjects are found in all Mahāpurāṇas. Although there are ten subjects discussed, there is at the same time only one subject about which the *Bhāgavatam* speaks, *advaya-jñāna*, nondual consciousness. How then can this apparent contradiction be resolved? In the two verses cited by Śrī Jīva, the first lists the ten topics of the *Bhāgavatam*, the second describes how all of them are actually only describing this *advaya-jñāna*, listed here as the tenth subject, *āśraya-tattva*.

"Śukadeva Goswāmī said: In the *Śrīmad-Bhāgavatam* there are ten characteristics: creation of the universal constituents, subcreation of the planetary systems, maintenance, protection by the Lord of his devotees, the creative impetus, the Manus, the Lord's incarnations, annihilation, liberation, and the shelter of these nine categories—the *āśraya-tattva*, Śrī Kṛṣṇa. Through Vedic reference, great sages describe the first nine characteristics both directly and also indirectly through the narration of histories, in an effort to shed light on the tenth category, the *āśraya-tattva*."[12]

---

12. *śrī-śuka uvāca*
atra sargo visargaś ca sthānaṁ poṣaṇam ūtayaḥ/
manvatareśānukathā nirodho-muktir āśrayaḥ//

In the above two verses, the ten subjects of the *Bhāgavatam* are mentioned. Nine of them are termed *āśrita-tattva,* or that which is sheltered, and one is termed *āśraya-tattva,* or the one who is the shelter of the other nine. The first nine are described for the single purpose of shedding light on the tenth, the ultimate shelter, *āśraya-tattva*. The true nature of the tenth subject will be understood by way of understanding those aspects of the ultimate shelter that are under its shelter.

The tenth subject, being Bhagavān Śrī Kṛṣṇa, is difficult to understand, absorbed as he is in *līlā,* or carefree activity, that resembles in outward appearance the activities of a young boy. Kṛṣṇa is dark like the rain cloud, wrapped in glittering golden dress, and crowned with a peacock feather. He carries a flute in his hand, and glances playfully with his lotus-like eyes at his *gopīs*. Kṛṣṇa is the friend of the cows, and the trees bow their branches in respect as he passes them in his forest pastimes. Those trees are the hair of the earth that stand on end at the thought of being touched by his tender soles. In the land of Vṛndāvana, the river Yamunā flows only for his sake, nourishing the land where animate and inanimate alike live a transcendent life of love, with him alone as their love's object. Surrounded with friends, lovers, and family members, Śrī Kṛṣṇa brings joy to all. Who is this Kṛṣṇa? A mere metaphor for divine love or a tangible reality more real than the illusory world of our experience? *Śrīmad-Bhāgavatam* stresses the latter—this ever-youthful boy is the ultimate shelter.

He is no ordinary boy. Thus to help us understand him properly, subjects relevant to our lives, such as creation and so on, all of which require his support, are also described in the *Bhāgavatam*. For this reason the Gauḍīya *sampradāya* insists that

---

daśamasya viśuddhy-arthaṁ navānām iha lakṣaṇam/
varṇayanti mahātmānaḥ śrutenārthena cāñjasā// (SB. 2.10.1–2)

one not jump to the tenth canto of the *Bhāgavatam* (where the *līlās* of the *āśraya-tattva* are the main subject and Kṛṣṇa's dancing with his *gopīs* is center stage) without understanding the other cantos. First let us understand this ultimate shelter through discussion of that which he oversees within our present world of experience.

Śukadeva Goswāmī utters seven consecutive verses following the two in which these ten subjects are mentioned to shed further light on the significance of the *āśraya-tattva*. In these verses, all ten of the subjects are described in greater detail.

"The creation of the elements *(bhūta)*, such as ether, sky, fire, water, and earth; the sense objects *(mātrā)*, such as sound, touch, sight, taste, and smell; the sense organs *(indriya)* such as ears, skin, eyes, tongue, and nose; the mind, intelligence, and *mahat (dhi)* is known as *sarga* (primary creation). The subsequent interaction of these constituents with the three modes of nature *(guṇa)* results in the secondary creation of moving and nonmoving creatures. All of this is ultimately done by the will of the Lord *(pauruṣaḥ)*"[13]

This verse describes both the primary creation of the elemental constituents of material creation and, once they are manifest, the creation of Brahmā using those elements to form the bodies of the various species, situate the planets, and so on. As mentioned, the backing of this is the will of the *puruṣa avātara* who is one of Kṛṣṇa's incarnations.

The next verse describes the subsequent task of the maintenance of the world order, the protection of the devoted, the virtues of those in a ruling capacity whose lives illustrate adherence to the will of God and are thus empowered by him, and the fruitive urge within the *jīva* that gives rise to the world again

---

13. *bhūta-mātrendriya-dhiyāṁ janma sarga udāhṛtaḥ/*
brahmaṇo guṇa-vaiṣamyād visargaḥ pauruṣaḥ smṛtaḥ// (SB. 2.10.3)

and again. "*Sthiti,* or *sthāna,* signifies the victory of the Lord of Vaikuṇṭha who maintains the world through creating fixed limits for those within it. *Poṣaṇa* indicates the Lord's grace and protection for his devotees who live in the material world. *Manvantara* indicates the virtues of those such as Manu who exemplify *dharma* during the periods known as *manvantaras. Uti* represents the desires and impressions, or *saṁskāras (karma-vāsanāḥ),* of the *jīvas.*"[14]

"*Īśa-kathāḥ* indicates the descriptions of the incarnations of the Lord and his devotees."[15] "*Nirodha* is the closing down of the manifest universe and the resting of the *jīva* in conjunction with the cosmic sleep of the Paramātmā. At that time everything is withdrawn back into the body of the Paramātmā. *Mukti* indicates that condition of the *jīva* in which it is free from ignorance owing to material identification and furthermore established in its own true nature as an eternal servitor of Bhagavān."[16]

Regarding *mukti,* it is significant here that the *Bhāgavatam* describes it as being characterized by both negative and positive results. Abandonment of one's foreign nature, material consciousness, is often considered to be the sum and substance of *mukti,* or liberation. *Śrīmad-Bhāgavatam,* however, takes this concept one giant step further. Not only is *mukti* characterized by renouncing one's material identification, it more importantly encompasses the establishment of one's true nature as an eternal servant of Bhagavān. *Mukti* is becoming free from

---

14. *sthitir vaikuṇṭha-vijayaḥ poṣaṇaṁ tad–anugrahaḥ/*
manvantarāṇi sad-dharma ūtayaḥ karma-vāsanāḥ // (SB. 2.10.4)

15. *avatārānucaritaṁ hareś cāsyānuvartināṁ/*
puṁsām īśa-kathāḥ proktā nānākhyānopabṛṁhitāḥ// (SB. 2.10.5)

16. *nirodho 'syānuśayanam ātmanaḥ saha śaktibhiḥ/*
muktir hitvānyathā-rūpaṁ sva-rūpeṇa vyavasthitiḥ// (SB. 2.10.6)

false ego and being situated in the pure ego of eternal service. In Gauḍīya Vaiṣṇava doctrine, the former, considered by the monists to be the goal, is but a by-product of the latter.

Thus nine subjects have been mentioned: 1) creation or the manifestation of the elemental constituents of the material world; 2) secondary creation involving the formation of planets, species, etc; 3) maintenance of the manifest world; 4) protection of those aspiring to serve God; 5) the nature of fruitive desire, which is in one sense the reason for the world; 6) the lives of pious rulers; 7) the *avatāras* of Godhead; 8) release from material existence; and 9) cosmic annihilation. All nine of these subjects are discussed in detail in *Śrīmad-Bhāgavatam.* However, they are all discussed with a view to shed light on that principle that is behind them, their shelter. These nine are but functions in relation to the world that are dependent upon one ultimate shelter. If we understand all these functions properly, we can understand their ultimate support—the tenth and only subject of *Śrīmad-Bhāgavatam.* This subject is the *tattva* of *Śrīmad-Bhāgavatam,* nondual consciousness also known as the *āśraya-tattva,* or ultimate shelter. Thus we must think twice when we see the beautiful portrait of Kṛṣṇa with his cows and cowherd girlfriends.

Having commented on the *āśrita-tattva,* or sheltered reality, Śukadeva Goswāmī next elaborates further on the *aśrāya tattva,* the ultimate shelter. "The *āśraya* is he from whom the origin *(ābhāsa)* of the manifest world emanates and by whom it is dissolved (*nirodha*). Because of him alone the world is perceived through the senses of the *jīvas.* He is that same nondual *tattva* mentioned earlier, who is designated as Brahman, Paramātmā, and ultimately *(iti)* Bhagavān, Śrī Kṛṣṇa."[17]

---

17. *ābhāsaś ca nirodhaś ca yato 'sty adhyavasīyate/*
sa āśrayaḥ paraṁ brahma paramātmeti śabdyate // (SB. 2.10.7)

Now in *anuccheda* fifty-nine, Śrī Jīva explains the last two verses of Śukadeva. He says that Śukadeva Goswāmī in uttering these last two verses seeks to explain the *āśraya-tattva* once again from the *vyaṣṭi,* or individual point of view, as well as from the *samaṣṭi,* or aggregate point of view. He does so by demonstrating that three *puruṣas, ādhyātmika, ādhibhautika,* and *ādhidaivika* are all interdependent upon one another, while the *āśraya-tattva* is in one sense the independent knower of these three *puruṣas*. In one sense, the *āśraya-tattva* is the pure *jīva,* but more accurately he is the very ground of the *jīva* itself—its source, the Paramātmā, who's fullest expression is Bhagavān Śrī Kṛṣṇa. He alone is fully independent, and thus the shelter of all.

The *ādhyātmika puruṣa* refers to the individual *jīva* embodied in the physical plane who identifies with the senses of the material body. The *ādhibhautika puruṣa* refers to the particular embodiment of the *jīva,* and the *ādhidaivika puruṣa* to the controlling deities of the senses that the *ādhibhautika puruṣa* is made up of. Both the *ādhyātmika* and *ādhidaivika puruṣa*s are embodied souls, one on the physical plane, the other on the psychic. The latter one presides over the former. What distinguishes the two is the *ādhibhautika puruṣa,* or the gross material body, which causes one to function as a controlling deity, the other to function under that control. All three of these *puruṣas,* or "persons," are interdependent aspects of the cosmic manifestation.

It may be questioned as to how the material body can be referred to as a "person." To this Śrī Jīva replies that it is justifiable on the basis of the *Taittirīya Upaniṣad*'s words, "This *puruṣa* (the body of a person) is the essence of food personified or embodied."[18] It is also our everyday experience that we re-

18. *sa vā eṣa puruṣo 'nna-rasamayaḥ* (Tai. U. 2.1.1)

fer to the body of a person as a person when we say, "Here comes Robin," when we see her body moving in our direction. Thus, it is proper to classify our embodiment as a "person," as the *Bhāgavatam* does.

Śukadeva Goswāmī says, "The *jīva* soul appears as both the *ādhyātmika puruṣa* (the possessor of the material body consisting of senses) and the *ādhidaivika puruṣa* (controlling deities of the senses). These two *puruṣas* are distinguished from each other by the *ādhibhautika puruṣa* (the gross material body). All three of these are interdependent. Without one, we cannot perceive the other. Because these three *puruṣas* are interdependent, none of them can be the shelter of the other two, nor of its own self. From this, the question naturally arises as to who their shelter (*āśraya*) is, who in turn must be the shelter of all *(svāśraya)?* Is it the pure *jīva*? Only in the sense that the *jīva* is identified with the whole, the Paramātmā, by which it becomes purified. The *jīva* is the witness and is thus the *āśraya* inasmuch as he is the Lord who having become many chooses to enter into an illusory relationship with the material energy consisting of the three *guṇas*. Otherwise, and more correctly, it is the Lord, the Paramātmā, a partial representation of Bhagavān Śrī Kṛṣṇa, and ultimately Śrī Kṛṣṇa Himself, who is the shelter of all."[19]

Both the *ādhyātmika* and *ādhidaivika puruṣas* are ultimately *jīva* souls constituted of nondual consciousness. They become materially distinguished from one another in terms of material duality through the agency of the physical body, which is termed the *ādhibhautika puruṣa*. Before the creation is manifest, the senses, having no dwelling place, are also unmanifest. At

---

19. *yo 'dhyātmiko 'yaṁ puruṣaḥ so 'sāv evādhidaivikaḥ/*
yas tatrobhaya-vicchedaḥ puruṣo hy ādhibhautikaḥ//
ekam ekatarābhave yadā nopalabhāmahe/
tritayaṁ tatra yo veda sa ātmā svāśrayāśrayaḥ// (SB. 2.10.8–9)

this time, within the Paramātmā, in accordance with their stored *karma,* both the *jīvas* who will be human and those who will become controlling deities are indistinguishable from one another in the material sense. That is, they are both *jīvas.* When the creation is manifest, in accordance with the *jīva*'s stored *karma,* each takes a respective position in the world. What then distinguishes the two is the physical body, the *ādhibhautika puruṣa,* the resting place of the sense organs. Most significant here is the statement that all of these essential aspects of the world are interdependent upon one another. On account of this, they cannot be the ultimate shelter, who is independent.

How are they interdependent? Jīva Goswāmī explains that without the presence of a visible sense object, it is impossible to verify the existence of either the sense organs such as one's eyes (whose existence is inferred from the perception of the object) or the seer himself. Similarly, without either the eyes or the seer, one cannot verify the existence of the presiding deity of sight, the sun (whose existence is inferred from the ability of the eyes to function). Without the presiding deity of the sun, the eyes cannot see. Without the senses the existence of the visible object cannot be verified. Therefore, if any one of these is missing in the equation, the others are rendered imperceivable as well. However, he who knows all three of these aspects of the cosmic manifestation, the pure *jīva,* who can cognize them through reflection and introspection, is their shelter, yet only inasmuch as he is identified with the Paramātmā, who is the shelter even of the *jīva*. It is thus the Paramātmā alone who is the *svāśraya,* the shelter of all. And that Paramātmā, as mentioned previously, is a partial manifestation of Bhagavān, who in his fullest expression is Śrī Kṛṣṇa.

Śrī Jīva explains further that, relatively speaking, one should not hesitate to identify the pure *jīva* as the *āśraya,* for he is described as being beyond the three *guṇas* and thus their support. As we heard in the description of Vyāsa's trance, "Though conscious like the Lord, and thus beyond the three *guṇas* (thereby the *āśraya*), the *jīva* due to the influence of the material energy considers itself to be composed of the three *guṇas* and consequently suffers (and is thus not ultimately the *āśraya*)."[20] Similarly, the fifth and eleventh cantos describe the *jīva* as the witness, who is thus beyond the world in its pure state: "The *jīva* is the pure witness of and transcendental to the three states of waking, dreaming, and deep sleep, all of which are modifications of the intelligence."[21] "The *jīva* conditioned by material energy in the form of the mind has many ideas and activities that it has been pursuing from time without beginning. These activities manifest in the states of waking and dreaming, and in deep sleep they seem to disappear. The *jīva* being the witness in all these states is considered distinct from them. When he realizes this *(jīvan-mukta)*, he can see all of this clearly."[22]

Although the *ādhyātmika*, *ādhibhautika*, and *ādhidaivika puruṣas* are also *āśrayas* of a sort, they are not so in an absolute sense. Taking the term *āśraya* in its primary sense, it cannot refer to any of them. Nor, as mentioned, does it ultimately refer to the *jīvātmā*, rather to the Paramātmā, as stated in the Haṁsaghuyastava of *Śrīmad-Bhāgavatam*, "Because they are only matter, the body, the life airs, the external and internal senses, the

---

20. *yayā sammohito jīva ātmānaṁ tri-guṇātmakam/*
paro 'pi manute 'narthaṁ tat-kṛtaṁ cābhipadyate // (SB. 1.7.5)

21. *jāgrat svapnaḥ suṣuptaṁ ca guṇato buddhi-vṛttayaḥ/*
tāsāṁ vilakṣaṇo jīvaḥ sākṣitvena viniścitaḥ // (SB 11.13.27)

22. *kṣetrajña etā manaso vibhūtīr jīvasya māyā-racitasya nityāḥ/*
āvirhitāḥ kvāpi tirohitāś ca śuddho vicaṣṭe hy aviśuddha-kartuḥ//
(SB. 5.11.12)

five gross elements, and the subtle sense objects cannot know their own nature, the nature of the other senses, or the nature of their controllers. But the *jīva,* because of its spiritual nature which makes it in one sense identical with the Lord, can know its material body, life airs, senses, elements, sense objects, and also the three *guṇas* that form these elemental constituents' roots. Nevertheless, although the *jīva* is completely aware of them, it is unable to understand the Lord who is omniscient and unlimited. I therefore offer my obeisances unto him."[23] Thus it is Bhagavān alone who is the ultimate shelter.

Śukadeva Goswāmī's description of the ten subjects of a Mahāpurāṇa is echoed by Sūta Goswāmī in the twelfth canto of the *Bhāgavatam.* Śrī Jīva in pointing this out in *anucchedas* sixty-one through sixty-three once again demonstrates the cohesive nature of the *Bhāgavatam.* Sūta Goswāmī's description is slightly different from that of Śukadeva's, but as Jīva Goswāmī masterfully explains, Śuka and Sūta concur both in terms of what the ten topics are and, most importantly, what the ultimate shelter is. Sūta's words cited in thirteen verses appear amidst a description of the Purāṇic literature.

"O *brāhmaṇa,* scholars understand the ten characteristics of a Purāṇa to be the creation of the universal constituents *(sarga),* the secondary creation of the planetary systems *(visarga),* maintenance *(vṛtti),* protection *(rakṣā),* the description of the Manus *(antarāṇi),* discussion of the dynasties of great kings *(vaṁśa),* the activities of these dynasties *(vaṁśānucarīta),* annihilation *(saṁsthā),* motivation *(hetuḥ),* and the ultimate shelter *(apāśraya).* Other scholars differ only inasmuch as

---

23. *deho 'savo 'kṣā manavo bhūta-mātrām ātmānam anyaṁ ca viduḥ paraṁ yat/ sarvaṁ pumān veda guṇāṁś ca taj-jño na veda sarva-jñam anantam īḍe//* (SB. 6.4.25)

they say that the lesser Purāṇas deal with only five of these characteristics."[24]

Several Purāṇas cite the following verse describing the characteristics of a Purāṇa to be fivefold: "*Sarga, pratisarga, vaṁśa, manvantara,* and *vaṁśānucarīta* are the five characteristics of a Purāṇa."[25] Jīva Goswāmī explains that these five characteristics are referring to minor Purāṇas, while the list of ten refers to major Purāṇas. Śrī Jīva makes an important point here regarding major, or *maha,* Purāṇas. He says that those Purāṇas that deal with the ten topics enumerated by Sūta and Śuka but stress only the five characteristics of a minor Purāṇa cannot be considered Mahāpurāṇas. In this connection he cites the *Viṣṇu Purāṇa* as an example. In doing so, Jīva Goswāmī does not intend to slight the *Viṣṇu Purāṇa,* an important *sattvic* Purāṇa even for the Gauḍīya Vaiṣṇavas, rather to emphasize further the glory of *Śrīmad-Bhāgavatam.* In effect, he says that the *Bhāgavatam* is really the only Mahāpurāṇa, all others, as we have heard from so many other angles earlier, are subordinate to it.

Just how these topics appear in *Śrīmad-Bhāgavatam* is a discussion in and of itself. Śrī Jīva takes this discussion up in brief. He says that the ten topics are not found in a sequence from one to ten, beginning with the first canto and ending with the tenth, for the *Bhāgavatam* consists of twelve cantos. Neither are these topics found sequentially from the third canto on (although the sixth topic does appear in the eighth canto). Śrī Jīva cites

---

24. *sargo'syātha visargaś ca vṛtti-rakṣāntarāṇi ca/*
vaṁśo vaṁśānucarītaṁ saṁsthā hetur apāśrayaḥ//
daśabhir lakṣaṇair yuktaṁ purāṇaṁ tad-vido viduḥ/
kecit pañca-vidhaṁ brahman mahad-alpa-vyavasthayā// (SB. 12.7.9–10)

25. *sargaś ca pratisargaś ca vaṁśo manvantarāṇi ca/*
vaṁśānucaritaṁ ceti purāṇaṁ pañcalakṣaṇam//

Śrīdhara Swāmī, who says that the tenth canto deals with *nirodha* by way of discussing the destruction of wicked rulers who came to power due to a decline in righteousness. It thus discusses *nirodha* to spread the fame of Kṛṣṇa, who killed the wicked rulers. This is an instance of how one of the nine *aśrīta-tattva,* or sheltered topics, is discussed to shed light on the significance of the *āśraya-tattva,* the tenth topic. Śrīdhara Swāmī states further that the tenth canto thus deals primarily with the *āśraya-tattva* directly, revealing that tenth topic to be Kṛṣṇa. Śrī Jīva concludes that all ten topics are discussed throughout all twelve cantos. He sees that this notion is confirmed by Śukadeva's statement cited earlier[26] in which he explains that these topics (the first nine) are described either directly or indirectly, since direct and indirect speech is found throughout the *Śrīmad-Bhāgavatam.*

Sūta Goswāmī discusses the ten characteristics of a Maha–purāṇa as follows: "*Mahat,* the great principle, originates from the agitation of the three modes of nature. From this *mahat,* false ego *(ahaṅkāra)* emanates. From *ahaṅkāra* comes the subtle elements, the senses, and the gross elements along with the presiding deities of the senses. This development is called *sarga.*"[27] "Brahma's assembling these elements with the help of the *puruṣa,* the Supreme Lord, on the basis of the dormant *karma* (described by Śukadeva as *ūti*) of the *jīva* is called *visarga.* This constitutes the creation of moving and nonmoving living beings. The entire affair develops just as one seed grows out of another."[28] "*Vṛtti* indicates the maintenance of the moving liv-

---

26. SB. 2.10.2

27. *avyākṛta-guṇa-kṣobhān mahatas tri-vṛto 'hamaḥ/*
bhūta-sūkṣmendriyārthānāṁ sambhavaḥ sarga ucyate// (SB.12.7.11)

28. *puruṣānugṛhītānām eteṣāṁ vāsanā-mayaḥ/*
visargo 'yaṁ samāhāro bījād bījaṁ carācaram// (SB. 12.7.12)

ing beings, who are sustained in general by that which is nonmoving, although in some cases one moving being is food for another. Humans are maintained either naturally, based on their natural drives, or by adherence to scriptural injunctions."[29] "*Rakṣā*, protection, indicates the *avatāras* of the Lord *(yaiḥ)*, who destroy the enemies of the Vedas. Thus the Lord's incarnations *(iśānukathā)* along with maintenance *(sthāna)* and protection *(poṣaṇa)* are described."[30] "*Manvantara* indicates six elements: the Manus themselves, the *devās*, the sons of the Manus, the ruler of the *devās* (Indra), the *ṛṣis*, and the partial incarnations of the Lord."[31] "*Vaṁśa* indicates the list of the dynasty beginning from Brahmā. The description of their activities is called *vaṁśānucarita* (these categories can be included in Śukadeva's category of *iśānukathā*)."[32] "*Saṁsthā* indicates annihilation, or *nirodha*. *Nirodha* is of four types: occasional, such as during the partial annihilation at the end of Brahma's day *(naimittika)*; elemental, or that which occurs at the end of Brahma's life *(prākṛtika)*; that which is ongoing at all times *(nitya)*; and that which is ultimate *(ātyantika)*. Ultimate annihilation *(ātyantika)* also indicates *mukti*. All of these are brought about by the energy *(svabhāvataḥ)* of the Lord."[33] "*Hetuḥ* indicates that the *jīvas* are the cause of the universe due to their desires born of igno-

---

29. *vṛttir bhūtāni bhūtānāṁ carāṇām acarāṇi ca/*
kṛtā svena nṛṇāṁ tatra kāmāc codanayāpi vā// (SB.12.7.13)

30. *rakṣācyutāvatārehā viśvasyānu yuge yuge/*
tiryaṅ-martyarṣi-deveṣu hanyante yais trayī-dviṣaḥ// (SB. 12.7.14)

31. *manvantaraṁ manur devā manu-putrāḥ sureṣvarāḥ/*
ṛṣayo 'ṁśāvatārāś ca hareḥ ṣaḍ-vidham ucyate// (SB. 2.7.15)

32. *rājñāṁ brahma-prasūtānāṁ vaṁśas trai-kāliko 'nvayaḥ/*
vaṁśānucaritaṁ teṣāṁ vṛttaṁ vaṁśa-dharās ca ye// (SB. 12.7.16)

33. *naimittikaḥ prākṛtiko nitya ātyantiko layaḥ/*
saṁstheti kavibhiḥ proktaś caturdhāsya svabhāvataḥ// (SB. 12.7.17)

rance in material identification. Some emphasize that the cause is the fact that the *jīva* is conscious *(anuśāyin)*, while others stress that it is owing to the *jīva's* material identification *(avyākṛta)*."[34]

The final three verses of Sūta Goswāmī describe the *āśraya-tattva*. As in the other of Sūta's verses, I have stated them in terms of Jīva Goswāmī's understanding. What follows this rendering of these verses is the considerable discussion that these verses merit in light of their being the concluding words of *Tattva-sandarbha*.

"The ultimate shelter is indicated by the word *apāśrayaḥ*. It is he who is both associated with and aloof from the states of waking, dreaming, and deep sleep. He is present throughout the entire manifestation of the material world, and he is the ground (*āśraya*) for the functioning of all *jīvas*. At the same time, he is separate from all of this *(apa)*, situated in transcendence."[35] "Just as the ingredient (such as clay) of an object (such as a clay pot) is one with that object, yet different from it when not considered in regard to the object, so the *jīva*, which is qualitatively one with Paramātmā, is associated through ignorance with the material body and its transformation in the three states of waking, dreaming, and dreamless sleep. When the *jīva* withdraws its mind, either through self-inquiry as Vāmadeva and others did, or through yoga *(bhakti)* as performed by Devahūti, refraining from all extraneous endeavors outside of the pursuit of the Lord, the result is that the *jīva* realizes the Lord who is the ultimate shelter as Brahman and Bhagavān respectively. The *jīva* realizes, that is, that the feature of itself that is one with

34. *hetur jīvo 'sya sargāder avidyā-karma-kārakaḥ/*
yaṁ cānuśāyinaṁ prāhur avyākṛtam utāpare// (SB. 12.7.18)

35. *vyatirekānvayo yasya jāgrat-svapna-suṣuptiṣu/*
māyā-māyeṣu tad brahma jīva-vṛttiṣv apāśrayaḥ// (SB.12.7.19)

the Lord is fully present in the Lord and thus the Lord is the *jīva*'s shelter."[36]

Sūta Goswāmī has described the *tattva* of the *Bhāgavatam* using the word *apāśraya,* which is analogous to the term used by Śukadeva, *svāśraya,* indicating the ultimate shelter. *Apāśraya* is the shelter (Bhagavān) of the shelter *(jīva-śakti)*. Bhagavān is aware of all dimensions of consciousness, as the *jīva* can be by his grace and thus realize oneness with him in love. This state of love, *prema,* the *prayojana* of the *Bhāgavatam,* is the fourth dimension of consciousness that is implied in these verses. That state lies beyond the three lower dimensions of consciousness, waking *(jāgara),* dreaming *(svapna),* and deep sleep *(suṣupti)*. Although the *āśraya-tattva* supports the three dimensions of consciousness, it is simultaneously aloof from them, ever existing independently, in Hegelian language, "for itself and by itself" in the fourth dimension *(turīya)*.[37]

Jīva Goswāmī's reference to Vāmadeva,[38] which he finds implied in this verse, indicates that this ultimate shelter can be

---

36. *padārtheṣu yathā dravyaṁ san-mātraṁ rūpa-nāmasu/*
bījādi-pañcatāntāsu hy avasthāsu yutāyutam//
virameta yadā cittaṁ hitvā vṛtti-trayaṁ svayam/
yogena vā tadātmānaṁ vedehāyā nivartate// (SB. 12.7.20–21)

37. *Turīya,* literally "the fourth," refers to transcendent consciousness, the ultimate reality. Exactly what this experience involves is something that various schools of Vedānta differ on. Vaiṣṇava Vedāntins agree that it is a dimension of transcendental love in which reciprocal dealings between Bhagavān and the *jīva* souls eternally take place. Monists, on the other hand, conceptualize *turīya* as that which is devoid of reciprocal dealings, a state of pure being. Although the Gauḍīya *sampradāya* is in agreement in general with the other Vaiṣṇava *sampradāyas,* they consider the experience of *svayaṁ bhagavān,* Śrī Kṛṣṇa, to be beyond even this fourth dimension, beyond God realization.

38. Vāmadeva, an Upaniṣadic sage, is mentioned in *Vedānta-sūtra* 1.1.30.

realized to some extent by the culture of devotion mixed with knowledge *(jñāna-miśrā bhakti)*. Such mixed devotees realize the Brahman feature of the absolute. His reference to Devahūtī indicates that the word *yogena* in this verse refers to *śuddha-bhakti*, or unmixed devotion, by which the ultimate shelter can be realized more completely as Bhagavān. In the latter case, one's efforts must be focused entirely upon realizing that shelter through the culture of utter dependence upon grace. Efforts outside of this pursuit that may be useful for the *jñānī bhakta* must be abandoned to rise above the three lower dimensions of consciousness and fully enter the fourth, the land of the soul.

We often hear that absence of experience of the soul is justification for its dismissal. For the Vedāntin, however, experience itself *is* the soul. Experience is the function of consciousness, and consciousness is that which cannot be dismissed, dismissal itself being a conscious act.

Gauḍīya Vedāntins and Jīva Goswāmī in particular have posited a beautiful picture of the soul, describing it and the Godhead as inconceivably one and different through a Vedānta of aesthetics. Who has not seen Śrī Jīva's ideal portrayed in art as the charming, flute-bearing cowherd, Kṛṣṇa, surrounded by his *gopī* lovers? Yet few have pondered the philosophy that serves as the canvas for this art of love.

Philosophizing about our worldly experience, *Śrīmad-Bhāgavatam* tells us that we do have experience of the soul in this world every night when we enter into dreamless sleep, and we have experience of something more as well if we but consider our worldly experience of love. Jīva Goswāmī points this out by analyzing all dimensions of consciousness as they are described in *Śrīmad-Bhāgavatam.*

Consciousness exists not as a one-dimensional point, a two-dimensional line, or a three-dimensional solid. It is four dimensional. Each of its dimensions are successively more profound experiences of itself. From waking to dreaming to the experience of deep sleep and beyond, the experience of the self deepens. Although in one sense the first three of these dimensions are material and the fourth alone transcendent, each of them, if analyzed in terms of the experience they afford, point us in the direction of deeper experiences of the experiencer, the self.

The waking state is a transformation of intelligence in the mode of goodness *(sattva-guṇa).* This is so because in this dimension of consciousness we can apply ourselves in pursuit of transcendence. Thus it is of greater value to us than those times at which we dream or enter into deep dreamless sleep. The dream state is a transformation of intelligence in the mode of passion *(rajo-guṇa),* wherein the mind predominates. Deep sleep is a transformation of the intelligence in ignorance *(tamo-guṇa).* How then can these material states of consciousness be seen as progressive stages of awareness of the nature of existence, ascending from waking to dreaming to deep sleep?

They can be seen as such if that which is experienced in waking, dreaming, and deep sleep is analyzed in terms of its philosophical and ontological ramifications. Otherwise, waking, dreaming, and deep sleep themselves are material conditions produced under the influence of the *māyā-śakti*. They have no bearing upon the reality of the self other than that they are conditions in which consciousness does exist although unaware of its nature. The answer to the question thus lies in analyzing what these states tell us about consciousness's capacity to exist in these dimensions.

If in the waking dimension of consciousness we can understand the three dimensions of consciousness in terms of their ontological status, we will find evidence grounded in experience, rather than mere theory. Basing our investigation on this evidence we can pursue the fullest experience of the nature of being that is realized in the fourth dimension. This fourth dimension, as with the other three, can be considered in the waking dimension of consciousness in terms of our experience. Experience, being at the very heart of consciousness, should guide us in the direction of ultimate consciousness.

The first two dimensions of conscious experience are those that we are all most familiar with. That consciousness exists beyond them, in the third and fourth dimensions, beyond the objective and subjective world, and ultimately beyond itself is harder to grasp. We are aware of the objective world of sense objects. We are also aware of the dream state, the realm of pure thought devoid of sensible objects. But do we exist beyond thought? Is there knowing without thinking? If there is, it must be the knowing that amounts to experiencing existence itself, as opposed to knowing that which is outside of ourselves (duality), namely thought and the objects of thought in the sense world of waking consciousness. If such knowing is possible, what then is that dimension of consciousness that lies beyond even self-knowing, and what in our experience would lead us to believe that it exists at all?

Let us first analyze the dimension of waking consciousness. This is the realm of sense experience. In this dimension we experience or feel material objects. Awake to this realm, we tend to minimize that which exists in the realm of thought, other than to the extent that such thought facilitates our ability to experience sense objects. Yet here we often fail to consider that any and all experience in the objective reality is dependent upon some form of thinking, however meager. We cannot experience any material objects save and except to the extent that our minds are attentive to them. If our minds are somewhere else, to that extent we will fail to experience sense objects even when confronted by them. It is no wonder therefore that idealists and Buddhists alike have stressed the subjective realm of ideas to such an extent that they doubt the validity of any objective world outside of the mind. Jīva Goswāmī would not agree with them as to the mere mental existence of the so-called physical world, but like them he and any Vedāntin place greater emphasis upon the realm of ideas than upon the realm of objects.

Drawing from the example of the *Bhāgavatam*, we can consider the thought world in terms of the dream state. In this dimension, thought alone exists unencumbered by the world of objects. This realm is freer. It is not constrained as our experience is in the objective world. In the thought world there are innumerable possibilities in comparison with our experience in the objective realm. Because of this, we often try to augment the physical realm in the form of fiction to make it more accommodating.

When we experience the realm of pure thought in dream, the entire objective physical world ceases to have any bearing upon our ability to experience. This psychic dimension of conscious experience is one in which we exist independent of the physical realm. Thus we may conclude that our existence is not ultimately dependent upon the physical realm. We exist independent of this realm, and the extent to which we diminish our physical needs, the mental realm becomes accessible to us. This is why to think deeply, one must sit down, free from physical commotion. When we sleep at night, we are active in dream, yet due to our ignorance we do not know how to make our way there. If somehow we could, we would have a more comprehensive vision of truth than that which we experience when dominated by the tyrannical reign of the objective realm. It is not that dreams are more real than waking life, they do, however, being examples of the realm of pure thought, reveal a possibility for greater self-knowing. In the realm of pure thought, philosophical introspection can be more consciously explored, as this writing and subsequent reading attest to. Consciousness unencumbered by the objective world's constraints is freer to consider itself.

Yet the example of the *Bhāgavatam* verses we are discussing takes us a step further. As we discussed earlier, we are a witness to the experience of deep sleep. This is the third dimension in which both the objective world and the subjective thought world cease to have any bearing. We witness its existence and in doing so witness that we ourselves exist independent of even the thought world.

Thought has a ground from which it springs. Thought and its object are experienced as distinct from one another, yet one has no meaning without the other. From this we can conjecture as to the existence of a realm from which they both arise and in which they cease to be distinct (nonduality). Thought itself is outside of the self, as is, and even more so, the objective world. Where thought meets object and the subsequent judgment causes us to "know," we may know everything but our own selves and our source. As we know from the example of our witnessing the existence of ourselves in deep sleep, consciousness itself, uninhibited by body and mind, is the ground from which thoughts and subsequently objects spring up producing the world of duality. We go beyond the psychic and physical dimensions of consciousness in deep sleep and it is peaceful. Yet we cannot stay in this reality, nor can we appreciate this reality in full awareness. Yet it leads us to know of the dimension of pure consciousness. It is a reality that can be demonstrated by more than Kant's practical reason. This dimension of pure consciousness is an ontological reality for the Vedāntin, the ground of being. It is a dimension we can reach after thorough exercise of the mind leads us to realize both the mental and physical world's futility. Going beyond the body, we realize the power of mind, and going beyond the power of thought we realize the self. Reaching the limits of reasoning, we are pointed in the direction of ourselves. We can only reach that self by not only ceasing to exercise the body in terms of its demands but ceasing to think as well. What the *Bhāgavatam* suggests is not irrational, rather it picks up where reasoning leaves off. It is beckoning us to experience the realm of consciousness proper, rather than merely to think about it.

Yet how shall we, and why should we, attempt to go beyond the third dimension, having found the self? What in our experience in the waking dimension of consciousness would lead us to believe that there exists a dimension of consciousness that is beyond ourselves? We all exist and in a sense unto ourselves as units of nondual consciousness. In this we are one, yet we cannot deny that we are not entirely the same either, for although we are one in that we are consciousness and possess will, we do not all will the same thing. If there is anything we do all seek, however, it is communion with one another, and that not at the cost of ourselves.

This communion involves acknowledging each others' common need. Furthermore, it involves understanding that this need will be realized only by acknowledging something greater than ourselves. We come together around a common cause that transcends our selfish needs. Living together requires that we give ourselves. This giving of the self reaches its zenith in love. Mysteriously, we find that in giving up ourselves, we ourselves are nourished.

This experience of the waking state should lead us to conclude that there is a dimension of experience, of consciousness, in which upon giving up ourselves, we get something greater. That greater experience is the unifying factor of existence. If this is so, we must look for it in the land of the self, beyond objects and thoughts. From the third dimension of consciousness we must go to the fourth. After finding ourselves, we must enter the domain of self-forgetfulness.

The fourth dimension is the ground of our existence. For the Vedāntin, it is perceived variously, either as undifferentiated consciousness, or a relationship with the divine. Regarding the latter, Śrī Jīva concludes that love is greater than ourselves and it is the greatest aspect of love of God, one that he himself is motivated by. For Śrī Jīva the nondual ultimate shelter of *Śrīmad-Bhāgavatam* is realized when we know that we do not belong to ourselves, what to speak of anything belonging to us. If there is any time at which we can accurately say that something belongs to us, it is when, having given ourselves in love to God, we can say that "he is ours."

If God realization is the fourth dimension of consciousness, Jīva Goswāmī's idea of love of God, in which God becomes ours, is revolutionary. It seems to take us beyond even this fourth dimension. If we resign ourselves to becoming God's own, he takes the role of our maintainer. However, if he is ours, he is then subordinated to our love such that his Godhood is suppressed by that love. This is the Kṛṣṇa conception of Godhead, one in which God appears not as God, nor *jīva* soul as *jīva* soul. Both interrelate intimately as lover and beloved, Kṛṣṇa and his *gopīs*, beyond any sense of each other's ontological reality, yet beyond the material illusion as well. This dimension of love of Godhead is thus justifiably termed by the Gauḍīya Vaiṣṇavas as the fifth dimension, *turyātitaḥ*,[39] the dimension of the soul's Soul.

This is the philosophy of Śrī Jīva Goswāmī. This is what he has indicated in his *Tattva-sandarbha* and developed in great detail in his subsequent five treatises that comprise *Ṣaṭ-sandarbha*. It is the experience that Śrī Caitanya, Śrī Jīva's deity, personifies. Śrī Caitanya is that ultimate shelter, supporting all exist-

39. Kṛṣṇa has also been described as beyond the "fourth"*(turyātīto gopāla)* in *Gopāla-tāpanī Upaniṣad* 2.96.

ence, yet aloof from it simultaneously. He is at the same time lost in the self-forgetfulness that Śrī Rādhā personifies, and thus represents the goal of life for all *jīvas,* Kṛṣṇa *prema.* This is what Śrī Caitanya taught and thus made available to us through the means of Kṛṣṇa *saṅkīrtana.* It reveals the inner depth of the soul of Kṛṣṇa. Śrī Caitanya is Kṛṣṇa, the *advaya-jñāna tattva,* and the ultimate shelter of *Śrīmad-Bhāgavatam,* celebrating his own ecstasy in eternity.

Completed on June 8th, 1995,
Śrī Gauḍīya Vedānta ācārya Baladeva Vidyābhūṣaṇa tirobhava.

PRONUNCIATION GUIDE

The system of transliteration used in this book conforms to a system that scholars have accepted to indicate the pronunciation of each sound in the Sanskrit language.

The short vowel **a** is pronounced like the **u** in b**u**t, long **ā** like the **a** in f**a**r.

Short **i** is pronounced as in p**i**n, long **ī** as in p**i**que, short **u** as in p**u**ll, and long **ū** as in r**u**le.

The vowel **ṛ** is pronounced like the **ri** in **ri**m, **e** like the **ey** in th**ey**, **o** like the **o** in g**o**, **ai** like the **ai** in **ai**sle, and **au** like the **ow** in h**ow**.

The *anusvāra* (**ṁ**) is pronounced like the **n** in the French word *bo***n**, and *visarga* (**ḥ**) is pronounced as a final **h** sound.

At the end of a couplet, **aḥ** is pronounced **aha**, and **iḥ** is pronounced **ihi**.

The guttural consonants—**k, kh, g, gh, and ṅ**—are pronounced from the throat in much the same manner as in English. **K** is pronounced as in **k**ite, **kh** as in Ec**kh**art, **g** as in **g**ive, **gh** as in di**g h**ard, and **ṅ** as in si**ng**.

The palatal consonants—**c, ch, j, jh,** and **ñ**—are pronounced with the tongue touching the firm ridge behind the teeth. **C** is pronounced as in **ch**air, **ch** as in staun**ch-h**eart, **j** as in **j**oy, **jh** as in hed**geh**og, and **ñ** as in ca**ny**on.

The cerebral consonants—**ṭ, ṭh, ḍ, ḍh,** and **ṇ**—are pronounced with the tip of the tongue turned up and drawn back against the dome of the palate. **Ṭ** is pronounced as in **t**ub, **ṭh** as in ligh**t-h**eart, **ḍ** as in **d**ove, **ḍh** as in re**d-h**ot, and **ṇ** as in **n**ut.

The dental consonants—**t, th, d, dh,** and **n**—are pronounced in the same manner as the cerebrals, but with the forepart of the tongue against the teeth.

The labial consonants—**p, ph, b, bh**, and **m**—are pronounced with the lips. **P** is pronounced as in **p**ine, **ph** as in u**ph**ill, **b** as in **b**ird, **bh** as in ru**b-h**ard, and **m** as in **m**other.

The semivowels—**y, r, l,** and **v**—are pronounced as in **y**es, **r**un, **l**ight, and **v**ine respectively.

The sibilants—**ś, ṣ,** and **s**—are pronounced, respectively, as in the German word **s**_prechen_ and the English words **sh**ine and **s**un. The letter **h** is pronounced as in **h**ome.

GLOSSARY

abhidheya — the means to attain the goal.

ācārya — one who teaches by example; a spiritual master who is a pure devotee and can guide his disciples to spiritual perfection.

acintya-bhedābheda — inconceivable simultaneous oneness and difference between the living entity and Godhead.

adhibautika puruṣa — the particular embodiment of the *jīva.*

adhidaivika puruṣa — the controlling deities of the senses.

adhikāra — the qualification of a person.

adhyātmika puruṣa — the individual *jīva* embodied in the physical plane who identifies with the senses of the material body.

advaita-vedānta — doctrine of nonduality articulated by Śaṅkara.

anubandha — an indispensable element of Vedānta that gives the reader a brief acquaintance with the book.

anuccheda — section of a book, chapter.

anumāna — inference, logical conjecture.

āśīrvāda — offering or seeking blessings.

avatāra — a descent of Godhead to the material world.

avidyā — ignorance.

Bhagavān — the personal aspect of the Supreme Personality of Godhead, Kṛṣṇa; the possessor of all six opulences in full.

bhakti — devotional love and service to Kṛṣṇa.

bhāṣya — commentary.

bhāva — spiritual emotion.

bhāva bhakti — devotional service in ecstasy.

Brahman — the undifferentiated aspect of the Supreme.

darśana — a philosophical way of seeing.

dharma — religion, duty, inherent nature.

Gauḍīya Vaiṣṇavism — the disciplic succession of Śrī Caitanya.

gāyatrī — the prototype of all Vedic *mantras.*

guṇa — rope; the three modes of material nature which bind and control the embodied *jīva;* viz. *sattva-guṇa,* the mode of goodness, *rajo-guṇa,* the mode of passion, and *tamo-guṇa,* the mode of ignorance.

guru-paramparā — an unbroken chain of disciplic succession.

īśvara — the supreme controller, God.

jīva — atomic soul.

Kali-yuga — the last and shortest of the four ages: the age of quarrel and hypocrisy.

karma — action producing a material reaction.

līlā — the transcendental pastimes of the Godhead.

maṅgalācaraṇa — prayers to invoke auspiciousness.

māyā-śakti — Śrī Kṛṣṇa's secondary energy which governs the affairs of the material world.

māyāvāda — doctrine of illusion.

monism — any doctrine advocating absolute oneness of the soul and God.

mukti — liberation from material life.

namaskara — offering obeisances.

nyāya — (1) logic. (2) the philosophy founded by Gautama.

paramārthika — absolute reality.

paramātmā — supersoul; the partial manifestation of Bhagavān who presides over the material universe.

pariccheda — limitation.

pramāṇa — evidence.

pramāṇa khaṇḍa — the section of a book that establishes the evidence by which one's thesis will be proven, epistemology.

prameya khaṇḍa — the section of a book in which one's thesis is presented.

prātibhāsika — apparent reality.

pratibimba — reflection.

pratyakṣa — sense perception.

prayojana — the goal to be realized.

prema — pure love for Kṛṣṇa.

prema-bhakti — devotional service rendered in pure love of God.

pūrṇa-puruṣa — the complete or perfect predominator.

rajo-guṇa — the material mode of passion.

rasa — aesthetic expression of relationship with God in transcendence.

śabda-pramāṇa — evidence by revealed sound.

sādhana-bhakti — devotional service in the stage of apprenticeship.

samādhī — spiritual trance; the highest attainment of yoga.

sambandha — knowledge of relationship.

sannyāsa — the renounced order of spiritual life.

śāstra — revealed scripture; sacred literature spoken by the Lord.

sattva-guṇa — the material mode of goodness.

siddhānta — conclusion.

smṛti — that which is recollected (after hearing the *śruti*); the supplementary scriptures to the Vedas.

śruti — scriptures spoken directly by God; the original Vedic literatures, the four Vedas and the Upaniṣads.

svāgatabheda — difference within a particular object.

svajātīabheda — difference between objects of the same class.

svāṁśa — the category of God as opposed to *vibhinnāṁśa.*

svarūpa-śakti — Śrī Kṛṣṇa's own internal potency.

svayaṁ bhagavān — the original Personality of Godhead.

tamo-guṇa — the material mode of ignorance.

upādhi — material designation.

Vaiṣṇavism — devotion to Viṣṇu (Kṛṣṇa).

vastu-nirdeśa — the subject of the book.

vedānta — the conclusion of Vedic knowledge.

vibhinnāṁśa — the category of the living entities.

vidyā — knowledge.

vijātīabheda — difference between objects of different classes.

vyāvahārika — practical reality.

yuga — an age of the cosmic time cycle. The four *yugas* are Satya, Treta, Dvāpara, and Kali.

yuga-avatāra — a descent of Godhead in a particular *yuga*.

yuga-dharma — the recommended religious duties in a particular *yuga*.

Bibliography

A. C. Bhaktivedanta Swami Prabhupāda. *Bhagavad-gita As It Is.* Los Angeles: Bhaktivedanta Book Trust, 1985.

———. *Śrī Caitanya-caritāmṛta,* Vols. 1–17. New York: Bhaktivedanta Book Trust, 1975.

———. *Śrīmad-Bhāgavatam,* Vols. 1–30. New York: Bhaktivedanta Book Trust, 1972.

Adams, George C. Jr. *The Structure and Meaning of Badarāyana's Brahmā-sūtras.* New Delhi: Motilal Banarsidass Publishers, 1993.

Beck, Guy L. *Sonic Theology: Hinduism and Sacred Sound.* Columbia: South Carolina University Press, 1993.

Darling, Gregory J. *An Evaluation of the Vedantic Critique of Buddhism.* New Delhi: Motilal Banarsidass Publishers, 1986.

Dasgupta, *A History of Indian Philosophy IV.* Cambridge, England: Cambridge University Press, 1949.

De, Sushil Kumar, *Early History of the Vaishnava Faith and Movement in Bengal.* Calcutta: Firma KLM, 1986.

Haberman, David L. "Divine Betrayal: Krishna-Gopal of Braja in the Eyes of Outsiders." *Journal of Vaishnava Studies,* Vol. 3 No. 1 (1994).

Houston, Vyāsa. "Language of Enlightenment." *Clarion Call,* Vol. 2 No. 3 (1989), p. 43.

Journal of Vaishnava Studies: Focus on the Bhāgavata Purāṇa, Vol. 2. No. 3 (1993).

Kapoor, O. B. L. *Philosophy and Religion of Śrī Caitanya.* New Delhi: Munshiram Manoharlal Publishers, 1977.

———. *The Gosvāmīs of Vṛndāvana.* Caracas, Venezuela: Sarasvatī Jayaśrī Classics, 1995.

Lipner, Julius. *The Face of Truth.* Albany, New York: State University of New York Press, 1986.

Mahanamabrata Brahmachari. *Vaiṣṇava Vedānta.* Calcutta: Das Gupta & Co., 1974.

Prasad, S. S., *The Bhāgavata Purāṇa: A Literary Study.* Delhi: Capital Publishing House, 1984.

Rocher, Ludo, "The Puranas," Vol. 2, *A History of Indian Literature,* ed. Jan Gonda. Wiesbaden: Otto Harrassowitz, 1986.

Rosen, Steven. *The Six Goswamis of Vrindavan.* Brooklyn, New York: Folk Books, 1990.

Tridandi Sri Bhakti Prajnan Yati. *Twelve Essential Upanishads,* Vols. 1–4. Madras: Sri Gaudiya Math, 1984.

Sharma, B. N. K., *A History of the Dvaita School of Vedānta and its Literature,* Vol. 2. Bombay: Bookseller's Publishing Co., 1960.

———. *The Brahmasūtras and Their Principal Commentaries: A Critical Exposition,* Vols. 1–3. New Delhi: Munshiram Manoharlal Publishers, 1986.

Śrīla Jīva Gosvāmī. *Tattvāsandarbha,* trans. Stuart Elkman. New Delhi: Motilal Banarsidass Publishers, 1986.

Śrī Rupa Gosvāmī. *Bhakti-rasāmṛta-sindhuh,* Vol. 1, trans. Swami B. H. Bon Maharaja. Vrindaban, India: Institute of Oriental Studies, 1965.

Swami B. R. Sridhar. *Śrīmad Bhagavad-gītā: The Hidden Treasure of the Sweet Absolute.* Nabadwip, India: Śrī Caitanya Saraswat Math, 1985.

———. *Sermons of the Guardian of Devotion,* Vol 1. North Yorkshire, UK: The August Assembly, 1988.

Vasu, Rai Bahadur Srīsa Chandra. *The Vedānta Sūtras of Bādarāyaṇa with Commentary of Baladeva.* New Delhi: Munshiram Manoharlal Publishers, 1979.

The Vedāntasūtras with the Śrībhāṣya of Rāmānujācārya, Vols. 1–3, trans. M. Rangacharya and M. B. Vardaraja Aiyangar. New Delhi: Munshiram Manoharlal Publishers, 1989.

VERSE INDEX

ābhāsaś ca nirodhaś ca 164
acintyāḥ khalu ye bhāvā 41
agneḥ puraṇaṁ gāyatrīṁ 82
ajñānenāvṛtaṁ jñānaṁ 114
ambarīṣa śuka-proktaṁ 72
ambuvad agrahanāt 127
anarthopaśamaṁ sākṣād 112, 135
anena jīvenātmanā 152
anyārthaś ca parāmarśaḥ 154
aprārabdha-phalaṁ pāpaṁ 137
ārādhyo bhagavān 111
artho'yaṁ brahma sūtrāṇāṁ 73
āsan varṇās trayo hy asya 17
aṣṭādaśapurāṇāni 139
ataeva avaśya āmi 94
ātmārāmaś ca munayo 112
atra sargo visargaś ca 160
avatārānucaritaṁ 163
avyākṛta-guṇa-kṣobhān 171
bhagavān iti śabdo 'yam 109
bhakti-yogena manasi 107
bhārata-vyāpadeśena 51
bhayaṁ dvitīyābhiniveśataḥ syād 115
bhūta-mātrendriya-dhiyāṁ 162
catur-lakṣa-pramāṇena 47
daivī hy eṣā guṇa mayī 116
daśamasya viśuddhy-arthaṁ 161
deho 'savo 'kṣā manavo bhūta-mātrām 169
dharmaḥ projjhita-kaitavo 'tra 66, 92
dhyānena puruṣo 'yaṁ ca 82
dvaipāyanena yad buddhaṁ 51
etac chrutvā tathovāca 70
ete cāṁśa-kalāḥ puṁsaḥ 26
evaṁ vā are 43
gāyaty ukthāni śastrāṇi 83
grantho 'ṣṭādaśa-sāhasro 68
harer guṇākṣipta-matir 141

hetur jīvo 'sya sargāder 173
idaṁ śata-sahasrād dhi 76
īkṣater nāśabdam 56
itihāsaḥ purāṇaṁ ca 45
itihāsa-purāṇābhyāṁ 43
itihāsa-purāṇanāṁ 46
itihāsa-purāṇāni 44
jāgrat svapnaḥ suṣuptaṁ ca 168
kalau naṣṭa-dṛśām eṣa 86
kālenāgrahaṇaṁ matvā 47
kaliṁ sabhājayanty āryāḥ 87
kasmai yena vibhāsito 85
kathaṁ vā pāṇḍave yasya 92
kṣetrajña etā manaso vibhūtīr 168
kṛṣṇas tu bhagavān svayam 138
kṛṣṇa-varṇaṁ tviṣākṛṣṇaṁ 14
kṛṣṇe sva-dhāmopagate 92
madhuram-madhuram etan 50
mahā-muni kṛte 38
manvantaraṁ manur devā 172
mathyate tu jagat sarvaṁ 20
māyā paraity abhimukhe ca vilajjamānā 112
muktiṁ dadāti karhicit 108
munir vivakṣur bhagavad-guṇānāṁ 78
naimittikaḥ prākṛtiko 172
nārāyaṇād viniṣpaṇṇaṁ jñānaṁ 53
nārāyaṇa-parāyaṇāḥ kvacit 95
nātmā jajāna na mariṣyati naidhate 'sau 156
nigama-kalpa-taror galitaṁphalaṁ 90
nirṇayaḥ sarva-śāstrāṇāṁ 77
nirodho 'syānuśayanam 163
nitayaṁ śuddhaṁ paraṁ brahma 80
padārtheṣu yathā dravyaṁ 174
pahile dekhiluṅ tomāra 16
pañca-dīrghaḥ pañca-sūkṣmaḥ 4
pañcāṅgaṁ ca purānaṁ syād 55
pitṛ-deva-manuṣyāṇāṁ 42
prāyeṇālpāyuṣaḥ sabhyāḥ 42
prāyeṇa munayo rājan 105

prītir na yāvan mayi vāsudeva ... 137
pṛthivīte āche yata ... 21
purāṇaṁ pañcamo vedaḥ ... 45
purāṇaṁ tvaṁ bhāgavataṁ ... 71
purā tapaś cacārogam ... 44
puruṣānugṛhītānām ... 171
pūrvam evāham ihāsam ... 111
rājñāṁ brahma-prasūtānāṁ ... 172
rājya-kāmo manūn devān ... 110
rakṣācyutāvatārehā ... 172
rātrau tujāgaraḥ kāryaḥ ... 71
ṛg-vedaṁ bhagavo ... 45
ṛg-vedo 'tha yajur-vedaḥ ... 50
ṛg-yajuḥ-sāmātharvākhyān ... 44
sad eva saumyedam agra āsīt ... 152
sāeva hi satya-ādayaḥ ... 56
samādhinānusmara tad-viceṣṭitam ... 109
saṁkṣipya caturo vedāṁś ... 47
sargaś ca pratisargaś ca ... 170
sargo'syātha visargaś ca ... 170
sarva-dharmān parityaja ... 76
sarva-vedānta-sāraṁ hi ... 89
sa saṁhitāṁ bhāgavatīṁ ... 138
sa saṁvṛtas tatramahān mahīyasāṁ ... 91
śāstrāntarāṇi saṁjānan ... 96
śāstra-yonitvāt ... 41
śāstre yuktau ca nipuṇah ... 5
satāṁ prasaṅgān mama vīrya-saṁvido ... 116
śataśo 'tha sahasraiś ca ... 84, 86
sattvaṁ yad brahma-darśanam ... 57
sattvāt sañjāyate jñānaṁ ... 57
satyaṁ jñānam anantaṁ brahma ... 152
sa vā eṣa puruṣo ... 165
śreyaḥ-sṛtiṁ bhaktim udasya te vibho ... 136
śrīdharera anugata ... 15
srīmad-bhāgavataṁ bhaktyā ... 72
śrutes tu śabda-mūlatvāt ... 41
sthitir vaikuṇṭha-vijayaḥ ... 163
strī śūdra dvija bandūnaṁ ... 78

śuci-śravāḥ satya-rato dhṛta-vrataḥ 109
śuddha-sattva-viśeṣātmā 108
śuko vetti vyāso vetti 94
sva sukha-nibhṛta-cetās 103
tac chuddhaṁ vimalaṁ viśokam 80
tad acchāyam aśarīram 128
tad aikṣata bahu syām 152
tad idaṁ grāhayām āsa 89
taj jhotir bhagavān viṣṇur 80
taj jotiḥ paramaṁ brahma 79
tamāla-śyāmala-tviṣi 138
tarko 'pratiṣṭhānāt 41
tataś ca vaḥ pṛcchyam imaṁ 91
tato 'tra mat-suto vyāsaḥ 52
tatrābhavad bhagavān vyāsa-putro 91
tatropajagmur bhuvanaṁ punānā 90
tat tu samanvayāt 58
tene brahmā hṛdā 38
tumiha kariha bhakti 21
tvam ādyaḥ puruṣaḥ sākṣād 111
upakramopasaṁhārāv 81
vadanti tat tattva-vidas 25,146
vedāḥ purāṇaṁ kāvyaṁ ca 92
vedārthād adhikaṁ manye 53
vedavān niścalaṁ manye 54
vede rāmāyaṇe caiva 84
vedyaṁ vāstavam atra vastu 146
vṛttir bhūtāni bhūtānāṁ 172
vyāsa-citta-sthitākāśād 52
vyatirekānvayo yasya 173
yad advaitaṁ brahmopaniṣadi 27
yaḥ svānubhāvam akhila śruti sāram ekam 90
yasyāṁ vai śrūyamānāyaṁ 136
yat karmabhir yat tapasā 135
yatrādhikṛtya gāyatrīṁ ityādi 64, 67
yayā sammohito jīva 113, 168
yenāśrutaṁ śrutaṁ bhavati 152
ye 'nye 'ravindākṣa vimukta-māninas 109
yo 'dhyātmiko 'yaṁ puruṣaḥ 166

INDEX

A

Abhidheya 104, 132–133
Acintya-bhedābheda 101–103, 117, 123, 129–131
Ādhibhautika 165–169
Ādhidaivika 165–169
Adhikāra 23, 43
Adhikaraṇa 31
Adhyātmika 165–169
Advaita-vedānta 118–120
  guru as God 19
  jīva as God 118
  jīva rejected 114
  mutual dependence 125–126
  propagated by Śiva 87
  theory of limitation *(pariccheda)* 120–127
  theory of reflection *(pratibimba)* 120–128
  three levels of reality in 119
  world as dream 124
Advaya-jñāna 25–26, 146–150, 160
Agni Purāṇa
  on *gāyatrī* 80–83
  on SB. 66–68
  on Viṣṇu 79
Ahaṅkāra 171
Akbar 8
Anubandhas 13, 24
Anumāna 34–36
Ambarīṣa Mahārāja 71
Apāśrayaḥ 173–174
Āśraya-tattva 160–168
Aśvinī-kumāras 69–70
Avatāra
  Caitanya as 2
  nondiff. from Kṛṣṇa 149
  puruṣa 162
  yuga 15–17, 172

B

Baladeva Vidyābhūṣaṇa 14, 73, 89
Beauty 118
Berkeley 150
Bhagavad-gītā 71
  on *jīva* 114
  on *māyā* 116
  on *sattva* 57
Bhakti 107–110, 153
  Kṛṣṇa *bhakti* 20
  prema-bhakti 107–109
  sādhana-bhakti 135–137
  śuddha-bhakti 175
Bhakti Rakṣaka Śrīdhara Deva Goswāmī 77, 141
Bhakti-rasāmṛta-sindhu 107
Bhakti-ratnākara 8
Bhaktivedanta Swami 20, 22, 61
Bhārata-tātparya 96
Bhargam 81
Bhāvārtha-dīpikā 15, 94, 103, 109–110
  on *gāyatrī-mantra* 65
Bhrama 32
Bible 36
Brahmā 172
  creation through sound 37–38
  heard SB. 85
  in relation to *śāstra* 44
  on *Mahābhārata* 77
  sampradāya 88

spoke fifth Veda 45
Brahmā Purāṇa 45
Brahma-vidyā 68–70
Brahman
Chāndogya Upaniṣad on 152–153
nirviśeṣa 55
relation to *jīva* 151–153
saguṇa 127–128, 56
Brahmavaivarta Purāṇa 104, 141
Buddhism 150–151, 177

C

Caitanya
ācārya-līlā 18
as *avatāra* 2, 13–17
as God 14–16, 182
as *svayam bhagavān* 17, 26
on SB. and Vs. 73
sannyāsa of 16, 94
Caturvarga-cintāmaṇi 86
Chāndogya Upaniṣad 152–153
Chattopadhyaya, Rampada 75
Cheating 33
Confusion 32
Consciousness 175
as conditioned 32
as covered 130
as ultimate reality 147–148
Buddhist approach to 151, 154–159
form constituted of 148–149
joyful by nature 149
knowledge as having 49
nature of 39
dimensions of 175–181
Creation 162

D

Dadhīci 69–70
Darling, Gregory J. 119, 150
Dasgupta 93
De, Sushil Kumar 1
Defects, in people 32–34
Deities 39, 54–59
Devahūti 173–175
Devi-Bhāgavatam 64, 69
Dharma 66, 76
Dhīmahi 80
Dimock, Edward 131
Dreams 178–179
Dvāpara-yuga 47

E

Evidence. See *Pramāṇa*

F

Fifth dimension. See *Turyātitaḥ*
Form 148–149
Fourth dimension. See *Turīya*

G

Gargamuni 17
Garuḍa Purāṇa 72–73, 83
Gaura-gaṇoddeśa-dīpikā 19, 89
Gautama 53, 71
Gāyatrī-mantra 63
Agni Purāṇa on 82–83
assoc. with Sarasvatī 83
'bhargo' discussed 79–80
Bhāvārtha-dīpikā on 65
meditation on Bhagavān 78–83
on *savitur* 65
in SB. 64–65

Śrīdhara Swāmī on 64–65
Gopāla Bhaṭṭa 21–22
Gopāla-tāpanī śruti 85
Gopī 2, 181
Govinda Bhāṣya 74, 89
Govinda mandir-aṣṭakam 8
Govindajī 74
Govindajī Mandir 7
Guru 7, 19

H

Haberman, L. David 21
Hayagrīva 68–70
Hegel 174
Hopkins, Thomas 60
Houston, Vyāsa 52
Hudson, Dennis 61

I

Illusion, self 32
Inattentiveness 32
Inference. See *Anumāna*
Intellect 38
Īśa-kathāḥ 163
Itihāsas 46

J

Jīva
as per trance of Vyāsa 113–117
Buddhist conception of 151
conscious nature of 154–159
relation to Brahman 151–153
Vedānta-sūtra on 154
Jīva Goswāmī 1–10
Jñāna 103

K

Kali-yuga 13–14, 42, 84
Kant, Immanuel 179
Kapoor, O. B. L. 89
Karabhājana Muni 14–15
Karaṇāpāṭava 33–34
Karma 103, 124, 158–159, 167, 171
Kaṭha Upaniṣad 48
Kavikarṇapūra 19, 89
Knowledge 49
Kṛṣṇa
appearance in other millennia 17
as God 25, 138
as Nārāyaṇa 25–26
as nondual 148–150
as source of all *avatāras* 17
as *svayam bhāgavan* 25–27
as ultimate object of love 133–134
holy name of 50
outward appearance of 161–162
senses of 33
speaker of SB. 84–85
three features of 146, 164
Kṛṣṇa *līlā* 94, 104–105, 130, 140
Kṛṣṇa-varṇam 16
Kṛṣṇadāsa Kavirāja Goswāmī 14, 21

L

Laghu-vaiṣṇava-toṣaṇī 1
Lakṣmī 95
Līlā smaraṇam 109
Logic 34, 41

M

Mādhavendra Purī 89

Madhusūdana Vācaspati 5
Madhvācārya 88–89, 95–96
Mahābhārata 77
  chronology of 139
  essence of Vedas 51
  on reason 41
  on supplementing Vedas 43
  offers highest knowledge 75–78
Mahapuruṣa, bodily symptoms 4
Majumdar, A. K. 88
Maṅgalācaraṇa 13
Manvantara 163, 172
Material manifestations 156
Mathurā 20–21
Matsya Purāṇa
  on condensation of Purāṇas 47
  on *Mahābhārata* 139
  on nature and necessity of Purāṇas 47
  on Purāṇas in the modes of nature 55
  on Purāṇic deities 55
  on SB. 64
Māyā 107, 109, 112–117, 176
Mithyā 119, 123
Modes of nature 162, 176
  Matsya Purāṇa on 55
  Purāṇas in 55–59, 92
Monism. See Advaita-vedānta
Muktāphala 92
Mukti 163–164
Mysticism, Eastern 36

N

Nārada Purāṇa 53
Narahari Cakravartī 1
Nārāyaṇa-varman 69–70
Narottama dāsa 7
Newton, Sir Issac 49
Nimi, Mahārāja 154
Nirodha 163, 171, 172
Nityānanda dāsa 1
Nityānanda Prabhu 5
Nyāya 41

P

Padma Purāṇa
  on *Bhagavad-gītā* 71
  on *karma* 137
  on *puruṣa* 109
  on *sampradāya* 88
  on SB. 71
  on Vyāsa 51
Pāṇini 81
Parama puruṣa 110, 137
Paramātmā 154, 158, 166–169
  as *parama puruṣa* 110, 112
Paramātmā-sandarbha 74
Pariccheda. See Advaita-Vedānta
Parīkṣit, Mahārāja 90–91, 108
Pippalāyana 154
Poṣaṇa 163
Pramāda 32–33
Pramāṇa 31. See also *Śāstra*
  śabda pramāṇa 35, 42–48
Prameya-ratnāvalī 89
Prāṇa 155, 158
Pratibimba. See Advaita-vedānta
Pratyakṣa 33–36
Prayojana 104, 132–133
Prema 135–137
  Kṛṣṇa *prema* 17–18, 76, 104, 133, 182

prema-bhakti 107–108
turiyā as 174
Prema-vilāsa 1
Puṇyāraṇya 88
Purāṇas
accessibility of 50
advocacy of numerous deities 54–60
as identified with different sages and demigods 48
as more important than Vedas 54
as *śruti* 46
as Vedic 43, 46–47, 50–54
divine origin of disputed 48–50
five elements constituting 55
in modes of nature 55, 57–59
maha–purāṇa 171
Skanda Purāṇa on 44
ten characteristics of 169–171
Pūrṇa-puruṣa 137
Puruṣa 165–169
Pūrvaṁ 110

R

Rādhā 111, 134, 182
Rādhā-Ramaṇa temple 22
Rāmānanda Rāya 16
Rāmānuja 95
Rasa 9, 97
Reader, qualification of. See *adhikāra*
Reality, nondual. See *advaya-jñāna.*
Reason 33–34, 41
Rocher, Ludo 60
Rūpa Goswāmī 3, 6–7, 20–21

S

Saṁskāra 163
Śakti 147–148
Sāma Veda 83–84
Sambandha-jñāna 132
Sampradāya 88–89
Gauḍīya 73, 88, 101
Śrī 74
Sāmudrika 4
Sanātana Goswāmī 3, 6–7, 14–15, 20–21
Śaṅkara
as Śiva 87
concept of nonduality 147
in relation to SB. 87–88
on explanation of Purānic deities 55
on *sampradāya* 88
saguṇa Brahman 127–128
stressed Upaniṣads 45
Saṅkīrtana 13, 87, 182
Sannyāsa 94
Sanskrit 43, 52, 76
Sarasvatī 67, 83
Sārvabhauma Bhaṭṭācārya 5
Śāstra 37
as eternal 37, 39
as experience 38
as independent 36
as perfect knowledge 36, 38, 40–41
as Veda 37
Brahman as subject of 37
in relation to *anumāna* 36
in relation to *pratyakṣa* 36
means of determining meaning 81
more than book 39

Vedānta-sūtra on 41
word order of 39–40
Śāstrī, Haridas 75
Ṣaṭ-sandarbha 8–9, 22–26
Sense perception. See *Pratyakṣa*
Senses, imperfect. See *Karaṇāpāṭava*
Shah, Nawab Hussain 2
Sheridan, Daniel P. 61
Siṁhāsana 68
Śiva 87, 94
Śiva Purāṇa 47
Six Goswāmīs 6–7, 14, 20
Skanda Purāṇa
on holy name 50
on *Mahābhārata* 139
on manifestation of Purāṇas 44–45
on Purāṇas as shelter of Vedas 53
on SB. 66–68, 72, 84, 86
on Vyāsa's mind 51
on *yuga* cycle 53
Sleep, deep 155, 158, 175–176, 179
Smṛti 42
Soul, qualities of 32
Sound, sacred 36
Śrī-Bhāṣya 95
Śrīdhara Swāmī 15
covert writing of 93–95
on *gāyatrī* 64–65
on SB. 171
Śrīmad-Bhāgavatam
as natural commentary on *Vedānta-sūtra* 75
as spotless *pramāṇa* 60
chronology 102
commentaries on 86
digests on 86
embodies religion 86
expanded by Śukadeva 85
on creation 162
on *gāyatrī-mantra* 63, 65–66
on *sattva* 57
on trance of Vyāsa 106–107
on Vedas 42
ten subjects of 160
Śruti 42–43
Śukadeva
as self-realized 139–142
as speaker of SB. 89–91
birth of 141
expanded SB. 85
Sūrya Nārāyaṇa 82
Sūta Goswāmī 103
given charge of Purāṇas 50
on fifth Veda 46
Sūtras 59
Svarūpa-śakti 111–113
Śyāmānanda 7

T

Taittirīya Upaniṣad 165
Tat tvam asi 122, 128–129, 152
Turīya 174, 177–181
Turyātitaḥ 181

U

Uddhava 85
Uttara Mīmāṁsā 58–59

V

Vaiśeṣikas 146
A Vaiṣṇava Interpretation of the Brahma-sūtras 75
Vāmadeva 173–175

Vaṁśa 172
Varṇavāda 39–40
Vastu-nirdeśa 26
Vedāṅgas 44, 54
Vedānta 35, 101
Vedānta Darśana 75
Vedānta-sūtra 58–59
  on *adhikaraṇa* 93
  on *jīva* 126, 154
  on logic 41
  on *saguṇa* Brahman 56
  on *śāstra* 41
  on system of argument 31
  SB. as natural commentary on 75
Vedas 42
  divine origin of disputed 48
  Śiva Purāṇa on 47
  fifth 44–45
    Sūta Goswāmī on 46
    Vayu Purāṇa on 46
  qualification for study of 43
  SB. on 42
  understood through Purāṇas 43
  Yajur 46
Vijñānavādin 150–151, 154–159
Vipralipsā 33
Viśiṣṭādvaita 95
Viṣṇu 79
Viṣṇu Purāṇa 50, 78–79, 95, 170
  on Vyāsa as incarnation 52
  Vedas found in Purāṇas 51
Viśvanātha Cakravartī Ṭhākura 74, 75
Vopadeva 92
Vraja 77
Vṛndāvana dāsa Ṭhākura 21
Vṛtrāsura 64, 68–69, 70
Vṛtti 171–172
Vyāsa
  as incarnation 47
  concerning *Mahābhārata* 51, 78
  covert writing of 15
  glories of 51–52
  Padma Purāṇa on 51
  Viṣṇu Purāṇa on 52
Vyāsasūnuṁ 104

Y

Yājñavalkya 81
Yogācāra Buddhists. See Vijñānavādin
Yogī, realization of 26
Yuga cycle 15
  in day of Brahmā 67
  position of knowledge in each 53
Yuga dharma 17, 87